RELIGIOUS PLURALISM

BOSTON UNIVERSITY STUDIES IN
PHILOSOPHY AND RELIGION

General Editor: Leroy S. Rouner

Volume Five

Volume Four
Foundations of Ethics
Leroy S. Rouner, Editor

Volume Three
Meaning, Truth, and God
Leroy S. Rouner, Editor

Volume Two
Transcendence and the Sacred
Alan M. Olson and Leroy S. Rouner, Editors

Volume One
Myth, Symbol, and Reality
Alan M. Olson, Editor

Contents

v

Library of Congress Cataloging in Publication Data

Main entry under title:

Religious pluralism.

(Boston University studies in philosophy and
religion ; vol. 5)
Includes index.
1. Religious pluralism—Addresses, essays, lectures.
2. Religion—Addresses, essays, lectures.   3. Religions—
Addresses, essays, lectures.   I. Rouner, Leroy S.
II. Series: Boston University studies in philosophy and
religion ; v. 5.
BL85.R38 1984   291.1'72   84-7431
ISBN 0-268-01626-7

Religious Pluralism

Edited by
Leroy S. Rouner

UNIVERSITY OF NOTRE DAME PRESS
Notre Dame, Indiana 46556

Preface

Boston University Studies in Philosophy and Religion is a joint project of the Boston University Institute for Philosophy and Religion and the University of Notre Dame Press. While these Studies may eventually include occasional volumes by individual authors dealing with critical issues in the philosophy of religion, it is presently focused on an annual volume edited from the previous year's Institute lecture program. The Director of the Institute, who also serves as editor of these Studies, chooses a theme and invites participants to lecture at Boston University in the course of the academic year. These public lectures are on Wednesday evenings, chaired by faculty from the various schools and departments within the university which jointly sponsor the Institute. There is a critical respondent to each paper and general discussion by the audience. The papers are then revised by their authors, and the editor selects and edits the papers to be included in these Studies. In preparation are volumes on nature, and on problems of religious epistemology.

The Boston University Institute for Philosophy and Religion is sponsored jointly by the Graduate School, the School of Theology, the Department of Philosophy, and the Department of Religion at Boston University. As an interdisciplinary and ecumenical forum it does not represent any philosophical school or religious tradition. Within the academic community it is committed to open interchange on questions of value, truth, reality, and meaning which transcend the narrow specializations of academic life. Outside the university community it seeks to recover the public tradition of philosophical discourse which was a lively part of American intellectual life in the early years of this century before the professionalization of both philosophy and religious studies.

Our themes are intentionally broad and inclusive in order to provide a home for a variety of views and projects. Our essays focus on the analysis of quite specific issues within the theme, however, and we encourage our authors to make an autobiographical connection with their analysis. We also emphasize the need for comparative studies. Religious and cultural pluralism is now the inescapable context for all work in the philosophy of religion.

The administration of Boston University and Deans Geoffrey Bannister, Michael Mendillo, and William Carroll of the Graduate School provide continuing budget support, which makes the Institute program possible. Bill Carroll, in his role as Director of the Humanities Foundation at the university, has helped arrange for a special grant to the Institute program from the Foundation. To all these friends and supporters we wish to express our continuing appreciation.

It is our hope that these volumes will provide a resource for critical reflection on fundamental human issues of meaning and value both within academic communities and beyond.

For WALTER G. MUELDER,
extraordinary Dean, exemplary scholar, a
founding father of the Institute for Philosophy and Religion, and a firm friend in our
developing years. His lectures and critical responses for the Institute have given renewed
intellectual integrity and moral seriousness to
the Personalism which he both espouses and
embodies.

Acknowledgments

The editor wishes to express his appreciation to those who have helped in the preparation of this book, especially to the authors of our essays, for their participation in the Institute's lecture program and their work readying their manuscripts for publication. I also wish to thank the editors of *Religious Studies* for their permission to reprint John Findlay's Institute lecture, and the editors of *Theological Studies*, who have previously published an earlier version of Eugene Borowitz's paper.

Irena Makarushka has done her regularly careful and prompt work in copyediting. Barbara Darling Smith has once again taken final responsibility for the Institute's manuscript preparation. She does it with increasing skill and continuing enthusiasm. Without her neither the Institute program nor these publications would be possible.

Our friends at the University of Notre Dame Press are a joy to work with as individual people, and an inspiration as professional colleagues. Ann Rice has given the manuscripts their final form with an easy expertise which is now legendary; and Jim Langford, whose adventuring spirit made the series possible, continues to provide creative ideas and continuing encouragement.

Contributors

EUGENE B. BOROWITZ is founder and Editor of *Sh'ma, A Journal of Jewish Responsibility* and author of several books, including *The Mask Jews Wear* (1974), for which he was awarded the National Jewish Book Award, *Choices in Modern Jewish Thought* (1983), and *Liberal Judaism*, vol. 10 (forthcoming). He was ordained Rabbi by Hebrew Union College and holds doctoral degrees both from Hebrew Union College and from Teachers College at Columbia University. In 1983 he was the first Albert A. List Professor of Jewish Studies at the Divinity School of Harvard University. He is Professor of Education and Jewish Religious Thought at the New York School of Hebrew Union College–Jewish Institute of Religion. He has been visiting professor at Columbia University, Princeton University, Temple University, Woodstock College, and the Jewish Theological Seminary.

MILIĆ ČAPEK, Professor of Philosophy, *Emeritus*, at Boston University, was born in Czechoslovakia and received his Ph.D. from the King Charles University of Prague in 1935. He studied at the Sorbonne in 1940 on a scholarship from the French Foreign office. In 1941 he came to the United States to study at the University of Chicago. He has taught at the University of Nebraska, at Carleton College, and at Boston University, where he was Professor of Philosophy between 1962 and 1975. He has also been a Visiting Professor at the University of California, at Yale University, and at Emory University. He is on the editorial board of *The Encyclopedia of Philosophy* to which he has also contributed many articles. Among his books are *The Philosophical Impact of Contemporary Physics* (1961, 1969), and *Bergson and Modern Physics* (1971). He is also the coeditor of *T. G. Masaryk in Perspective* (1981).

JOHN B. COBB, JR., is Ingraham Professor of Theology at the School of Theology at Claremont and Avery Professor of Religion at Claremont Graduate School, as well as Director of Process Studies there. Born in Kobe, Japan, Professor Cobb received M.A. and Ph.D. degrees from the University of Chicago. Among his books are *A Christian Natural Theology* (1965) and *The Structure of Christian Existence* (1967). More recently he coauthored (with David Ray Griffin) *Process Theology: An Introductory Exposition* (1976) and (with Charles Birch) *The Liberation of Life: From the Cell to the Community* (1981).

ELIOT DEUTSCH is Professor of Philosophy at the University of Hawaii and Editor of *Philosophy East and West*. He studied at the University of Wisconsin, the University of Chicago, and Harvard University, receiving his Ph.D. from Columbia University in 1960. As a Faculty Fellow of the American Institute of Indian Studies, he studied in India 1963–64. He has also been the New York State Faculty Scholar in International Studies (1965–67), and Senior Fellow of the National Endowment for the Humanities (1973–74). Among his many guest lectureships are those at the University of Chicago, the University of London, Lucknow University, Oxford University, and Harvard University. His books include: *Ādvaita Vedānta: A Philosophical Reconstruction* (1969); *Humanity and Divinity: An Essay in Comparative Metaphysics* (1970); and *Personhood, Creativity, and Freedom* (1982).

J. N. FINDLAY is University Professor and Borden Parker Bowne Professor of Philosophy at Boston University. He has studied at Transvaal University College, South Africa; and at Balliol College, Oxford. His doctorate is from the University of Graz, Austria, in 1933. Professor Findlay has written numerous books, including *Meinong's Theory of Objects* (1933), *Hegel: A Reexamination* (1958), *Values and Intentions* (1961), two series of Gifford Lectures entitled *The Discipline of the Cave* (1966) and *The Transcendence of the Cave* (1967), *Ascent to the Absolute* (1970), *Plato: The Written and Unwritten Doctrines* (1974), and *Kant and the Transcendental Object* (1981). Professor Findlay is a Fellow of the British Academy and of the American Academy of Arts and Sciences.

JOHN HICK was born in England and educated at Edinburgh University, Oxford University, and Westminster Theological College, Cambridge University. Presently the Danforth Professor of Religion at Claremont Graduate School, he has also taught at Cornell University, Princeton Theological Seminary, where he was the Stuart Professor of Christian Philosophy; Cambridge University; and Birmingham University. Professor Hick has written numerous books, among them: *Faith and Knowledge, Evil and the God of Love, God and the Universe of Faith,* and *The Second Christianity.* With Brian Hebblethwaite he is the editor of *Christianity and Other Religions.* He has lectured at several universities in India, Sri Lanka, Holland, and Sweden, as well as in the United States, Canada, and Britain.

RAIMUNDO PANIKKAR has lived and studied in Spain, Germany, Italy, and India. He holds a Ph.D. and a D.Sc. from the University of Madrid, and a Th.D. from the Lateran University (Rome). Since 1971 he has been Professor of Comparative Philosophy of Religion and of the History of Religions at the University of California at Santa Barbara. He is the author of more than nine hundred articles and twenty-eight books written in several languages, including *La India: Gente, Cultura, Creencias* (1960), *Religion and Religions* (1964), *The Unknown Christ of Hinduism* (1964), *Kerygma*

*und Indien: Zur heilsgeschichten Problematik der christlichen
Begegung mit Indien* (1967), *The Vedic Experience* (1977),
and, most recently, *Blessed Simplicity: The Monk as Universal Archetype* (1982).

JOSEPH PRABHU received his B.A. and M.A. in Economics from
Delhi University (1966, 1968), his M.A. in Philosophy from
Cambridge University (1976), and his Ph.D. in Philosophy
from Boston University (1982). He has also studied at the
University of Munich and at Heidelberg University. Presently
he is Assistant Professor of Philosophy at California State University at Los Angeles. He has taught at the United Theological College in Bangalore, at the University of California at
Santa Barbara, and at the University of New Hampshire.
His articles have been published in such journals as *Man and
World, Bangalore Theological Forum*, and *Negations*. Currently he is working on a project titled "Yoga and the Quest
for Wholeness."

LEROY S. ROUNER is Professor of Philosophical Theology at Boston University, Director of the Institute for Philosophy and
Religion, and general editor of Boston University Studies in
Philosophy and Religion. He graduated from Harvard College (A.B., 1953), Union Theological Seminary (B.D., *summa
cum laude*, 1958), and Columbia University (Ph.D., 1961).
He was Assistant Professor of Philosophy and Theology at
the United Theological College, Bangalore, India, from 1961
to 1966. He is editor of the Hocking Festschrift, *Philosophy,
Religion, and the Coming World Civilization* (1969), and (with
John Howie) of *The Wisdom of William Ernest Hocking*
(1978), as well as author of *Within Human Experience: The
Philosophy of William Ernest Hocking* (1969). He was Visiting Professor of Philosophy at the University of Hawaii in 1982.

GEORGE E. RUPP is Dean of the Divinity School at Harvard
University and John Lord O'Brian Professor of Divinity. He

studied at the University of Munich and at Princeton University as an undergraduate and pursued his graduate studies at Yale University and at Harvard, where he received his Ph.D. in 1971. In 1969–70 he studied Buddhist thought at the University of Sri Lanka. He has been the recipient of several awards, including the Danforth Graduate Fellowship, the Dwight Fellowship, and the Daggett Prize. His books include: *Christologies and Cultures: Toward a Typology of Religious World Views* (1974); *Culture and Protestantism: German Liberal Theology at the Turn of the Twentieth Century* (1977); and *Beyond Existentialism and Zen: Religion in a Pluralistic World* (1979).

NINIAN SMART, Honorary Professor of Religious Studies at the University of Lancaster and Professor of Religious Studies at the University of California at Santa Barbara, was born in England and educated at Queen's College, Oxford. In 1968 he was awarded an honorary doctorate from Loyola University in Chicago. He has taught at London University and was the H. G. Wood Professor of Theology at Birmingham University. Professor Smart has written and reviewed extensively for numerous journals, and his books include: *Reasons and Faiths* (1958), *Philosophers and Religious Truth* (1964, 1969), *The Religious Experience of Mankind* (1969, 1976), *The Science of Religion and the Sociology of Knowledge* (1973), and, most recently, *World Views: Cross-Cultural Explorations of Human Beliefs* (1983). He has also served as editorial consultant for the British Broadcasting Company's television series *The Long Search*.

FREDERICK E. SONTAG is Robert C. Denison Professor of Philosophy at Pomona College and chairs the Department of Philosophy. He was educated at Stanford University (B.A. 1949) and Yale University (M.A. 1951, Ph.D. 1952). He is a member of Phi Beta Kappa and a Kent Fellow of the Society on Religion in Higher Education. His visiting professorships include positions at Union Theological Seminary (New York),

Collegio di Sant' Anselmo (Rome), the University of Copen-
hagen, and the University of Kyoto. He has also been the
Fulbright Regional Visiting Professor for India, East Asia,
and the Pacific areas. The numerous articles and books he
has written reflect his wide interests. He is the author of *Divine Perfection* (1962), *The Problems of Metaphysics* (1970),
The American Religious Experience (1972), *Sun Myung Moon
and the Unification Church* (1977), and *A Kierkegaard Hand-
book* (1979).

DAVID TRACY is the author of *The Achievement of Bernard
Lonergan: The New Pluralism in Theology* (1970), *A Blessed
Rage for Order* (1975), and *The Analogical Imagination*
(1982). He is also coeditor of the *Journal of Religion* and is
on the editorial boards of various publications, including the
Journal of Pastoral Psychology, Concilium, and *Theology
Today.* Having taught at Loyola University, the North American College in Rome, and Catholic University of America,
Professor Tracy is presently Professor of Theology and a member of the Committee on the Analysis of Ideas and Methods
at the University of Chicago.

Introduction

LEROY S. ROUNER

RELIGIOUS PLURALISM, AS A historic fact, poses the fundamental philosophical problem of the One and the Many in regard to religious truth. It also poses social and political problems. Inter- and intra-religious conflict is responsible for much current warfare; and even benign forms of religious diversity present major difficulties for nation building in the third world. Our focus here, however, is on the philosophical and theological truth question which underlies the social, cultural, and political problems which religious pluralism currently presents. We have not, of course, dealt with every aspect of this critical issue. We have only begun a sketch of the problem and some possible avenues of solution. The Institute for Philosophy and Religion is persuaded, however, that there is no issue more critical for religious believers today than finding a *modus vivendi* with those who trust a different God. The authors of the essays which follow are in the forefront of that quest.

From 1800 to 1970 the people most involved in this issue were Christian missionaries, and it is not incidental that a number of our authors have some connection with missionary thinkers and workers. Prior to the mid-nineteenth-century surge in missionary activity there had been an academic interest in what we have sometimes called the history of religion or comparative religion, but those scholars were usually Christian and were strongly influenced by a deep desire that Christianity should come out on top, as it regularly did. A good example is the early pages of Schleiermacher's book *The Christian Faith*. Primitive religions were at the bottom of the scale, and since there was no readership in that group there was no argument about that. Then there were the other world

1

religions — for Europeans that usually meant Islam and Judaism, although Hinduism was later included in this group of better religions — but they were not historical and incarnational in quite the way Christianity was. So our religion was the best.

The early missionaries weren't even as generous as the scholars. From Greenland's icy mountains to India's coral strand they made it clear that even the other world religions were very bad news indeed, and that the only way to salvation was the version of Christian faith in which they believed. Unlike the scholars, however, the missionaries had the eventual advantage of vital contact. While the scholars were reading sacred texts in German and British university libraries, the missionaries were living cheek-to-jowl with believers in other Gods. In India, for example, the neo-Hindu movement of the nineteenth and early twentieth centuries had produced Ram Mohun Roy, Sri Ramakrishna, Swami Vivekananda, and Mohandas Gandhi, all of whom were in touch with missionary thinkers and activists, and all of whom eventually cooperated with missionaries to bring about social and religious reform. The relation between Gandhi and the Christian missionary Charles Andrews was distinctive but not entirely unusual. The missionaries had gradually discovered that other religious folk knew something crucial about the God who was really God, and were living in devotion to that knowledge.

At the International Missionary Conference in Jerusalem in 1928 there was, therefore, a call for cooperation among the world's living religions. A few years later William Ernest Hocking published *Rethinking Missions*, reinforcing that call. In Germany, however, the collapse of the Weimar Republic and the rise of National Socialism were forcing a radical distinction between those who were prepared to fight for authentic Christian faith and those who capitulated to the Blood-and-Soil tribalism of the Third Reich. This was the crucible from which the New Reformation theology of Karl Barth emerged. His distinctive and triumphant Christianity stood over against all the powers of this world. Among the missionaries, Hendrik Kraemer was Barth's most effective interpreter, and his study volume for the International Missionary Conference in Tambaram, India, ten years later, *The Christian Message in a Non-Christian World*, rejected Hocking's conciliatory thesis as lacking in authentic Christian faith. In the United States after World War

II, Reinhold Niebuhr showed the relevance of Christian faith to political problems, and Dietrich Bonhoeffer's *Letters and Papers from Prison* was a widely-read resource for a politically realistic Christian piety. But both Bonhoeffer and Niebuhr were critical of Barth's religious exclusivism. What had been so effective a rallying cry against Nazi tyranny now seemed unappreciative of the spiritual depth in other religions and unmindful of the need for common spiritual ground in a world threatening to destroy itself. By the mid-fifties, Ernest Hocking's sanguine liberalism had been tempered by existentialist philosophy and the war's confirmation of human sin; and Hendrik Kraemer's theological exclusivism had been softened by his reexamination of a biblical natural theology and a reappraisal of *World Cultures and World Religions*. The new question which both were asking was how Christian faith might fare in what Hocking called *The Coming World Civilization*.

It is this question which motivates many of the contributors to this volume. Most of our authors are Christian because it is the Christian community which has felt the intellectual threat of religious pluralism most keenly. The situation today is comparable in many ways to the threat which Darwinism posed to Christian truth claims in an earlier generation. The careful reader will find much reflection here that is troubled and somewhat anxious as Christian thinkers struggle to find some way of understanding religious truth which does not exclude believers in Gods other than their own.

We begin, however, with the Jewish theologian Eugene B. Borowitz, whose considerable expertise in Christian theology as well makes him an acute commentator on the differences current between the Christian and Jewish communities. Both are historical religions, yet Judaism seems to have been more influenced by historical events, and to have taken them more seriously, than Christianity has. Most current Christian thought, with the exception of liberation theology, seems to him academic and abstract. Jewish thought, on the other hand, especially in the past two decades, has been a response to historic events, especially the Holocaust and the founding of the State of Israel.

Why so? In a cautious conclusion Borowitz speculates that the different attitudes toward historic events derive from different understandings of God's Covenant with humankind. For Judaism God fulfills the Covenant promises to the patriarchs, delivering them from Egypt, giving them the Torah, and establishing them in the Promised Land. This Covenant relationship is understood as continuing, however, to include subsequent everyday historic events in which the people continue as active agents in the Covenant-making process. Perhaps most importantly, they agree to bear the personal and corporate responsibility of being God's Torah in history. In this way Judaism becomes peculiarly able to provide for a modernized religious interest in recent events such as the Holocaust and the founding of the State of Israel. That Christianity should put less emphasis on the revelatory nature of recent historic events seems to him to be in keeping with a rather different understanding of Covenant. God's redemptive activity in Christ is so overwhelmingly gracious as to make humankind more subordinate and passive in relation to God than is the case in Judaism. Further, God's relation to people is more emphatically with individuals than it is in Judaism. But most significantly for the sense of history of each religion, the gracious act of God in Christ is so extraordinary that God's action "cannot have the same sort of continuity in Christian lives that God's partnership has after God's gift of Torah at Mount Sinai." The Christ event has virtually completed the meaning of history, whereas for Judaism God's meaning in and for history is a more continuous unfolding of historic events. Borowitz's intent has been to help two religious communities which were once contentious to understand and live with one another despite their differences by trying to clarify why what seems so obviously critical to Judaism has not been so to Christianity, even though both have lived through the same history.

Frederick E. Sontag is concerned with a more recent American religious phenomenon than the fundamental Protestant-Catholic-Jewish matrix of the traditional melting pot. What of those heretical fringe sects, like the Mormons, the Christian Scientists, and now the Unification Church, which have more recently moved into the mainstream of American religious life? His interest is in the process whereby minority religions come to be an accepted part of the mainstream, and the Unification Church is his primary example. He points out that controversy now surrounding the so-called Moonies is comparable to that of earlier fringe groups, and he anticipates that they will eventually be an accepted part of the American religious scene.

Sontag's brief sketch of Unification life and theology will interest those who know the movement only through media reports. It is characteristic of the movement that it both recaptures elements of traditional Christianity which mainline groups have neglected or abandoned — in this case the expectation of a Second Coming of Christ — and, at the same time, blends in new emphases, such as a focus on the family as the vehicle of salvation. Many Americans found the mass wedding of Unification followers bizarre, especially when the new couples were often virtual strangers. Others, however, have seen this family emphasis as an intra-Christian vehicle for relating to other world religious communities. While Sontag does not make this specific reference, I have a Chinese colleague who refers to the Unification movement approvingly as "the Confucianization of Christianity." Sontag, for his part, is concerned that a much criticized contemporary American religious movement be seen in a historic context, and therefore better understood. Readers may well not be any more enthusiastic about the Moonies after reading Sontag's careful exposition of their history and theology, but this is a good example of an instance where better understanding at least increases one's serious regard.

Borowitz and Sontag were both concerned with comparative studies of American religious life, attempting to understand the ways in which differing religious communities make their claim to religious truth. Milić Čapek shifts the focus of the discussion from the religious community as such to the history and phenomenology of a specific religious and philosophical idea, that of determinism. He shows that determinism has been characteristic of later Hellenized Judaism, early Christianity, Islam, and the thought of the high Middle Ages, as well as the Protestant Reformation. He argues further that modern liberal theology has extended its influence through a secularized scientific version of the older theological determinism. He has three main theses: that theological determinism is a conceptualization of the original religious experience; that this intellectualization of the experience conflicted with other essential aspects of the same experience; and that strict theological predestination and philosophical predetermination are not only morally unsatisfactory but counterempirical and irrational.

Of particular note is Čapek's excursus in defense of his third thesis, wherein he examines the relationship between philosophical and theological determinism, on the one hand, and scientific determinism, especially in physics, on the other. The determinism of modern physics gave support to philosophical and theological determinism in the modern world. Čapek argues, however, that contemporary physics no longer provides a decisive support for classical determinism and that its sole continuing support comes from those logicians who invoke the formal law of the excluded middle as a basis for belief in the eternal truth of some propositions. Quine's doctrine of "eternal sentences" is, in Čapek's view, only predestination without God, and he finds it without either rational or empirical justification.

We conclude this first section of essays on religious pluralism in Western culture with Joseph Prabhu's discussion of modernity as a philosophical and theological tradition. An Indian philosopher who has studied and now teaches in this country, Prabhu questions the philosophical assumptions underlying the equation of modernization with westernization and attacks cultural imperialism. He distinguishes between the humane and the barbarous in Western culture. Countries like India must develop models of modernization appropriately adapted to their own cultural and historical traditions.

The primary vehicle for Prabhu's analysis is the nature of reason itself as it shaped the Western conception of modernity. He focuses on Hegel because of his enormous influence on our understanding of reason. His analysis of Hegel is generally sympathetic, primarily because Hegelian reason is bound to the reality of Spirit. Once that bond is broken, however, and reason becomes purely instrumental, it leads to the seemingly cogent irrationality of planning for nuclear war. This divorce of reason from the good or any notion of value beyond the utilitarian one is the focus of Prabhu's critique of Western modernization. At the end of his essay he returns to Hegel, arguing that Hegel's deification of history and his deification of reason are both the glory and the failure of Hegel's system. It was Hegel's excess in this regard which made Hegel's wisdom concerning the relation of reason to Spirit eventually unavailable to modern consciousness in the West. Prabhu concludes with the suggestion that Hegel's major insight can be maintained only when allied with a religious mythos. He quotes Roberto Unger's statement that philosophy must finally pass into politics and prayer. Prabhu's model for a modern consciousness viable for a country like India is a philosophic wisdom which integrates theory and practice, and grounds both in a religious ultimate.

These initial essays show diverse attitudes toward both history and reason. For Borowitz, the distinctive Jewish attitude toward history is to find God working in present secular events. He finds Christian thought generally more abstract and less historically oriented than Jewish thought. Sontag's sympathetic treatment of new religious movements, however, implies at least that the events of recent religious history are significant for American Christian life. Neither Borowitz nor Sontag is primarily concerned with religious rationality, however, whereas the nature of religious reason is the primary concern for both Čapek and Prabhu. They both point out that obsessive concern for rationality in matters religious leads to a distortion of the religious reality.

With these preliminary excursions as background, our second group of essays deals directly with the theoretical problem of religious rationality. What, after all, *is* religion? What does it claim to know about the human condition and the human prospect? How can it best be studied? What is its relation to other cultural enterprises, such as art? And how is a religion such as Christianity to be understood in relation to a religion such as Buddhism?

This section begins with an essay from Raimundo Panikkar, who argues that truth itself is pluralistic. He points out that most civilizations have been built on a correlation between thinking and being. The metaphysical challenge of pluralism is to break that correlation, confess that thinking is not the controller of being, and assess ways in which various religious traditions, as expressions of being, become what he calls "ever new adventures into the real." Thinking alone does not help much in dealing with reality. We need a new "cosmotheandric confidence" whereby we may be active participants in the life of reality.

Panikkar argues that each religion is distinctive in its features and insights, which must be evaluated in context, since truth itself is pluralistic and each religious community participates in that pluralistic truth. This view may seem to restate an older and discredited syncretism, but syncretism argued that all religions were saying essentially the same thing. His point is that the truth of a religion is not its symbols, myths, and practices, but the interpretation of them. So a true religion is, first of all, pragmatically effective; or, as he puts it, it must "deliver the promised goods to its members." More than that however, it must also be intelligibly coherent. So pluralism is not a supersystem of religious truth. It emphasizes that none of us has an all-encompassing view of reality.

Panikkar's pluralism is a nondualistic philosophy. What he calls the cosmotheandric experience does not have to be totally intelligible in itself. Neither a monism nor a dualism, the pluralism of nondualism is not sheer relativism, because it accepts the view that things *are* only insofar as they are in relation to one another. Pluralism celebrates this relatedness. The nondualistic metaphysics of pluralism is not a static conclusion of a single conceptual truth, but the dynamic interrelationship of varied religious creativities.

David Tracy continues many of these same lines of thought. Religion is not only pluralistic but ambiguous. All definitions of religion inevitably represent a particular and therefore partial perspective. Tracy defends his view with an extensive examination of Kant's notion of limit as it applies to religion. Limit is that which can be thought but not known. As with Panikkar, limit emphasizes that ordinary life experience and the revelatory religious experience of the whole are both cognitively and ethically ambiguous. Religious classics are always in need of new interpretation. Relative adequacy is possible through a discipline which Tracy calls a hermeneutics of religion, and much of his paper deals with directions for developing such an interpretation of religion.

Panikkar's purpose had been to establish pluralism as a metaphysical principle. Tracy's purpose is to apply that metaphysical conviction to methodology in the study of religion. His method would be hospitable to varied schools of interpretation, whether semiotic, structuralist, literary-critical formalist, or whatever, as long as each has its own inner consistency and can acknowledge its partial and limited perspective on the total reality which is religion. Tracy insists that each interpretation is a legitimate moment of explanation in the fuller process of interpretation. The notion of limit makes him particularly sympathetic to the hermeneutics of suspicion, as in Marx, Freud, and Nietzsche.

Eliot Deutsch also works within a nondualistic metaphysical framework and here turns to the relation between art and religion as a way of understanding the place of religion in culture. Art and religion are bound together by a common concern for moral value, but Deutsch notes that this morality has nothing to do with the artist's social behavior or even the artist's motive in creating any particular artwork. It has to do rather with that special celebratory lovingness which informs imagination and intuition and is at the heart of artistic creativity. Without this goodness, art is impossible.

Art and religion also share a common capacity to remake the self. The theistic experience of self-surrender to the divine results in self-transformation. By the same token, Deutsch argues that the aesthetic experience also has transformative power. To experience a work of art, he points out, one must be fully open to it. "Theists may assert God's need for them as well as their need for God, and transfiguration through the relationship; aesthetic experiencers also find themselves to be new beings when they are truly with that artwork whose excellence may rightfully call for rejoicing."

For the most part, Deutsch finds art and religion informing one another through a common spirituality of celebratory lovingness. This extends even to the level of mystical religious experience where religion and art meet, interrelate, and finally separate, for religious mystics dispense with artworks entirely in that abysmal aloneness where they realize Reality itself.

We conclude this section with Ninian Smart's proposal that religious study should not be separated from the study of those other aspects of culture, such as economics and politics, with which it is so closely interwoven. His proposal is that we need a wider category of interpretation for the religious reality, so that its bond with other value-laden and loyalty-invoking culture ventures may be clearly stated. For this purpose Smart suggests that religion is essentially a world view, and that religious study should think of itself as world-view analysis and evaluation.

Having thus broadened religious study and integrated it with other studies of contemporary life, he turns to the problem of conflicting ideologies in the modern world, suggesting that Buddhism and Christianity, as distinct but sympathetic world views, can jointly offer a critique of secular ideologies. He calls for a blend of Christian and Buddhist values in order to promote understanding in the global city: the Buddhist capacity to still those feelings which prevent empathy with others, and a Christian capacity to generate positive feeling toward those who are different from our-

selves. With Panikkar and Tracy he points to the limitation of any
particular world view. He offers this specific analysis of two great
missionary faiths and ways in which they can act jointly in service
of the human community based on what he calls "a new transcendental pluralism."

Our final group of essays continues the exploration of metaphysical pluralism but focuses more specifically on the theological problem which this new perspective poses for Christian thought.
Three of our four authors are teachers in Christian theological semi-
naries, and the fourth, John Findlay, analyzes the theology of Saint
John's Gospel in relation to the spirituality of other world religions.

John B. Cobb, Jr., wrestles with the theological legacy of Ernst
Troeltsch, who forced the issue of religious pluralism on the attention of theologians. His question is this: "How is one to understand
the Christian faith in light of the challenge to its claim to absoluteness constituted by Troeltsch's life work?" He examines the views
of Küng, Pannenberg, Moltmann, Hick, and Wilfred Cantwell
Smith prior to making his own constructive suggestions. Too often,
he finds, there are partly hidden presuppositions in these various
appeals to common ground, particularly in the professed openness
of liberal Protestant thought, with which he is much in sympathy.
His goal, in the words of Dorothee Sölle, is "the indivisible salvation of the whole world." He takes his stand as a Christian, but
he understands Christianity as a living movement. With Panikkar,
he eschews relativism, but embraces a dynamic relationalism in
which all religions are being transformed. He is not afraid of the
Buddhization of Christianity, for example, since to believe in Christ
as "the way, the truth, and the life" is bound up with creative
transformation. Although he does not emphasize the Christian doctrine of the Holy Spirit and its leading into new truth, Cobb's view
has much in common with Ernest Hocking's vision in an earlier
generation.

Spirit, on the other hand, is the focus for John Findlay's reading of Saint John's Gospel. If one conceives of Saint John's God as
a particular among particulars, then his Gospel reads as a hard-
line particularism which Findlay scorns as "a repugnant form of
heteronomous idolatry." But conceive of God as transcending particularity in the same way that God also transcends any form of
abstract universality, and religion and worship acquire perfect sense

and reverence for Findlay. His interest in Saint John continues a tradition among philosophical idealists who have found this Gospel a major resource for spiritual philosophy.

While Cobb, Hick, and Rupp are specifically concerned with historic Christianity and its interaction with other religious communities, Findlay's presupposition is that all religion is grounded in spiritual perception, and that John's Gospel gives voice to that perception. He is mindful that such an interpretation may be "spurned as Gnostic or Alexandrian or Hegelian or simply good old-fashioned New England 'transcendental,'" but Findlay is persuaded that "it remains one that gives the 'good news' of Christianity some purchase on the contemporary mind, and which ensures that its glorious myths, rites, and disciplines will not become 'mere fragments of a faith forgotten.'" With that we are whisked through the text in a spirit of appreciative delight and celebratory wonder which Eliot Deutsch would recognize as a meeting of art and religion. Findlay's indirect challenge to his coauthors is whether their Protestant seriousness may not be missing the point. If worship or celebration is the essence of religion, Findlay could probably make a case that nondualists are closer to the heart of the matter. And if his style is indicative, they seem to have more fun.

John Cobb's interest centered on the dynamic historic life of religious communities, and the thinking which arises from historic experience. John Findlay was not at all concerned with historic experience *per se* but with a perennial insight into the nature of humankind's religious experience. John Hick is concerned with rational analysis of various religious views. Analysis can help us see what is really at stake in various theologies. His is a commonsense approach to the empirical reality of religious life and thought.

In a pragmatic metaphor reminiscent of Panikkar, Hick speaks of religion's concern for salvation or liberation as "the goods conveyed," and he argues that no currently available package of religious goods warrants the term *absolute.* Rather, he suggests, our various religions are products of a large-scale ethnicity. We believe the religion into which we are born. Religious loyalty is therefore much like loyalty to the nation into which we are also born. Hick is less concerned to structure a new basis for Christian loyalties than he is to show that past presuppositions do not bear scrutiny. Focusing on the uniqueness of Christ as central to Christian absolutism,

Hick surveys the views of Geoffrey Lampe and Donald Baillie especially and concludes that reinterpretation of the doctrine of Incarnation no longer necessarily involves the claim to the unique superiority of Christianity.

Hick concludes his review of recent Christologies with a plea that we should develop a theology of religions, and an observation that recent Christologies make it possible for Christians to think without basic inconsistency in terms of religious pluralism.

We conclude with George Rupp's essay on the question of commitment. Christian thinkers are concerned to do justice to those folk whom an imperial Christianity has previously ignored, neglected, and put down. Unless it represents something both valuable and true, however, the easiest way to solve the problem of interreligious conflict would be to give up religion altogether, as many are doing. Rupp confronts the issue of commitment, acknowledging that the foundations for faith have been severely shaken. With the collapse of traditional authorities, Rupp recognizes the same pragmatic concern voiced earlier by Panikkar, Hick, and others. For him, however, the "goods" are less in terms of individual spiritual fulfillment and more in terms of "commitment to more inclusive causes." He gives voice to the concern which Josiah Royce had for the spirit of loyalty, and Ernest Hocking discussed under the general theme of human morale. He develops his thesis with specific reference to feminist concerns for more inclusive religious imagery and institutions, and the ecological concern for limiting growth in our biosphere in order to preserve a viable planet.

Rupp's call is for an inclusive commitment rather than the narrower traditional ones. Like Cobb, he is concerned for a religious life which seeks the salvation of the whole world, but he is especially mindful that this comes only from a commitment within particular communities, where the full range of contemporary experience is taken seriously.

In the thirty years since the Hocking-Kraemer debate, several things have happened. Most obvious is the growth of interest in the philosophical and theological problem posed by religious pluralism. Many more people are writing on the issue than was the case then, and the issue is much more in the popular mind since Vietnam, Iran, and the continuing crisis in the Middle East. While the missionary movement is over, world travel has made it possible for an increasing number of people to have a living experience of different cultures and religions, and this has generally increased empathy for other world views. The new generation of scholars are also folk who combine academic expertise with lived experience in different cultures and among different communities. While Arthur Waley, the distinguished scholar of Chinese philosophy and religion, did all his work in the British Museum and never visited China, most of our authors have had extensive experience in Asia.

For all that, our authors would readily admit that their work is sketchy, preliminary, and subject to much continuing revision. Schleiermacher and his colleagues in the nineteenth century were the last generation to claim an authoritative schema of religious truth. Today we have all gone back to school. There are no experts. The most helpful ones are those who know how much they have to learn.

PART I

Religious Pluralism and Western Culture

1

On the Jewish Obsession
with History

EUGENE B. BOROWITZ

FOR ABOUT TWO DECADES now, Jewish religious thinkers have centered most of their attention on the theological implications of recent historic events. Five distinct interests can be delineated. The first two, the "death of God" and the State of Israel, aroused far more participation than the three other topics I shall explicate.

The early novels of Elie Wiesel and the first group of Richard Rubenstein's theologically revisionist articles appeared in the late 1950s. Yet it was not until the mid-1960s that large-scale Jewish discussion of the meaning of the Holocaust began. I remain convinced that an important factor in finally legitimating this topic was the emergence of the Christian death-of-God movement then. In any case, the debate continued vigorously for about ten years and still sporadically resumes, though in rather ritualized fashion.

What moved the Jewish theoreticians was less the classic issue of theodicy than responding to the actual, awesome events under Hitler. Rubenstein's argument and title (*After Auschwitz*) made Auschwitz the symbol for the new form of an old problem. He, Wiesel, and Emil Fackenheim asserted that the Holocaust was unique in the history of human evil. It therefore demanded totally new responses from Jews. It was, for all its negativity, our Mount Sinai. Wiesel insisted that its singularity took it far beyond our ability even to frame proper questions about it, much less to provide answers. Rubenstein demanded a radical rejection of the received God of Judaism, in whose place he now saw the Holy Nothing. Fackenheim, after years insisting that God's revelation must be

17

the basis of modern Judaism, could no longer speak of God's presence in history. Instead, he built his Jewish commitment on the unconditional command to nurture Jewish life which came to the Jewish people from Auschwitz, though no commander was discernible. The responses to these views were based on new ways of restating the old defenses: it is good that people are free and responsible, even to be Nazis; God is finite; having some reason to have faith, we can trust in God even though we do not fully understand God.

The second major discussion arose out of the Holocaust controversy as a result of the 1967 Israeli Six-Day War. In the weeks prior to and during the news blackout of its first two days, the possibility of another "holocaust" loomed before world Jewry. This mood was intensified by our first experience of war by television. Those experiences were sufficient to arouse Jewish ethnic concern to levels previously unprecedented. They were then heightened by the details of an incredible victory — deliverance — and, even more miraculously, by seeing Jews enter old Jerusalem and, for the first time since the State of Israel had been established, being permitted to pray before the Temple Mount Western Wall.

The effect of those weeks on American Jewry was profound, lasting, and utterly unanticipated. Our new affluence and success in an expanding American economy had made us lukewarm to our ethnic identity and rather indifferent to the State of Israel. The frightful threat and wondrous triumph of the Six-Day War made us realize how deeply Jewish we were and wanted to be, and how organically we were bound to the State of Israel. The growing urban strife in America and the consequent burgeoning of ethnic consciousness in all groups undoubtedly influenced us. And the ensuing years of international isolation for the Israelis and the rise of a new international anti-Semitism strengthened a post-Holocaust community's determination to make Jewish survival primary.

Theologically, the issue became what spiritual weight one should attach to the State of Israel. To Irving Greenberg it was, with the Holocaust, the second irresistible imperative transforming Jewish modernity into a new pluralistic traditionalism. Fackenheim went further. He proclaimed the State of Israel the contemporary absolute of Jewish life. This followed logically on his evaluation of the Holocaust. The Commanding Voice of Auschwitz had laid an unconditional obligation upon the Jewish people to deny Hitler a posthumous victory. The State of Israel was Jewry's collective, life-affirming fulfillment of that commandment. Hence keeping it alive and flourishing was the unimpeachable, overriding Jewish responsibility.

Opposition to this Israelocentrism faced the difficulty of communicating the difference between the extraordinarily important and the essential or indispensable. Specifically, the protagonists of the opposing view sought to establish that, on the biblical model, Jewish statehood must be subordinate to other beliefs, certainly in God, but also in the Jewish people itself. Two political tangents of this discussion deserve mention. The one had to do with the right and criterion of criticizing the Israeli government. The other considered the long-term viability of Diaspora Jewry should the State of Israel disappear.

A third recent theme, notable mainly because our Orthodox writers rarely debate theology, centered about the possible eschatological implications of Old Jerusalem coming under Jewish sovereignty for the first time in nearly two thousand years. Some thinkers, taking seriously their daily prayers for God's return to Jerusalem, saw the spectacular events of 1967 as possibly the first glimmers of the messianic redemption. Other thinkers, chastened by the long, bitter Jewish experience of premature messianism, cautioned against this view, despite its special appeal in explaining our recent experience of terrible travail as "the birth pangs of the Messiah."

Fourth, a broader segment of our community has seen the Vietnam War, Watergate, and other socially disillusioning events requiring them to rethink the old alliance between Judaism and modernity. This has a social as well as an intellectual aspect. American Jews have long considered themselves fully at home here. Some thinkers now suggest that we must revive the category of Exile. To a considerable extent, they argue, Jews are aliens in this society. They propose utilizing the term *Exile* not merely in its existentialist, universal connotation of alienation but in a particular Jewish fashion, in the Bible's nationalistic usage, without thereby yielding to the Zionist secular definition, which is purely political.

A rather more compelling question addresses the balance between the authority of American culture and Jewish tradition. If, in our new realism, our culture is less worthy of religious devotion, then our tradition newly commends itself to us. Not only does it suggest itself as the antidote for our society's ills but it also presents us with an independent source of human value we have long ignored. We therefore need to be "more Jewish" in belief and practice than we have been. The two most exciting spiritual phenomena in our community during the past decade have been the new traditionalism of liberal Jews and the ground-swell founding of *havurot*, small communities for Jewish celebration and experience. Unexpectedly, too, Orthodoxy has emerged as an option for modern Jews desirous of living an authentic Jewish existence. Both movements have parallels in the general American turn to the right. The specific Jewish contours of our developments arise from considering the failures of America and the reemergence of anti-Semitism against our memories of the Holocaust.

Fifth, our most recent issue has come out of our everyday experience in these years. Not long ago many writers were saying that our entire Jewish way of life must now be rebuilt around the Holocaust. With most of us day by day finding normality the basic condition of our lives, that older view seems faulty. Frightful disasters occur and dreadful horrors are still regularly perpetrated. We must never be blind to the hells about us or to the potential of their occurrence. But our lives are very far from a recapitulation of Auschwitz; they are not even greatly illuminated by its uniqueness. Even God, who in Rubenstein's formulation was absent to us— "we live in a time of the death of God"—has reappeared in the living search of at least a minority of the Jewish community.

This transition can most readily be seen in the thought of Irving Greenberg, who has devoted himself wholeheartedly to the intellectual and communal tasks imposed by the Holocaust. In his earliest writing it was not clear whether he seriously dissented from Wiesel, Rubenstein, and Fackenheim, that Auschwitz had taken the place of Sinai for us. Before long he not only gave it equal rank but began speaking of moment-faiths and the continuing place of God in our lives. Most recently he has given further prominence to Jewish continuity, though with the radical revisions required by living in a post-Holocaust age.

It seems to me that abstract, academic themes dominate contemporary Christian theology, save for liberation theology (of

which more later). By contrast, Jewish thinking overwhelmingly
centers on living social questions prompted by recent historical
events. In theological language, my Jewish colleagues are asking,
"What is God saying in what has happened to us?" To be sure, we
do not hear that question articulated in those words. Jews retain
a certain traditional reticence about speaking directly of God.
Surely, too, some of our thinkers remain so sensitive to the agnostic Jewish environment in which they grew up and continue to move
that they habitually bracket out the God-question, preferring instead to speak about the Jewish people or Jewish duty. Nonetheless, our debates involve more than ethnic interests or social concerns. They inevitably reach down to our ultimate convictions
about Jewish responsibility. In the typical selectivity of a secular
generation, we tune out the most important frequencies of our sig-
nals of transcendence.

Before asking how Christian theologians approach recent
events, I think it important to test and thereby try to strengthen
the comprehensive hypothesis I have sought to establish. Let us in-
quire to what extent historic events are a long-term or only a recent Jewish religious interest. The evidence from biblical-Talmudic
Judaism is unambiguous. One might even argue that this religious
concern with history is as unique to Hebrew tradition as is monotheism. The prophets and rabbis regularly sought God's hand in
the major historic occurrences of their time. While the theophany
at Mount Sinai may ground and limit Jewish life, the Bible spends
comparatively little time on what transpired there and devotes itself in great detail to what happened in later centuries when Jews
sought to live by the Torah. Though the rabbis restrict where revelation may be found, they quite organically react to the destruction
of the Temple or to rulers such as Hadrian by indicating what God
is teaching the Jewish people through these calamities.

This pattern of interpreting the triumphs and trials of Jewish history as the operation of God's justice continued until Jewish modernity. Characteristically, it now surfaces among us only
in the speeches of one or another of our European-oriented *yeshi-
vah* heads, that is, the leaders of that part of our community which
has resolutely refused to modernize. For the rest of us, as early as
the nineteenth century, modernization meant secularization, sub-
stituting a scientific world view for a religious one. Those mod-

ernized Jews who maintained some effective belief in God quickly gave up the old mechanistic, Deuteronomic reading of history. The modern concepts of God made history almost entirely the domain of social forces and human moral decisions, not God's direct action.

This modern demythologization of history is of some importance for our theme. Consider, for example, the response of Jewry to the Holocaust of its time, the 1903 Kishinev massacre. Jews worldwide could not imagine such an act occurring among civilized people, and the conscience of much of Western civilization motivated almost universal protest. Despite the pain, the modernists did not try to explain this tragedy in terms of theological verities they had long given up. Rather, the outrage was blamed, variously, on a failure of conscience and reason, a cynical governmental diversion of the masses, a capitalist plot against the proletariat, or a result of the Jews not being expected to stand up in self-defense. Rubenstein's charge, half a century later, that the Holocaust made it impossible to believe in the old God of history may have applied to the Jewish traditionalists who still affirmed Deuteronomic justice in history. However, this interpretation of the death of God simply did not apply to the mass of modernized Jews. They had secularized long before the Holocaust and were largely atheistic or agnostic. Those who had liberal concepts of God knew nothing of a God who was the ultimate omnipotent actor in history.

If so, did secularization mean the end of the classic Jewish perception of history as a continuing scene of God's self-manifestation? A surface examination of liberal Jewish theologies in the early decades of this century bears out that surmise. Hermann Cohen, whose neo-Kantian, philosophic reinterpretation of Judaism set the standard and problem for most of the succeeding thinkers, described Judaism in terms of its central, regulative idea: ethical monotheism. His younger German compatriot Leo Baeck yoked religious consciousness to the master's rationalism and spoke of the essence of Judaism. Both notions derived from German idealism, in which the empirical is radically subordinated to the rational — as good as dissolving history into concept.

I wish to argue that, on a deeper level, this seeming ahistoricalism is itself their response to what God was doing in their history. Their idealistic Judaism arose, though they do not remind us of it, as a means of coping theologically with Jewish Emancipation. The political and social enfranchisement of the Jews in the general society was not one event but, by their time, a century-long process. While most Jews enthusiastically accepted their new human equality, many doubted they could adopt a way of life determined by their society and yet remain authentically Jewish. The decades of experiment in worship, observance, and rationalization finally reached maturity in the thought of Hermann Cohen. If the University of Marburg philosopher did not discuss his system as a response to Emancipation, it was only because he took that move for granted even as he exemplified its benefits. Note that his philosophy of Judaism elevates Judaism's eternal idea against the books tradition says were given at Sinai. He thus validates the authority of contemporary reason in Judaism, making rational relevance the criterion of Jewish authenticity. Baeck employed a similar strategy to reach similar goals. He only expanded the dimension of the immediate experience which Jews would now make sovereign.

As the twentieth century moved on, the succeeding philosophers became more historically self-conscious. Our other great rationalistic system builder, Mordecai Kaplan, is a good case in point. Kaplan justifies his radicalism by pointing to the reinterpretations brought on by the prior major turning points in Jewish history, the Exile and the destruction of the Second Temple. He argues that the Emancipation is another of these, requiring us to rethink and reshape Judaism stringently to our democratic social situation. Since our cultural ethos is scientific, Kaplan reconstructs Jewish institutional life, practices, values, and ideas in naturalistic terms. In this system, American naturalism replaces German philosophic idealism but the function of reason remains the same: to establish the emancipated Jew as the master of the Jewish past, though also its beneficiary. This, once again, is a philosophy of the revelation given by historic events.

A decade earlier in Germany, Martin Buber had reached his unique insight about the reality and authority of genuine interpersonal encounter. In this nonrationalist system, history has renewed importance. The homogenized chronology of rationalism now is accompanied by the personalistic experience that some moments are far richer in meaning than others. By this theory Buber reached the same goal as the rationalists: he had acknowledged the revelatory authority of the Emancipation and met it by giving the present encounter hegemony over tradition.

At the same time, Buber had provided modernized Jews with

a non-Orthodox understanding of how God might be speaking in contemporary events. Israel, the people, can today, as in the past, encounter God, this time in the wilderness of contemporary history. Buber responded to events in his lifetime from this perspective. Zionism was to be the modern counterpart of the ancient Hebrews' corporate relationship with God; the *kibbutz* was the noble Jewish effort to live community in full dimension; the Israeli need to reach out and make common cause with the Arabs was the test of Zionism's Jewishness; though Eichmann was guilty of the most heinous crimes against the Jewish people, Buber argued that it did not befit our character to take his life. The Holocaust so troubled him that he rethought his theory of evil, acknowledging now the terrifying biblical truth that, on occasion, God withdraws from us and God's face is hidden from us.

The other two distinctive system makers of this century, Franz Rosenzweig and Abraham Heschel, would seem the exceptions to my hypothesis. Since I believe I can somewhat mitigate the refutation by way of Heschel, I shall speak first about him, though Rosenzweig wrote nearly half a century earlier.

Heschel interpreted Judaism as a religion centered on time rather than space. But he did not initiate the contemporary Jewish theological interest in historic events. Before 1967, the opposite was actually the case. In his system, which was fully elaborated prior to that fateful year, contemporary history has no role, except perhaps as secularizing villain. I read Heschel's work as a religionist's protest against the desanctification of the world and, in particular, against the liberal secularization of Jewish faith. In quite classic fashion, therefore, Heschel made the recovery of revelation the goal of his apologetics. He thereby returned Sinai and the prophets to their authoritative place and made the rabbis their legitimate interpreters. In his Judaism contemporary history was only another arena for the application of these eternal truths. At that stage his attitude to recent history merely involved him in reversing the liberal Jewish manner of accommodating to modernity, though he retained its ethical thrust.

The return of Old Jerusalem to Jewish sovereignty changed that. Heschel's book *Israel, An Echo of Eternity* movingly describes what this place, Jerusalem, means to him as a Jew, and therefore what this event of return means to Judaism. Intriguingly for so traditionalistic a thinker, he makes no messianic argument. Rather, he limits himself to the theological significance of geography. He provides a phenomenology of standing on the sites which constitute some of the people of Israel's most sacred symbols. Thus, though Heschel's thought was based on the classic tenet that ancient revelation determined contemporary Judaism, he too was religiously overcome by a modern event.

We cannot say the same for Rosenzweig, though it must quickly be noted that he died in 1929 after a meteoric intellectual career, in the last few years of which he was incapacitated by an almost total paralysis. Like Heschel, he saw revelation as the heart of Judaism, though Rosenzweig posited a nonverbal, contentless encounter with God. As a result, Rosenzweig too had no significant doctrine of the Jewish people and, alone of all twentieth-century Jewish thinkers, turned his back on contemporary events. He made history a Christian domain, with authentic Jews already participating in eternity by living the Torah. They thus had no religious interest in what passes for history.

Rosenzweig's thought clearly counts against my argument concerning the centrality of history to modern as to ancient Jewish theology. If he is correct, the concerns of my generation are an accident of our situation, but not Jewishly essential. I think it fair to rejoin that this aspect of Rosenzweig's thought has been an embarrassment to those who would follow him. On the issue of eternity, not the moment, he has been almost totally rejected by the Jewish community on the basis of its lived experience. Any theory that would render the Holocaust and the State of Israel peripheral to being a Jew cannot be right. I suggest that Rosenzweig came to his extreme stand because of his heavy polemic agenda against the opposing views of Judaism, the Orthodox, the liberal, and the Zionist. This caused him to emphasize God and contentless revelation to the detriment of the folk and human aspects of Judaism. Consequently, the philosophical idealism which Rosenzweig was seeking to escape managed to reassert itself and frustrate the proto-existentialism he had creatively initiated to take its place.

Let me sum up my Jewish case by adducing one further piece of evidence. With the exception of Buber, the great system builders give almost no attention to the Mount Sinai experience. The rationalists as good as dissolve it into mind and conscience. Heschel assimilates it to his general theory of revelation as *sym-pathos*, despite his commitment to Sinai's uniqueness. Rosenzweig, describing revelation as love, speaks of Sinai only symbolically. Buber, applying the I-thou relationship to the national level, searches the Exodus account with intriguing personalistic openness. But having devoted one chapter of one work to the topic, he does not return to it. Thus the Jewish concern for history in these thinkers is not attention to a unique occurrence in the past but to the events of their time.

It may well be countered that this is so because the thinkers I have analyzed, except Heschel, are liberal Jews. If only Orthodoxy can be Judaism, my argument again fails. But I see no useful way of debating the issue of what constitutes authentic Judaism. I would only point out how Orthodoxy itself has changed as a result of events. Particularly notable is its about-face toward Zionism. What was almost a complete rejection of this irreligiosity when modern secular Zionism arose, has now become almost total support, mainly enthusiastic but partially grudging. This transformation was not the result of a changed philosophy of history but of a realistic response to what happened. Moreover, I cannot here treat any Orthodox Jewish philosopher because there are no twentieth-century systematic expositions of traditional Jewish faith comparable to those of the liberals. The least that can be said of my hypothesis, then, is that it characterizes such Jewish theology as we have. I gladly acknowledge that I am speaking about liberal Judaism. I must add that the systems I have described raise to the level of academic reflection the beliefs of the overwhelming majority of concerned American Jews.

In turning now to contemporary Christian theology, let me identify a methodological problem. The differing Christian attitude toward recent events I perceive is not totally distinct from that of the Jewish theoreticians. Polemicists prefer to draw battlelines sharply. They force a decisive choice — and then the advocate is tempted to delineate the two stands so as to make the decision well-nigh irresistible. I think no false sense of ecumenism secretly makes me see only indistinct lines of dissimilarity between us. Even in disagreement the positions partially overlap. Living in the same culture, brought ever more closely into contact by democracy, media, and travel, utilizing the same repertoire of civilization symbol-structures, we are bound to be alike. That does not rule out genuine, fundamental opposition, but it explains why seeking to discern where our disagreements begin and leave off is a most subtle and often frustrating task.

To some extent, the greatest similarity in dealing with recent events may be seen in the attitudes of some evangelical Christians and Orthodox Jewish thinkers. Both can discern in the happenings around them signs that the eschaton is breaking in. I do not know how much weight to attach to the different historical valences they consider meaningful. The Christian thinkers work with the negative aspects of events and resonate with vibrations of the power of the Antichrist. Because of Jerusalem, the Jews are overwhelmed by a positive indication the Messiah may be nigh.

Even in this convergence I detect somewhat contrary evaluations of the pre-messianic history in which we stand. The evangelicals seem to me to esteem the Second Coming and its salvation so highly that present events are, by comparison, of small significance. Accepting the Christ and remaining steadfast in one's faith, while devotedly awaiting, even anticipating, his speedy return are the religiously desirable virtues. Obviously, these will affect one's everyday life. But the time frame radically distinguishes between the value of this era and that which was when Jesus walked this earth and that which will be when he returns.

Jews, for all their commitment to the coming of the Messiah, are less eschatologically oriented. God's Torah directs them to the here-and-now, not to the life of the world-to-come, though it awaits them. Their sense of the Messiah remains so human that figures as ordinary as Bar Kochba and Sabbetai Zevi could be taken for the Shoot of Jesse. Though the great eschatological drama of resurrection, judgment, and eternal life ensues in due course, the advent of the Messiah will occur in profane, not transformed, history. I suggest, then, that even on the right we can distinguish between the faiths on this theme. With some hesitation, I find here what I see more clearly elsewhere: the Jewish thinkers can be deeply moved by specific happenings, while the Christian theologians seek to read the signs of the times in general.

The contours of difference emerge more readily when I read less orthodox thinkers. The most dramatic confrontation with contemporary history would seem to occur in the European praxis

theologians like Moltmann and Metz, and the South American lib-
erationists. In the late 1960s I would have described the European
movement as a response to the student revolution and the prospect
of great social change. But for more than a decade now, no particular occurrence — the Polish workers' revolt, for example — has
had anywhere near similar impact. And Hispanic liberation theology likewise seems far more socially than historically oriented.

Something also must be said now about the power of events
to reshape theology. For the Jews, the Emancipation, the Holocaust,
the State of Israel, the gaining of Old Jerusalem, and, potentially,
other happenings can cause fundamental revisions in our thought.
These events changed the thinkers' teaching concerning God and
Torah and, most markedly, their doctrines of the people of Israel.
I do not see historical incidents impinging as strongly on Christian thinkers. Recent experiences may transform Christian witness
and the tone of Christian existence, as in recent years, but I do not
see events causing so fundamental a rethinking of faith among
Christians as among Jews. Somewhat less hesitantly now, I would
identify the Christian concern as responding to the culture generally, while the Jews have reacted more directly to specific historic
occurrences.

Perhaps I can go a step further. The socially oriented Christian theologians seem to me to be answering the Marxists' legitimate criticism of the society and the church. The leftists co-opted
and perverted the church's social ethics. Now that the ethical du-
plicity of the secular critics is plain, the church can reclaim its social values, challenge the Marxists for their institutional failure,
and, by co-opting the Marxist social analysis, renew its mandate
of stewardship. My ethical admiration for that stance does not
change my judgment about our diversity in theologically confront-
ing our time.

Somewhat similar attitudes emerge in two lesser themes of
Christian writing. One is the continuing effort to create a theology of culture. While this activity seems less lively to me in recent
years than it did in the exciting days of H. Richard Niebuhr and
Paul Tillich, little similar work surfaces among Jews. Far less pre-
dictable is the outcome of contemporary Christian thinkers' en-
gagement with Asian religions, now freshly seen as dialogue partners rather than as objects of missionary zeal. I read this as a

broadening of contemporary Christian theology's cultural horizon from barely beyond the West to include the whole globe. Accompanying it has been an enlarged sense of the equality of humankind and the universality of genuine spirituality. This poses a new challenge to Christian as to other faiths' particularity. But these activities fit in well with my earlier speculations about the central orientation of Christian thought.

Even clearer insight is yielded by a retrospective look at the Protestant death-of-God agitation of the mid-1960s. The four theoreticians who formulated the issues under discussion then — Paul Van Buren, Thomas J. J. Altizer, Gabriel Vahanian, and William Hamilton — based their positions, different as they were, on cultural considerations. Altizer's cyclical view of opposing spiritual epochs, based vaguely on Mircea Eliade's view of religion, yielded a negative judgment about Western civilization and contemporary religion. Van Buren called for demythologizing the Son to conform to the philosophic temper of the times. Vahanian and Hamilton examined immediate religious experience and found it empty. In our culture, they proclaimed, God was dead. Not until Richard Rubenstein's writing came to their attention did it occur to them to argue that an event in their lifetime, the Holocaust, was an immediate refutation of the existence of a good and omnipotent God. And the Nazi experience never did play much of a role in their subsequent discussion.

In the near twenty years since those days, some Christian thinkers have acknowledged that, at the least, this event requires some reconsideration of theologies formulated before evil like the Holocaust could be imagined. Roy Eckardt, Franklin Littell, John Pawlikowski, and others have tried to rethink their Christianity in terms of this human and Jewish horror. Paul Van Buren has gone even further and now has begun to study what it might mean to think rigorously of Christianity as an offshoot of Jewish religious experience. Such Christian theologians are doing very much what Jews have done, but I shall not further consider their work. I cannot tell to what extent they are responding to what happened or to the challenge of Jewish colleagues for whom attention to this matter is a condition of dialogue. How such an event might find a proper place in Christian thought remains unclear to me. My doubts arise from the fact that the overwhelming majority of Christian theologians do not yet consider the Holocaust a sufficiently significant event to merit much attention in their thinking.

I have come across only two Christian thinkers who have responded to historic events somewhat as Jews have. Karl Rahner has pondered the theological implications of the declining world influence of Christianity and its potential fall to a minority impulse in Western civilization. To Jews, long accustomed to Christian apologists arguing that the success of Christianity demonstrates its truth, the change in Christian power over the past two decades has been striking. Rahner resolutely rejects all such temporal criteria of worth as contrary to the kenotic traditions of the church. To the contrary, Christianity most authentically fulfills its mission as a servant church. It may now well be required by God to become a church in diaspora, serving in the humility befitting a relatively powerless, scattered institution. But that will only confirm, not contradict, its central truth.

Rahner's effort here is comparable to the reconsideration forced on Jewish thinkers by the Emancipation which drastically changed their social status. But where their experience could compel them to rethink radically the nature of their Jewishness, Rahner's reaction to this apparently substantial historical shift barely impinges upon his central understanding of Christianity. The notion of a church in diaspora is only hinted at in his comprehensive volume *Foundations of Christian Faith.*

A far more direct investigation of the meaning of historical events in Christianity may be found in Wolfhart Pannenberg's *Human Nature, Election, and History.* Pannenberg's interest in history is well known, since he contended in *Jesus — God and Man* that an academic historical approach to the evidence available validates the factual occurrence of Jesus' resurrection. In the last three of these lectures he probes the meaning of historic events since the Christ. He deplores those tendencies in Christianity, from Augustine through Luther and beyond, to separate the true domain of Christian existence from the commonplace realm of sociopolitical affairs. This led, after the collapse of the medieval effort to establish a proper Christendom, to the secular modern state, where religion is reduced to a private activity. Pannenberg calls for a proper recognition of the social dimension of Christianity. He emphasizes the importance of the "people of God" motif in the New Testament and Christian belief, holding it to be more important even than the notion of church, but, in any case, equally significant a doctrine as that of individual salvation.

I was particularly curious to see what he made of this as he applied it to our time. In a paper on contemporary Christologies, I had excoriated Pannenberg for his religious anti-Semitism. He had continued the old Christian-Protestant-Lutheran charge that with the crucifixion the religion of the Jews died. I was outraged that he, a post-Holocaust theologian, in Germany of all countries, seemed to have no consciousness of the social consequences of centuries of such teaching. The anti-Semitism of Christian theology had made it possible for secularists to transform "Judaism is dead" into "Jews should be killed." While reworking this material into book form,[1] I learned that in a work of the early 1970s Pannenberg had modified his earlier view. He then described his prior statement as "the resupposition of a view widespread in German Protestantism, that the religion of the Law and the Jewish religion are identical."[2] But when Richard John Neuhaus kindly brought us together to discuss this matter, Pannenberg could not understand why I should assess his thought in terms of the previous German generation's actions, which, plainly enough, he considered totally reprehensible. I therefore was particularly interested in what he might say about recent historic events.

In his final lecture Pannenberg devotes one long paragraph to the meaning of the two World Wars, which he discusses in terms of modern nationalism. Because it has been secularized, nationalism has been affected for evil as well as for good, as has the other chief organizing principle secularism utilized: liberalism. (Both nationalism and liberalism have Judeo-Christian origins, he argues.) The evil effects on nationalism have been most pronounced, leading to World War I's orgy of European self-destruction and an end to Europe's world domination. Worse, "it meant that the divine vocation that was perceived earlier in experiences of national chosenness had been forfeited by nationalistic self-glorification." He then continues:

> That judgment became definitive with World War II. Among the hardest hit was the German nation. The single most serious reason for that in theological as well as in historical terms

may have been the persecution and attempted annihilation
of the Jewish people. This attempt disclosed to the world the
radical nature of that nationalism. The German case demonstrated in a particularly decisive way the dangerous potential of nationalism, but it is uncertain whether the general
significance of that experience has yet been properly understood in the contemporary world.[3]

The ethical import of this passage is admirable. But it leaves
a Jewish reader troubled. Events can apparently teach a Christian
theologian something about nationalism, in this case particularly
about German nationalism, though here that instance is sublimated
to the world's problem with it. Events do not, in this instance, cause
this theologian to take a hard look at his own religious tradition.
Surely, that such an evil made itself manifest in the birthplace of
Protestant Christianity and still one of its most important intellectual centers is not a trivial matter. How could a nation with such
a vigorous church life, Catholic as well as Protestant, have become
so demonic? Should there not be a thorough critique and rethinking of the intellectual factors in the church which made this
possible?

If we follow the Talmudic dictum of judging others by looking only at the scale of merit, we may say that Pannenberg's lectures, for all that they do not say so explicitly, are a judgment on
and a reconstruction of Christian theology. While Pannenberg
does not discuss Christian theological anti-Semitism here, he does
isolate and correct the basic error he sees in prior interpretations
of Christianity: it was too individualistically oriented and now
needs to take more direct responsibility for the nation in which it
functions. If that is the proper understanding, Pannenberg is one
of the few Christian thinkers I have encountered who have allowed
their basic faith to be modified by recent events.

Can we now provide some reasons for the dissimilar interests
of contemporary Jewish and Christian theologians?

Let us say the simplest yet most important thing first: we do
not know when or where or why God acts. All religions know moments highly charged with meaning and long stretches when memory must take the place of revelation. Who is to say that perhaps

in recent years God chose to act toward the Jews with a directness and significance God did not in the same period manifest to Christians? In other centuries one might have made the same observation the other way around. Let us therefore proceed with great humility. We may be seeking to fathom matters which radically exceed our depth of penetration. But let that not keep us from seeking to explore that which mind and soul make available to us.

In this spirit of tentativeness, two sociological caveats ought to be introduced. To begin with, the distinctive Jewish theological concerns may reflect the situation of those who do it rather than Judaism's essential faith. Most Jews writing in this area are not professional theologians. Their agenda is not set by a well-established guild and they are not centrally concerned with the academic challenges one's seminary or university colleagues may raise. Even those of our writers who are academics work in disciplines other than Jewish theology. As a result, we are far more likely to attend to the realities faced by our community than to the abstract issues made significant by generations of learned, abstract, academic debate.

Second, our community is small, conscious of being a tiny minority everywhere but in the State of Israel and sensitive to the perils to its survival. We magnify every trauma, and having recently undergone previously unimaginable pain — even in terms of the long, anguished history of Jewish suffering — we have been humanly and spiritually changed. But we have also been overwhelmed by several unbelievable triumphs in our time. We can, therefore, often find ourselves quite confused as to how such extremes as we have known can testify to one ultimate reality.

By these familial Jewish standards we find it almost incomprehensible, for example, that when the Christian Lebanese were under severe assault by their Moslem Lebanese brothers and their Syrian allies, there was no Western Christian outcry. Perhaps the vastness of Christianity simply gives a different scale to any individual event. Thus, for all Rahner's genuine humility, he can know that even a diminished church will contain some hundreds of millions of remaining believers. That should surely keep it alive until the Spirit manifests itself again in the church's social status. We do not have this numeric assurance. Nonetheless, Jews may well ask what God is saying to them in keeping them so few and so imperiled. However, with this question about the theology of Jewish sociology, we have moved on to the more important level of our analysis.

I wish to suggest that the differing responses of Jewish and Christian theologians to recent historic events is largely due to their different paradigms of religious reality. For Jews, that is the Covenant with the people of Israel begun at Mount Sinai; for Christians, it is the New Covenant made through the life and death of Jesus the Christ and carried on through the church. If we contrast these two religions to Asian faiths, the many similarities between Judaism and Christianity quickly stand out. The structure and content of the relationships with God clearly show a family resemblance.

Yet there remain major differences between them. For our purposes, let me point to the rather diverse balance each faith gives to God's role and to that of God's human partner in the covenants. I believe we will find this theological divergence determinative of the phenomenon to which I have been calling attention.

In Judaism God initially fulfills the Covenant promises to the patriarchs by expanding Jacob's family to a populous nation, by taking them out of Egypt, giving them the Torah, and setting them as a people on their own Land. The act of receiving the Law-and-Teaching climaxes the early relationship and sets the conditions of all that is to follow. But it includes a commitment to the everyday history which will come after Sinai, in which God's care will regularly make itself felt. Then, too, the people of Israel, though utterly subordinate to their King/Lord/Creator/Only God of the universe, are active agents in the Covenant-making process. More, by assenting to being yoked to this God, they agree to bear the personal and corporate responsibility of living out God's Torah in history. By rabbinic times and the emergence of the doctrine of the Oral as well as the Written Law-and-Teaching, the rabbis become the effective shapers of the continuing meaning of Torah. They then richly endow the ordinary Jew with duties to sanctify life as perhaps only priests had thought of doing in prior times.

With secularization, modern Jewish thinkers transformed the ancient notion of the Covenant. Under the impact of science, God's providence was reinterpreted as less active, while the formerly limited role of human agency in the Covenant was extended almost

to the point of dominance. As I analyze it, this transition did not
negate the old covenantal faith that God was continually involved
in the people of Israel's efforts to live by Torah. Thus, despite modernization, Jews could remain open to the possibility that contemporary history might be revelatory. To put this in the less tortured
language of a simpler age, they could still ask what God was saying to them in their history.

It seems to me that Christianity's New Covenant does not as
easily provide for such a modernized religious interest in recent
events. What is involved, I am suggesting, is a sense of time which,
for all its similarity to Judaism, here exposes its difference.

At the heart of the New Covenant lies God's utterly gracious
and incomparable generosity in sending the Son and thereby assuming personal responsibility for atoning for human sinfulness. God's
act-of-love in the Christ is so extraordinary that God's action cannot have the same sort of continuity in Christian lives that God's
partnership has after God's gift of the Torah at Mount Sinai. To be
sure, when the Parousia comes, all that was promised and foreshadowed in the life of the Christ will be gloriously fulfilled in ways
beyond our imagining. In the interim God does not, of course, for-
sake the newly called-forth people of God. The Holy Spirit is with
them, acting in their lives, their institutions, and their history. But
I am suggesting that the interim work of the Spirit, though real
and powerful, is of a different order than that of the God who gives
a Teaching rather than a person of the triune Godhead. For the
God of the Sinaitic Covenant remains personally involved with
those who, alone in all the world, seek to live by God's Torah.

To better understand the differentiating thrust which will influence contemporary Christian theologians who seek to modernize the classic doctrine of the Holy Spirit, we must first seek what
the traditional notion of the New Covenant makes of the role of
the human partner. To Jewish eyes, Christianity's overwhelming
sense of God's graciousness renders human beings in the New Covenant more thoroughly subordinated and passive in relation to God
than are the Hebrews of the Covenant of Sinai. To be sure, there
are major differences here between Catholic and Protestant teaching. Yet, in terms of the Jewish religious self-perception, Christianity as a whole seems to create a rather different balance between God and humankind. Christianity does call on us to open

our hearts to faith and be ready to receive God's truth. In various interpretations it stresses the importance of the church and the life of sacraments as crucial to salvation. Yet, as Jews view it, in classic Christianity the balance is radically weighted toward God's side by the incomparable act-of-love God once did. Moreover, it should be noted that Christian salvation is primarily directed to the individual by God, though in varying interpretations the group, that is, the church, plays a role in it. Hence what happens to individual Christians is likely to have more significance to them than what happens to their community. Thus, Rahner appears to be predominantly occupied with the individual human being and God, and only secondarily with the church. By contrast, when Pannenberg needs models for his newly socialized Christianity, he draws them almost entirely from Hebrew Scripture.

The modernization of the New Covenant pioneered the radical activation of the human role and the deemphasis on God's providence which is typical of liberal religion What happens to the Holy Spirit in this, and where it is now seen to operate, I am speculating, keeps contemporary theologians from envisioning recent events as revelatory. This is not to argue that events can never play such a role in Christianity. In a previous time, when Providence was strongly activist, the Holy Spirit might be seen in happenings as varied as the Crusades or the Reformation. Today, with our scientific view of existence making the Holy Spirit less likely to be seen as objectively active, historic events retreat in importance for Christians. Rather, with salvation understood in primarily personal terms and religion now conceived of largely in experiential terms, the Holy Spirit is more likely to be seen acting in the inner life of individuals than in the occurrences which befall the church as a whole or some significant part of it. But I have now strained my thesis to its limit. In extenuation, I ask you to remember my intention: I have been trying to clarify why what seems so obviously critical to one faith, Judaism, has not been so to another faith, Christianity, though both lived through the same history.

Perhaps in the clash of all the other factors which affect our perception, understanding our theological lenses does not explain very much. But if it helps enable once contentious religions to understand and live better with one another despite their differences, that will be accomplishment enough.

NOTES

1. Eugene B. Borowitz, *Contemporary Christologies: A Jewish Response* (New York: Paulist Press, 1980).

2. Wolfhart Pannenberg, *The Apostle's Creed in the Light of Today's Questions*, trans. Margaret Kohl (Philadelphia: Westminster Press, 1972), p. viii.

3. Wolfhart Pannenberg, *Human Nature: Election and History* (Philadelphia: Westminster Press, 1977), pp. 104–5.

2

New Minority Religions As Heresies

FREDERICK E. SONTAG

I. THE GENERAL SITUATION AND ONE EXAMPLE

IT IS OBVIOUS THAT all religions must begin as minorities and equally obvious that existing religions must consider the new religion to be a heresy. Either the religious movement is not new, or else it will differ in its belief and practice from established groups. If it did not, there would be no need for the leader to separate himself or herself and call for the formation of a new order. Of course, no existing major religion remains always the same. The question is how the inevitable change takes place. If the established body maintains order internally and is able to moderate the pressure exerted on it to change, the reforming minority can stay within the traditional group and still accomplish its purposes. The difference is that between democratic change within a constitutional framework and a revolution which overthrows an existing order and substitutes a new one. The issue is one of the internal moderation of change versus the disruption of the existing order by a dissident group.

Religious history shows periods of relative calm. Existing religions go unchallenged for a time and then come periods of considerable disruption when a number of new religious groups are born. Anyone aware of the internal workings of a major religion knows that a wide variety of beliefs and practices are tolerated within every sizable religious body. Only small groups can hope to retain conformity and enforce a purity of practice and belief. Dissidents who stay inside existing bodies may be ignored and even remain largely unknown. The group which separates itself from

38

an established community becomes highly visible and thus is a greater source of irritation. Religions vary, of course. Some are by nature less concerned with conformity of practice and orthodoxy of belief. Hinduism and Buddhism are more easily able to accept a wide variety of beliefs than either Western Christianity or Judaism.

Most new groups split off because they become critical of the religious life from which they originate. They seek to restore a purer form of practice or to revise a belief. The new minority religious group will probably be objectionable to its parent body. It will draw fire because it begins by criticizing the existing majority and by claiming to be a vehicle to achieve a purer religious life. The new group may appeal to the unchurched, but the odds are that it will attract its members from already existing religious groups. The original churches then react strongly, because the departure of any member is an implicit criticism of their practice. Defections in any number are based on the claim that the new group is in possession of a superior religious insight. This resulting irritation is heightened if the established group is, for any reason, insecure, and this is likely to be the case since in turbulent religious times new groups emerge primarily because they find existing religions cold and unsatisfying.

The challenge of the new heresy can reawaken enthusiasm and incite reform in the religion which finds itself threatened. This happened when Protestantism spawned the Counter Reformation within Catholicism, which later admitted many of the original Protestant criticisms and incorporated the reforms demanded. This also happened within Judaism after the rise of Christianity. Christianity arose in a time of Jewish laxity, not in opposition to a mainstream of vibrant orthodoxy. Groups which are alive, attractive, and growing in size are not bothered by competing sects. But internal insecurity or uncertainty on the part of the older group exaggerates the reaction and aggravates the conflict. Furthermore, a few new groups do arise quietly and then withdraw from public view. In this case they can be overlooked and are little noticed, until they either establish themselves and receive de facto acceptance or else disappear. However, most new groups are zealous to convert others and vociferous in their criticism of existing religions. In this case, the reaction they draw can be violent.

The Unification Church is an interesting example of such new

religious movements. It began in Korea as a split from the existing Protestant evangelical groups originally transplanted there by
missionary effort from the U.S.A. In this case the situation is complicated by the inclusion of elements of folk religion, Confucianism, and some Buddhist influence. Such a blend of East and West
is not unusual. As a matter of fact, recent scholarship indicates that
much the same situation existed in the blend of locally prominent
religious strains we find incorporated into early Christianity.
Neither Jesus' nor Paul's words represent a pure, untouched strain
of central Judaic belief, but rather they reflect the inclusion of other
religious notions popular at the time. In the nature of the case, a
new religious movement must represent elements other than the
orthodox traditions of its time. Unless it did, it would not have been
called forth and could not distinguish itself.

New movements inevitably center on a new leader, in this case
the Reverend Sun Myung Moon. Neither dissatisfaction nor a new
spirituality can arise disembodied, and the leading figure must be
charismatic in order to attract an original following. The leader
is bound to be controversial too. Sometimes, but not always, new
scripture is written. A new or significantly modified belief must
emerge, but this can take the form of a novel reading of existing
scriptures. Protestantism is of this type. Arguing that existing scripture had been distorted, it called for a return to a primitive and
pure reading. Some reform movements call for a return to an original purity of lifestyle. Others, like Mormonism or Christian Science or Unificationism, involve the receipt of new scriptures, and
this challenge to the authority of tradition makes them even more
disruptive.

When common scriptures are accepted, the return or reunion
of dissenting groups remains possible. When new authoritative texts
arise and are accepted, little is possible except apostasy or conversion, since there is no common basis of appeal to establish religious
authority. In the case of the Unification movement, as long as adherents accept the principle outlined in *The Divine Principle*,[1] they
have a different court of appeal from Protestants, Catholics, or
Jews, and the conflict seems irreconcilable. *The Divine Principle*
claims to be a "completed revelation" that casts existing scripture
in a new light, or reveals the principle of God's operation hidden
within scripture until these later days. As long as adherents accept

this claim, their understanding of traditional scriptures is bound to vary and will contain novelties unacceptable to existing groups.

Converts to the new group, however, often join for quite other than theological reasons. They leave for reasons other than theological disagreement too. They may be attracted first by a person or a lifestyle and so accept novel teachings for extraneous reasons. The disillusionments which force the recent convert out may be a disappointment in the leader or a discovery of the leader's failings. Or, defection may simply come about because the original ecstatic mood that incited the conversion fades or cannot be sustained under the pressures of life's everyday demands. Still, systematically speaking, the position of the new scriptures is key in forming and sustaining the new religion and it explains the hostility which existing religions instinctively feel toward the intruder. The rise of a new leader or a new scripture casts a shadow over existing authority. Both cannot be true. The new movement attracts attention precisely because it casts aspersions on the adequacy of existing leaders, practices, and scriptures. Otherwise, no new movement is called for.

Unificationism understands neither Judaism nor traditional Christianity exactly as they understand themselves, although it is nearer to certain practices within its parent religion (Protestantism) than to others. It might seem that as heretical movements arise they would be radically divergent from the group they protest against. Closer examination reveals that, like the conflict between a parent and a child who are too much alike, the dissident religion does not deny everything its parent belief asserts. In fact, the new set of beliefs is very close to the old set, except for certain central and perhaps determinative changes that are made. We do not object as much to anyone who accepts totally different religious beliefs as we do to one who claims to accept common central doctrines but alters them. We react more strongly to things close to us which are changed by persons who claim to understand them better than we, than we do to new beliefs so esoteric that they bear no relation to existing beliefs.

Consider *The Divine Principle*'s teaching on the Second Coming and the mission of Jesus. Many mainstream Christian groups have either modified, given up, or put out of mind the belief in the Second Coming of Christ which had been traditional since

Jesus' departure. The Moonies, as they are often called, are another in a long line of millennial groups, each announcing in a later day that the time has come for God's intervention now. Of course, there are novelties in the new doctrine, since *The Divine Principle* rejects the notion of Jesus' physical return. Adherents to Unificationism expect another one elected by God to assume that function. Where Jesus' mission is concerned, they believe he was not fated in advance to die. His mission was to marry and establish the restored family which was lost to us in Adam and Eve's fall and banishment from the Garden of Eden. This focus on the family as the vehicle of salvation is an Eastern addition to Western Christianity and is not supported by either scripture or tradition in the West. However, the new interpretation draws objection because it is a change in a long-standing doctrine, not because it is totally novel or unlike any established belief.

II. SOME EXAMPLES IN THE AMERICAN SITUATION

One of the more interesting minority groups to arise in American history, and who have now become established, are the Mormons, or the Church of Jesus Christ of the Latter Day Saints. Though their development will not necessarily follow the same course, the Moonies show many similarities to the Mormons, who began as a "despised and persecuted minority whose existence was considered a national problem."[2] The Mormons were driven across the continent to the wastes of Utah, which they actually felt God had prepared for them by providential action. Joseph Smith began the movement in New York state in his claim to combine a modern revelation with a restoration of primitive Christianity. At that time, New York was the scene of considerable religious agitation. Smith was troubled by the religious controversies of the day and worked hard to study the Bible. The result was his conviction that Mormonism came as a divinely established vessel by God's intervention in American history.

Religious conditions and the state of morals had reached the lowest ebb in our national history at that time.[3] New movements are often born of discontent and a revolt against chaos, whether consciously so or not. America, of course, represents a different religious scene from Europe. "Dissent, enthusiasm, and emotional expression, anti-authoritarianism, anticlericism, and experimentation with new theological ideas characterized much of the American scene."[4] The same could be said of Protestantism as it was transplanted to Korea or to China. Revivalism tends to foster innovation and division at the same time that it sets up an effort to restore lost unity and authority. Mormonism was new and at the same time it claimed to be a basis for uniting all Christians, since it was the restoration of an ancient ideal. Every novel group seems forced to claim that its novelty can overcome the very divisions which it intensifies.

Mormonism represented a growing recognition of free will and the efficacy of human effort versus the absolute sovereignty of God which Calvinism had stressed. Thus, it may be an ancient ideal restored, but it reflects modern sentiments. The West revolted against the denial of human freedom. Mormonism made the meaningfulness of human striving a part of its basic beliefs. The widespread secular optimism of the time was reflected in a religious counterpart, Mormonism, just as *The Divine Principle* is a counterpart for Marx's intention to reform the world and build an ideal order. New religious notions are inspired by secular change, even if their basic impetus is a new spiritual search. It is an oversimplification to think that new religions are born out of this search, then draw a violent reaction, but eventually are accepted whole and unchanged. Mormonism underwent changes in response to the opposition it encountered. This made it acceptable at the same time that it gained recognition. New doctrine is seldom held to wholly as it is first proposed. Circumstances force some parts to be downplayed and other parts to be stressed, perhaps in variously interpreted forms. There is every indication that the Unification Church is going through this same process now as a result of widespread attack.

New spiritual religions attempt to widen the scope of existing religions which the reformer feels has been narrowed, and sometimes they involve an effort to carry religion into the whole of life. When this is the case, the new group risks calling forth just as strong a reaction from secular society as from the established church, since it opposes the cultural mores of the day. The Mormon practice of polygamy, for example, might be more acceptable today but certainly was unacceptable then.

If one starts from inward spiritual experience, that becomes the only spiritual authority for the new convert. Those who follow this religious path naturally become exponents of free will and as such are not open to compromise with either society or existing churches. Their new freedom seems as certain as life itself and cannot be denied. Quakerism is built on such an experience. Along with the Mormons and other dissenting groups, it has always bred hard-core individualists on the American scene. The Anabaptist movement, which became important in America, stressed inward freedom and the denial of any attempt to make Christianity a legislated religion. Anabaptists fought against any effort to subject religion to state control. The need for a revolution in consciousness thus becomes a religious task. All revolutions, whether religious or political, consist in this struggle to be free.

Not all American religious reform movements have resulted in separation as the Mormons and the Quakers did. The social gospel which Walter Rauschenbusch[5] launched had wide impact, but it stayed largely within the confines of existing denominations. Although Rauschenbusch seems to have responded to a spiritual unrest in the day and was in revolt against the growing identification of religion with the culture of his time, he gave voice to a majority opinion, or to one which rapidly became so. In this case, the pressure did not arise to expel the leader and his followers, since they quickly became heroes within the church. Rauschenbusch also wanted to bring God's purpose to a worldly realization, but, unlike Mormonism or the Unification Church, he thought this program could be carried out by existing institutions. Just as Protestantism demanded different institutional forms from those of the Roman church, so the issue with any minority movement is whether its host institution can continue to house it.

Rauschenbusch wrote during the flood tide of progressivism, so his reforming spirit captured a mood of the day more than it opposed it. This congruity between religious message and cultural mood spells the difference between popularity and persecution. Furthermore, Rauschenbusch argued that the institutional church was the best instrument to carry out the needed reform, so he supported rather than opposed existing structures. He brought out a new interpretation, but it did not involve a claim to a new revelation of scripture, a fact which moderated his conflict with existing authorities. He was optimistic about the ability of existing religion to accomplish great reforms. Since it was not a demand that the present religious forms must change, the new movement did not directly challenge existing church hierarchies so fundamentally. They had to respond, but their very existence was not challenged. Rauschenbusch based his campaign on an Old Testament prophetic demand for righteousness,[6] and he cast Jesus in the role of the social reformer.[7] However, he did claim that Jesus had been misunderstood, since the regeneration of social life is at one with the life of religion. The church must carry out the Christian reconstruction of social life, but no revolution in existing institutions or hierarchies is needed to accomplish this reconstruction.[8]

Rauschenbusch links the church with the goal of a "just and even distribution of wealth."[9] It might seem that the introduction of an economic and social issue would draw strong opposition, as it did for other groups. But at least in American society, where social reform schemes are common practice, a proposed theological change or a demanded religious alteration is likely to be more controversial than a new social program. Rauschenbusch linked the church to the fight against poverty. Social welfare was to become the work of the church. "The social movement could have no more powerful ally than religious enthusiasm,"[10] he said. Faith, for him, meant the possibility of a new social order. The common aim of church and state should be to transform humanity into the kingdom of God.[11] Rauschenbusch reflected the growing demand for reform that followed the abuses of the industrial revolution. The minority who is ahead of its time, or against its time, or who must fashion its own social acceptance, faces a more difficult or even negative response.

In the late twentieth century, when Asian religions have begun to attract American youth, the response of the general public is bound to be more puzzled, because of our unfamiliarity with these new attractions. The new groups do not reflect an aspect of American culture past or present. They advocate a total way of life more or less at odds with the mores of middle America. Whereas the gospel of Rauschenbusch could be preached in Protestant pulpits, the Moonie who drops out to live in a communal center and who will work and marry in different ways is another matter altogether. The very legitimacy of the established order is called into question, and this virtually assures that the deviating minority will be persecuted in some way.

The persecution of deviating minorities is not confined to Christianity by any means. Gershom Scholem has written a fascinating account of the Sabbatian movement, "the most important messianic movement in Judaism since the destruction of the Second Temple."[12] Vitality, boldness, and radicalism broke out with surprising strength wherever Sabbatianism appeared, which ought to make us ask what amazing sources of strength it tapped. The Sabbatian movement shook the house of Israel to its very foundations. How can such a heretical minority cause such an impact or draw such a reaction unless it touches something of fundamental concern? All the more surprising in this case is the fact that the new Messiah eventually apostatized (embraced Islam) and publicly betrayed his mission. But the movement spread wide and deep through all classes in Judaism. Evidently such reform calls forth untapped spiritual energies which need to focus on a leading figure but quickly move beyond that need to embrace whole groups.

The utopian and messianic spirit must be deeply embedded in human nature, so much so that it needs an outlet and focal point from time to time. A full examination of the causes of the rise of the Sabbatian messianic movement, and the reasons for its suppression and censorship on the part of the rabbinical tradition, would require a book even larger than Scholem's one thousand pages. My purpose is merely to use it as a dramatic illustration of the need that calls forth these heresies, the power with which they arise and attract, and the strength of reaction they draw from the existing religious establishment. Heresies seem to tell us more about the depth of our religious interests and needs than do more sedate and accepted majorities. This is something like Freud's notion that understanding psychic illness is the best avenue to understand the structure of the normal psyche. Those who preside over orthodox institutions would not have it so, since part of their success lies in the claim to be the authorized version. To say this does not mean that the minority religions are right, or that all majority religions are somehow wrong. But it does say that the new minorities often provide us with the back door to truth.

Viewed in a Jewish perspective, Jesus did not fit a universal image of the Messiah widely held at the time. Rather, as a result of its own experience of the messianic personality of Jesus, Christianity shaped its image of the Messiah after the fact. This being the case, we can understand the violent reaction that anyone who comes after him with messianic claims is likely to receive. Christian messianic hopes have become concretized and poured into the mold of a historical figure. Human messianic hopes are generalized and unspecific as they arise in the depths of the human soul. The challenge of a new messianic claim threatens the security of any fixed mold by awakening us to the realization that what we have settled on is only one among the many ways in which our inherently vague yearnings can be focused. Since part of the religious yearning is to find a solution to the human problem, any challenge to the solution we have accepted is a threat to such stability as we have found. Our situation is inherent instability and we prefer not to acknowledge that directly. In fact, the vagueness of the human longing probably cannot be faced directly, because it has no specific face until we give it one.

"Scripture has seventy faces," an old rabbinic adage tells us. But this is an uncomfortable situation, so that even the modern movement of higher criticism in biblical scholarship can be seen as a messianic movement. It hopes to provide a definite focus to our human longings at last, this time based on a scholarly method rather than on a person.

In the case of the Sabbatian messiah, he gave himself up to evil, just as Faust and the People's Temple did. However, we know that many powerful small movements flourish because they offer a way to deal with the traditional problem of evil. Established religions do also, but their notions have grown cold or overly optimistic, whereas the power of evil constantly threatens us with new destruction.

Thus, the connection powerful new minorities have with evil is close, not distant. This may explain some of their power, the ease with which new converts defect and turn bitter, and the tendency of new groups to commit excesses or even to become destructive. To confront evil is never an easy or a safe matter, and those who are comfortable in existing religions do not like to be disturbed by this news. Where God is close the danger is the greatest. It is quite possible for a new heretical minority to bring its followers closer to God than sedate, correct religions. But it also thrusts the follower into danger.

III. PAUL TILLICH'S ASSESSMENT OF RELIGION

If the above analysis is at all correct, we should come to understand religion better from examining its minority heresies than from studying established orthodoxies. (Of course, to use the term *heresy* is meaningless without reference to some orthodoxy.) This is not so strange where heresies are concerned, except that orthodoxies exhibit the characteristics of any in-power group and would prefer to be understood alone. Tillich has commented on this point in *What Is Religion?*[13] Religion for Tillich is merely one concern alongside other human concerns, not something separate. He argues, however, that the meaning of the concept of religion must be derived from the concept of God, not the reverse. Thus, any orthodoxy inherently claims to have understood God perfectly, while new minorities challenge the completeness of any existing understanding of God.

Tillich uses the concept of the "unconditional" when he speaks about God. Though the unconditioned can be grasped in the religious act, by nature it cannot be rendered into finished systems. The impossibility of this task in itself explains why new attempts spring up: each is trying to achieve the impossible. "Religion is directedness towards the unconditioned,"[14] so that we know its results cannot be finalized but only expressed. "The intention to speak unsymbolically of religion is irreligious,"[15] Tillich says. There cannot be a final statement of orthodoxy as against heresy, since any claim to a final formulation of doctrine is a blasphemy against God. It would reduce the unconditioned to a humanly manipulable object. Minority religious groups spring up as protests against the claims of established groups to finality and thus a lack of openness. Faith, then, is not the acceptance of uncertain objects as true, as it is sometimes said to be; it is a turning toward the unconditioned. There is no way of telling what new movements genuine faith may yet produce, since by nature faith cannot be fixed.

For Tillich, the divine and the demonic always form a polarity in the sphere of the holy. There can be no rest in orthodoxy, much as we might wish it could be so.[16] If we remain unconscious of the demonic, this causes a split in our awareness of God. Since all religion is based on such awareness, there can never be a final form of religion. Early Christianity opened itself to become all-inclusive, whereas only later as it became successful did it consider itself as exclusive. This question arises for Christianity again whenever it encounters other world religions, this time perhaps on a more equal footing.[17] The leaders of the Enlightenment measured Christianity by its reasonableness and wanted to judge all other religions by the same criterion.[18] But Tillich wishes to include the mystical as a key ingredient in religion.[19] If we do that we must give up the notion of a single rational standard for religion by which all may be judged. The idea which was so long accepted — that our goal is to merge all religions into one universal — must be brought into question.

Tillich ends by saying that "a mixture of religions destroys in each of them the concreteness which gives it its dynamic power."[20] If this is true, we must abandon the search for a universal religion and likewise the attempt to place one orthodoxy over others. The continual outbreak of minority religious heresies is a natural outcome of the impossibility of relegating religion to one universal mold. Minority religions spring up to remind us what the life of religion is all about in contrast to the comforting conformity of established religious practice. There can be no single form of practice which sums up all religion, since God cannot be summed up. But there will be constant attempts to do so as humans search for greater security. Heresy is as natural a tendency as orthodoxy, since the religious experience which remains fixed is not authentic.

IV. FROM RELIGION TO THEOLOGY

When new minority movements spring up, we cannot help approaching them from the point of view of some existing theology. That is, we look over each new intruder and point out its excesses and defects and its unfamiliar doctrines. Then, we pronounce it a heresy according to existing theologies which have been neatly worked out. What we forget is that all existing theologies represent later human reflection, philosophically refined, that systematizes and clarifies what did not start out in that form. First, we experience the outbreak of emotion and religious zeal with all its disturbing side effects. Only later do we form a revised standard version. Thus, we are bound to fault any new minority religion for its birth defects, forgetting that all new religions are strange at their inception and gain respectability only after a long process of refinement. Powerful religious movements are not born of careful theological reflection, although that stage is equally necessary if the youthful enthusiasm is to sustain itself to maturity.

If we take Tillich's view of religion as an example, no religion can begin as a rationally constituted system. Even Hegel, our strongest believer in system, recognizes that system is only produced at the end of the process, never at the beginning. In all origins there must exist contradictions and the birthmarks of chaos. For Hegel's opponent, Kierkegaard, there can be a system, but only for God. If religion means the search for God, and if God should turn out to be less structured by nature than even Kierkegaard thought, religions born in the search for such a God are bound to be less than systematic and perfect in their inception. The God they reflect is not perfect in Aristotle's sense of being complete, at rest, and fully formed. Only if God could finally be authoritatively defined could this process stop. But the history and multiplicity of our attempts to define God indicate that the attempt itself may be fruitful and challenging (if it does not become destructive), but the defining of God is never a finished matter.

Thus minorities may never cease to arise in religion so that one orthodoxy can go on unchallenged — indeed, this state of affairs is not even desirable. As with political and economic suppression, we can, of course, try to stop dissidents by violence or by restraining laws. The sad history of what has been called deprogramming in America is one example, the Inquisition in medieval times another. Wars have been fought to establish one religion and then to oust its challengers once it came to power. And it must be admitted that the history of religious conflict has been more destructive than positive. We should not yield to an all-too-American tendency to vaunt unrestrained pluralism as if this were always an unquestioned good. The tendency to enforce orthodoxy and to resist new religious movements undoubtedly grows partly out of the good motive of wishing to stop infighting and destructive competition between various religious groups. The human soul may yearn for an unknown, but its other half also appreciates the solidity of Aristotle's goals to achieve rest and completion.

In spite of the stability and peace which established orthodoxies provide, we must ask what a true reflection of the religious life means and what the search for God involves. Unless we project God in the image of our desire, and then go on to design God to satisfy our fear of what exceeds our capacities, God seems more compatible with a vast plurality of religions than with any single established approach. The ever-changing religious scene reflects the impossibility of finalizing either the definition of God or the human search for a dimension of meaning in our lives. The vast religious spectrum, with all its irreconcilable notions, tells more about God and the vastness of the religious task than any majority view could, no matter how refined.

This does not mean that we must accept every excess, every tragedy and insanity perpetrated in the name of God or under the authority of some new religion. Exactly the opposite. The multitude of new religious minorities which continually spring up tell us that God has not defined deity for us or offered any obvious path for religious expression. That refining, exploring, evaluating, and searching is left to us. But we must protest all censorship or harassment of dissenting groups and new heresies and do so in the name of the God who instituted this variety and gave it to us as the only authentic context for our religious search. This does not mean that all religions taken en masse somehow point to God. Some may be mistaken, demonic, or destructive. Nor does it mean that we are working toward the development of some world religion which will synthesize all. It is still possible that some messiah or one religious group has the right way. But we know that this can never be evident in advance to all.

It seems more likely that God has many faces and can be found by several routes, not one. Successful paths are made known by the good fruits they produce — healing the sick and feeding the hungry — whereas other paths lead to confusion and destruction. But if God has shown no tendency to produce only one scripture with one interpretation, we should learn to live with the risks and problems religious freedom brings. Any enforcement of orthodoxy is the usurpation of a power God denied in allowing so much di-

vergence among religions. Are some innocents destroyed if heresies in religion are not constrained? States have a duty and a right
to outlaw violence and physical coercion. But if we outlaw all the
risks to the individual which minority religions constantly pose,
we block the path to God we seek and misread the most important message God has sent us. We should never let the natural human yearning for security blind us to God's intent to launch us on
an odyssey.

Does this mean that we can never reach rest or find solace in
any religion, and that those who promise it and those who think
they have experienced it are living in an illusion? No, for new minority religions often promise us the peace they cannot secure from
an existing religion. The origin and the very existence of new minority religious groups testifies to the fundamental nature of this
human search to achieve final rest. It can be offered, and it is often
found momentarily within some one religious context. But durable
peace comes only if we face the plurality which God has given us,
and even then it arrives at the end of the odyssey and never at the
beginning.

Are we forbidden to believe the claim of any religion that it
offers us an exclusive way, or the assertion of any theology that it
has a correct doctrine? No, for a doctine may be correct. When
Jesus says, for instance, "I am the way, and the truth, and the life"
(John 14:6), that can be true and believable. But it is significant
that Jesus does not tell us that some particular religious group is
his sole authentic representative or that one theological system is
preferable. God and the persons God chooses to work through are
different from and prior to the various religious groups that rise
up after these theophanies. Theological doctrines come along even
later. Their task is to make the divine intrusion rational and re-
spectable, but God's appearance is always upsetting, difficult to
deal with, and hard to explain adequately. We must accept the fact
that religions are more unsettling than stabilizing when taken as
a whole.

NOTES

1. *The Divine Principle* (Washington, D.C.: Holy Spirit Associa-
tion for the Unity of World Christianity, 1973).

2. Thomas F. O'Dea, *The Mormons* (Chicago: University of Chicago Press, 1957), p. 2.

3. Ibid., p. 9.

4. Ibid., p. 12.

5. Walter Rauschenbusch, *Christianity and the Social Crisis* (New York: Harper Torchbooks, 1964).

6. Ibid., p. 4.

7. Ibid., p. 47.

8. Ibid., p. 198.

9. Ibid., p. 291.

10. Ibid., p. 348.

11. Ibid., p. 380.

12. Gershom Scholem, *Sabbatai Sevi: The Mystical Messiah* (Princeton, N.J.: Princeton University Press, 1973), p. ix.

13. Paul Tillich, *What Is Religion?* (New York: Harper & Row, 1969).

14. Ibid., p. 59.

15. Ibid., p. 71.

16. Ibid., p. 85.

17. Paul Tillich, *Christianity and the Encounter of the World Religions* (New York: Columbia University Press, 1961).

18. Ibid., p. 41.

19. Ibid., p. 58.

20. Ibid., p. 96.

3

Determinism in Western Theology and Philosophy

MILIĆ ČAPEK

I AM GOING TO DISCUSS the rigorous, strict form of determinism according to which every event in the world, including human thoughts, emotions, and actions, is unambiguously determined not only in its general character, but also in its most concrete details. If we take "Western religious tradition" in its broader sense, which would include not only Christianity but also late Judaism and Islam, the ubiquity of this theme is, indeed, striking. Whether it was called providence, predestination, or merely fate, it occurs in later Hellenized Judaism, early Christianity, Islam, the Middle Ages, the Protestant Reformation, and in a major part of modern liberal theology where it merged with the determinism of philosophers and scientists. In truth, modern philosophical and scientific determinism is in many respects a secularized form of the old theological determinism. Despite the terminological divergencies and differences in emphasis, the basic idea of complete predetermination of nature as well as of history remained the same through two and one-half millennia. In other words, what I am *not* going to speak about is the form of determinism which affirms the general dependence of the present on the past without claiming that this dependence is totally restrictive and altogether incompatible with the elements of novelty and individual initiative. If such distinction between what was called hard and soft determinism still appears rather vague, unconvincing, and basically unjustified, it only shows how great the prestige of the strict determinism, whether theological or naturalistic, still remains: the so-called soft determinism thus usually appears as an incomplete form of determinism, whose only true and consistent form is classical predestinationism.

In this essay I shall defend the following three main theses: (1) that strict theological determinism is a result of the accessory conceptualization of the original religious experience; (2) that this growing intellectualization of the original experience was in permanent conflict with the other essential aspects of the same experience; (3) finally, that the notion of strict predetermination was not only morally unsatisfactory and repulsive to the most sincere and sensitive minds, but in its ultimate consequences counterempirical and irrational. The last point will make necessary a brief excursion into the philosophy of science, since without a brief discussion of the present status of determinism in physical sciences our analysis would remain incomplete and unconvincing.

(1) Although the notion of fate or destiny has its roots in mythological and pretheistic thought, it still lacked the definiteness and clarity of the later philosophical and theological determinism. In the Greek tragedies only the final outcome is predestined; thus Oedipus cannot avoid the tragedy, even though he is free to try to avoid it. Apparently the intermediate events, separating the prophecy of the final inevitable tragic event from the fulfillment of the prophecy itself, are themselves not fated; in truth, the very essence of tragedy consists in a vain struggle of human will against fate. In other words, people are free to struggle against fate, but without success. In the later consistent theological determinism the very expressions "against fate" and "against the immutable divine decree" are devoid of meaning; every event is predetermined, including the illusory human feeling that one is free to resist destiny.

Similarly, there is hardly any indication of rigorous and total predetermination in the Old Testament. True, there is a constant emphasis on the overwhelming power of God which will ultimately prevail, but certainly not at once; the divine will is continually thwarted by human disobedience. Only a few passages, such as Exodus 4:21 and 7:3 according to which God "hardens the heart of Pharaoh," foreshadow vaguely the later notion of predestination; but, on the whole, the God of the Old Testament appears to be limited in power and even limited in knowledge, continually disappointed and painfully surprised by the lack of human cooperation which interferes with the realization of divine aims. Furthermore, God's will is far from being immutable; God regrets decisions and revises plans in a way altogether incompatible with the later doctrine of predestination. Election is understood in a collective sense. Israel remains a chosen people but its recalcitrance interferes with the fulfillment of its mission.

Only in the New Testament, specifically in Romans 8:29–30 and 9:11–24, the idea of predestination is stated fully and explicitly and with all consequences ruthlessly drawn out. The omniscience of God implies divine foreknowledge of the future and this implies predestination: "For whom he did foreknow, he also did predestinate to be conformed to the image of his Son, that he might be the firstborn among many brethren. Moreover, whom he did predestinate, he also called: and whom he called, them he also justified: and whom he justified, them he also glorified." Similarly, the First Epistle of Peter speaks of "the elect according to the foreknowledge of God the Father." But there are also in the New Testament other trends which are difficult to reconcile with a strict doctrine of predestination. Thus the famous passage of Matthew 23: 37 on Jesus weeping over Jerusalem rejecting his call; or Jesus' prayer in Gethsemane, which Albert Schweitzer regards as altogether incompatible with the very notion of the eternal and immutable counsel of God.[1] Here there is the main source of chronic conflict between two equally powerful trends in the Western religious tradition: on one side, a fearful awareness of the overwhelming divine power and glory which reduces the human to a mere inert, thing-like instrument of God's all-pervading will (let us recall Saint Paul's brutal metaphor of the potter shaping a lump of clay); on the other side, the persistent emphasis on human initiative, freedom, and responsibility without which every distinction between good and evil, virtue and sin, loses its meaning. This conflict remained unresolved through the whole history of Christianity — in truth, through the whole Western religious tradition. On the theological level it was the antagonism between the monarchic conception of God, with an almost exclusive emphasis on God's power and glory, and the notion of God-Charity, subject to time and even to suffering. All attempts to remove this conflict — sometimes very elaborate and ingenious, but intellectually often not entirely honest — remained unsuccessful and unconvincing.

The monarchic conception of God can be easily traced to the mythological, pretheistic religions. Greek mythology is a good example: a number of local divine kings and queens, each of them ruling over a certain province of nature, and with Zeus having the greatest but obviously not unlimited power. Thus the Greek religion was a henotheism rather than a polytheism; there was a visible tendency to subordinate the plurality of minor gods to one who was the most powerful. Even the early Hebrew religion was of a similar kind, although it is more accurate to characterize it as ethical henotheism. Yahweh was viewed as superior to the pagan deities not only in power, but also in moral character. But the existence of other deities, less powerful and morally inferior, was hardly denied before the period of the great prophets. The notion of the divine seat, still discernible in earliest Judaism, was gradually given up, and as the jurisdiction of Yahweh was extended beyond the mountains of Palestine, Yahweh's omnipresence and omnipotence were more and more explicitly emphasized. We can see it clearly in the magnificent Psalm 139: "Where could I go from thy Spirit, where could I flee from thy face? I climb to heaven — but thou art there; I nestle in the netherworld — and there thou art! If I darted swift to the dawn, to the verge of the ocean afar, thy hand even there would fall on me, thy right hand would reach me." Concomitantly with the ideas of omnipresence and omnipotence, that of omniscience begins naturally to emerge. God, being everywhere, knows everything that is and even what is not yet but will be. "All the days of my life were foreseen by thee, set down within thy book; ere ever they took shape, they were assigned to me, ere ever one of them was mine." Here we see that sadly famous notion of the Book of Life in which everything is written once and for all. It is this Book of Life which later on Saint Thomas identified with predestination (*Summa theologiae* 1.14.1).[2]

But this was one of the rare instances in the Old Testament where the idea of divine foreknowledge was foreshadowed. Despite the accumulation of all flattering attributes, Yahweh still retained a personal character, remaining Supreme Person rather than Supreme Being. We may well say that in Christianity God was at first Supreme Person before becoming Supreme Being. In this respect the philosophical thought of Greece had a decisive influence which began to affect even late Hebrew thought following the conquest of the Middle East by Alexander. Two centuries earlier, in Greece, Xenophanes sharply criticized the crude anthropomorphic ideas of divinity and was probably the first who tried to formulate a philosophical monotheism:

> There is one god, supreme among gods and men; resembling mortals neither in form nor in mind. The whole of him thinks, the whole of him hears. Without toil he rules all things by the power of his mind. And he stays always in the same place, nor moves at all, for it is not seemly that he wander about here, now there.[3]

Note again how omnipresence implies omnipotence; God's power is present everywhere since God by nature pervades the whole of space. But God is not yet beyond time; this last step was made by Parmenides. It is important to dwell on the thought of Parmenides since, as we shall see, it can be said without exaggeration that if geometry remained Euclidian for more than two thousand years, philosophy and, in particular, theology remained basically Parmenidian.

In the philosophy of the Eleatic school, which Parmenides founded, the monism of the previous pre-Socratic philosophers found its most radical expression. While his predecessors believed the single substance underlying the diversity of nature was a concrete or semiconcrete stuff such as water, air, or fire, Parmenides identified it with Being. It was not yet the purely abstract Being of philosophers, since it still possessed spatial characteristics. Parmenides regarded his Being as a homogeneous sphere. But the basic features of the Eleatic Being, its oneness, its homogeneity, its indivisibility, and its changelessness, were retained even when the concept of Being was stripped of its original spatial and materialistic connotations by a great majority of subsequent philosophers and theologians. Plato's Idea of the Good, Aristotle's *actus purus*, Plotinus's Ineffable One, the God of Saint Thomas, the infinite substance of Spinoza, the Absolute Ego of Fichte, the Absolute Idea of Hegel, the Absolute of Bradley, and the notion of Being in Paul Tillich are merely different terminological variations of the same basic theme, the Eleatic One. It is true that nobody after Parmenides went as far as to deny diversity and change altogether, although some of them, like Bradley, came rather near to it. In most instances the concrete realm of nature was not flatly denied but merely degraded to a lower, less dignified status of half-existence, a sort of shadowy reality, floating uncertainly between being and nonbeing. This can be seen in Plato, in Neoplatonism, and, with suitable terminological modifications, in Christianity. This was the only way Christianity could escape pantheism. It was obvious that the God of the prophets and Jesus cannot possibly be the Eleatic One and All, ἕν καὶ πᾶν, unless perhaps in the last eschatological phase of world history, as suggested in I Corinthians 15:28. But there was a lurking latent pantheism present not only in Western and Eastern mysticism, but in Christian theology as well, which more than once became almost explicit — as for instance in Johannes Scotus Eriugena, whose terminology is strikingly similar to that of Spinoza. The persistent conflict between the Eleatic conception of God and theism of the biblical kind is the most characteristic feature of Western religious thought.

Take as an example one of the most important representatives of medieval theology, Thomas Aquinas. His God has all the features of the Eleatic Being except spatiality. God is not only simple, but altogether simple (*Summa theologiae* 3.7); not only one (11.3), but supremely One (11.4). God is not only immutable, but altogether immutable (9.1); not only eternal, but eternal in the sense of Boethius's definition of eternity, "the simultaneously whole and perfect possession of interminable life" (*interminabilis vitae tota simul et perfecta possessio*, 10.1). Needless to say, God is also omnipresent, being present in all things and everywhere (8.1–2). God is thus viewed as an absolutely static and perfect Being whose essence and existence coincide and who is beyond change and time.

At the same time the reader of the first part of *Summa theologiae* can see the author's persistent and almost desperate efforts to breathe some life and religious meaning into the dead Eleatic conceptual framework. By an ingenious but tortuous dialectic Saint Thomas tries to graft ethical and mental qualities on his immutable and ethically neutral Being. He does it by identifying Being and Goodness and quotes Augustine's view that "inasmuch as we exist, we are good." But this device is much older, since it was used by Plato and, before him, by Euclid of Megara, who identified the Socratic Good with the Eleatic One. This leads to an almost Leibnizian optimism: "Every being as being is good" (5.3), and in different words, "All things are good, inasmuch as they have being" (6.4). Thus contrary to the intentions of the author, evil is regarded as either nonbeing or a lesser being and thus loses its serious and tragic character. In a similar fashion, Saint Thomas tries to transform his static and lifeless principle into a living being when he claims that "life can be properly attributed to God" (8.1). But all that his artificial and unconvincing argumentation shows is that he uses the term *life* as a mere metaphorical designation for the eternal self-identity of the same intrinsically lifeless entity. The very fact that Aquinas raises such a question shows that he is uneasily aware of the distance separating his Being from the God of the prophets and Jesus.

His attempts to introduce will and love into his Supreme Being meet with similar failure. Yes, God has the will (19.1) which is the cause of things (19.4) and is not subject to any external cause (19.5); but it is the will which is always fulfilled (19.6) and unchangeable (19.7). It is clear that Aquinas's term *divine will* is merely another name for the rule of the laws of nature, to use a modern term. It is the same old fusion of necessity and providence, of ἀνάγκη and πρόνοια, as we find it in the Stoics and later in Bruno, Spinoza, and modern pantheism in general. In vain does Saint Thomas insist that God's will does not impose necessity on the things willed (19.8) and that God "does not will evil" (19.9); philosophical and theological difficulties cannot be removed by juxtaposing mutually incompatible propositions.

Saint Thomas encounters similar difficulties when he introduces love into his Supreme Being. But this as much as the notion of divine will is closely related to Aquinas's theological determinism exposed in questions 22, 23, and 24 of *Summa theologiae*, where the concepts of providence, predestination, and the Book of Life are discussed.

In reading the specific articles of all these three questions, one must see how intransigent and implacable Saint Thomas's determinism is. Only occasionally is it moderated by what looks like an admission of spontaneity. This is blatantly inconsistent with the theses upheld by him only a few lines before. Thus, after having insisted that everything is subject to the providence of God (22.2), and that God has immediate providence over everything (22.3), he claims that providence does not impose any necessity on the things foreseen (22.4). In question 23 we see his rigorous determinism again with a tiresome repetitiousness: first, human beings are predestined by God (23.1); then, predestination does not place anything in the predestined (23.2); God reprobates human beings (23.3); the predestined are chosen by God (23.4); the foreknowledge of merits is not the cause of predestination (23.5); predestination is certain (23.6); the number of the predestined is certain (23.7); finally, predestination can be furthered by the prayers of the saints (23.8). Here his inconsistency is apparent, since prayers themselves are a part of the providential plan of God. The basic underlying motive is to elevate God's majesty as much as possible and to degrade or even eliminate human initiative and merits altogether. The Protestant Reformers of the sixteenth century are hardly more radical determinists. The most radical among them, Ulrich Zwingli, preaches in his book *De providentia* that God is not only the first cause, but the only cause. He goes even further than Aquinas in claiming that evil as well as good are the work of God, "since what is sin to men who are under his law is no sin to him."[4] True, Saint Thomas does not go so far (Duns Scotus and Occam did); but is not the same view implied when he says that the divine will is always fulfilled (19.6) and that God's power is infinite since God is omnipotent (25.2–3)? In truth, the only restriction which Aquinas imposes on divine power is of a logical kind. God cannot make the past not have been, since this would be inherently contradictory (25.4).[5]

The same metaphysical determinism is implied in Saint Thomas's doctrine of God's knowledge. If God's knowledge is the cause of things (14.8), it must be also the cause of human actions. It is true that he recognizes the contingency of some future events, which would open a place in his system for the freedom of human will. However, he unwittingly eliminates their contingent character by maintaining that God has the knowledge of future contingent things (14.13)! Furthermore, since he equally strongly stresses that God's knowledge is invariable, the alleged contingency of future events, fully anticipated by God, ceases to be genuine. When he still maintains that one can be struck off from the Book of Life, he is simply unaware of his own inconsistency (24.3).

(2) It does not require any particular moral sensitivity to recognize the harsh and cruel character of the doctrine of predesti-

nation. Calvin, one of its most intransigent defenders, explicitly concedes it when he writes *"decretum quidem horribile fateor"* ("I admit that it [predestination] is certainly a horrifying decree"). Nevertheless he does not give it up, since he regards any restriction on divine power and knowledge, including, of course, foreknowledge, as incompatible with the glory of God, as a blasphemy against the majesty of God. He is scandalized by the very thought of God "trembling and uncertain, waiting like a blind person for the decision of man." Like Saint Thomas he denies that God's election is due to foreknowledge of human merits or demerits, since this would make God dependent on humanity and this would be incompatible with omnipotence. Those who deny foreknowledge are mere "arrogant beasts who deserve to be spit upon." Even the fall of Adam was a part of the eternal divine decree. At the same time, Calvin, like Saint Thomas, asserts that God is the cause of everything except sin (*excepto peccato*). He seemingly admits human responsibility, though responsibility only for sin, not for human virtue, which should be always credited to the divine irresistible grace. This inconsistency is due to Calvin's fear of offending God by blaming God for anything. His contradictions show that he is vaguely aware of antagonism between God's moral attributes and God's alleged infinite power. He is visibly embarrassed by the story of Jesus weeping over Jerusalem and he wonders aloud about it: "Couldn't the Almighty have done everything that he wanted? . . . Who could be so foolishly impious to deny that God could not have turned the bad wills of men toward the good whenever and wherever he wanted?"[6] One modern critic of Calvin adds ironically: "Evidently, Jesus was wrong in speaking as he did. He then simply forgot to be a Calvinist."[7]

It is possible that Calvin's hatred and his persecution of his theological opponents was an unconscious defensive reaction against his own doubt. His treatment of Michael Servetus is well known. It is true that Servetus was burned alive because of his denial of the Trinity; but this was not his only heresy — he also rejected predestination in the strongest terms. Another opponent of Calvin, Jerôme H. Bolsec, compared the cruelty of Calvin's predestining god to that of pagan deities such as Moloch; he barely escaped the fate of Servetus. Equally appropriate was the way the unfortunate Servetus characterized the doctrine of predestination:

it reduces the human person to a log or a stone.[8] Yet the very same simile which Servetus and other opponents of predestination used as an objection, Saint Paul used as a favorable argument:

> Thus God has mercy on anyone just as he pleases, and he makes anyone stubborn as he pleases. "Then," you will retort, "why does he go on finding fault? Who can oppose his will?" But who are you, my man, to speak back to God? Is something man has molded, to ask him who has molded it, "Why did you make me like this?" What! has the potter no right over the clay? Has he no right to make out of the same lump one vessel for a noble purpose, another for a menial? What if God, though desirous to display his anger and show his might, has tolerated most patiently the objects of his anger, ripe and ready to be destroyed? What if he means to show the wealth that lies in his glory for the objects of his mercy, whom he has made ready beforehand to receive glory — that is, for us whom he has called from among the Gentiles as well as the Jews? (Rom. 9:18–24, Moffatt trans.)

Like Saint Thomas, like Calvin, like all those who uphold rigorous theological determinism, Paul is uneasy about it, as is evident from the question he raised a few lines before the passage quoted: "Then are we to infer that there is injustice in God?" But he silences this question by denying any human right to ask it. For a piece of clay or a log or a stone has no rights whatever. It is difficult to imagine a more extreme *Verdinglichung* of the human person, to use Jaspers's word, a more complete conversion of the human into a mere thing, than the passage quoted above.

It would be unfair, then, to blame Saint Augustine or Saint Thomas or Calvin for introducing the doctrine of predestination. Its source is clearly traceable to the Epistle to the Romans. In truth, its origin was even farther back in the past — in the philosophical determinism of Greeks, more specifically in Stoicism. It is extremely unlikely that Saint Paul, a highly educated Roman citizen, was unacquainted with the prevailing philosophy of his time. It is true that the old tradition about his contacts and friendship with Seneca has no historical basis; it is even possible that Paul's speech on the Aeropagus in Athens, which has such striking Stoic overtones, is not historically authentic, as Albert Schweitzer, among others, suggested.[9] Still, the affinity between some Stoic ideas and those of Paul is striking despite other important differences. The notion of strict foreordaining is certainly common to the Stoic deterministic pantheism and Paul's deterministic theism. It was via Saint Paul that the notion of strict predetermination penetrated into Western Judeo-Christian tradition.

It is significant that the moral protests against predestination are as old as the concept itself. Plutarch's diatribe against Stoic philosophy, in particular against Chrisippus, is one of the most eloquent and most cogent refutations of the idea of an omnipotent and all-ordaining God. He writes in *De Stoicorum repugnantis* 32–37: "The [Stoics] are always giving fine and human names to God, yet they attribute to him savage and barbarous deeds, yea, deeds worthy of Galatae. . . . It is a horrible thing that vice should be both produced and punished agreeably to the reason of Zeus. . . ." He ridicules the idea that evil is produced by God for some future benefit of the universe, and he remarks: "And to this most beautiful and holy end, I say, what need was there of robbers and murderers, parricides and tyrants?"[10] Evidently, nearly two thousand years before Dostoevski, Plutarch was indignantly "returning the ticket." His opposition to the idea of God as the source of everything, including evil, is of the same kind as that of the opponents of Calvin in Geneva, or that of Arminians to Calvinism in Holland, or that which led John Wesley to sympathize with the Arminians. It was the same attitude which at the time of the Enlightenment inspired Ethan Allen, that unjustly forgotten American popular philosopher, to write:

> To suppose the conduct and demeanor of mankind to have been predetermined by God, and affected merely by his providence, is a manifest infringement on his justice and goodness . . . and it is injurious to the divine character . . . as it would make God the author of moral evil . . . or exclude moral evil from the universe.[11]

Since the sixteenth and seventeenth centuries, when modern science and modern philosophy came into being and modern life became increasingly secularized, the influence of theological thinking generally receded. But theological determinism merely changed its name. It merged gradually with philosophical determinism, whose authority was so much greater since it was based — or at least appeared to be based — on the undeniable verdict of science. Since the times of Galileo, Kepler, and Newton, the concept of scientific, mathematically expressible law had become the very cornerstone of scientific thinking, and successful precise predictions of future events were regarded as triumphant confirmations of rigorous determinism. It is hardly surprising that philosophers in general accepted the determinism of modern science. Until Kant — in truth, until the coming of post-Kantian romantic philosophy — there was hardly any differentiation between science and philosophy. (There is no place here to document this view; let me only recall that the title of Newton's main work is *Philosophiae naturalis principia mathematica*, that as late as the time of Faraday physical experimental researches were called "philosophical investigations," and that one scientific periodical was given the name "Philosophical Magazine.") In the nineteenth century, philosophy, with a few exceptions, remained as deterministic as science even after its ways and the ways of science more and more diverged. It may be said that the concept of strict determination of every event was probably the only idea which philosophers accepted from science completely and without reservation.

The transition from theological determinism to its modern naturalistic form was gradual. I spoke of the lurking pantheism of medieval theology. This pantheism had little chance of becoming manifest as long as the dualism of God and nature seemed to have its justification in the Ptolemaic cosmology, as, for example, in the sharp distinction of the celestial and sublunar world. Giordano Bruno, in removing the last celestial sphere of the fixed stars still retained by Copernicus, Tycho Brahe, and even Kepler, eliminated the last barrier to the unity and infinity of nature and thus paved the way for Spinoza's *Deus sive natura* ("God or nature"), which thus replaced *Deus et natura* ("God and nature"). Pantheism replaced theism. What is even more significant is that Bruno's idea of God, despite his pantheistic reinterpretation, still retained the same Eleatic timelessness present in Neoplatonism and medieval theology. "The divine spirit," writes Bruno in his *Summa terminorum metaphysicorum*, "sees all things in one single act at once, that is, without distinction between the past, present, and future."[12] As before, the notion of divine foreknowledge implied inexorable, strict foreordaining. In this respect, Bruno's older contemporary Calvin would have been quite satisfied. The only thing which changed was that the immutable will of God became an immanent, but no less rigorous, determinism of nature which the nascent classical science began to discover.

This became even more obvious one century later in the thought of Spinoza. As with Bruno, Spinoza was influenced by medieval thought, Christian as well as Jewish; Neoplatonism; the mechanistic philosophy of Greek atomists, modified by Descartes; and, finally, the nascent deterministic science. Spinoza's basic thesis affirming the unity of nature and the rigid necessity of its immanent divine order agreed with that of Bruno. His exposition was far more rigorous, however, and, in the light of the triumphs of the nascent physical science, far more convincing. He ruthlessly drew consequences from these two basic ideas and his anticipations reached far deeper than Bruno's into the future. The spirit of Spinoza's philosophy pervaded the whole of classical science and I believe that it still pervades a larger part of the present scientific establishment. (It probably influenced Einstein's persistent opposition to certain aspects of quantum theory.) According to Spinoza, every contingency, spontaneity, or indetermination is merely apparent. The term *possibility* is devoid of meaning, since it merely betrays our ignorance (Spinoza, *Ethica* 1.33.1). The only meaningful dichotomy in a consistent deterministic scheme is that between necessity and impossibility: whatever happens is necessary and whatever does not happen is impossible. There is no middle ground, no genuine possibilities. He extended deterministic explanations to the whole of reality, including humankind. All teleological explanations were dismissed by him two centuries before Darwin, and his theory of mind and body as two coordinated aspects of the same underlying reality was revived two centuries later by physiological psychology. It exists under minor terminological modifications even today.

All these consequences followed from Spinoza's view of an implicative causal order which happened to coincide with the classical, mathematical, logical view of causality. According to Spinoza, everything follows from the infinite divine substance with the same necessity as the proposition about the internal angles follows from the nature of a triangle. But this "following" should not be understood, as Spinoza explicitly stressed, in a *temporal* sense. It is a tenseless, timeless implication — *ab aeterno et in aeternum sequitur* (Spinoza, *Ethica* 1.17). Spinoza thus, with the perspicacity of genius, discerned the coming trend in physics and in the sciences in general: an assimilation of causal order to tenseless logical implication, or what I would call the container theory of causality. His infinite divine substance became a mediating link between the medieval omniscient God and the "Universal Mind" of Laplace. In the same way as all future details of world history are present in the omniscient divine intellect (Augustine), all future events preexist in the impersonal mathematical order of classical physics. Spinoza still kept the name God, but it was hardly more than a name, especially when the words *sive natura* ("or nature") were added. It was Laplace who achieved its depersonalization and secularization; his answer to Napoleon is well known. Divine omniscience thus became immanent and depersonalized while it retained its rigorously predetermining character. In the minds of some scientists certain theological reminiscences were still present: "To such a mind [the Laplacean omniscient intellect] all the hairs on our head are counted and without its knowledge not a single sparrow falls to the ground."[13] The Laplacean all-embracing formula superseded the Book of Life of Aquinas in which everything was registered in advance once and for all. Although its language was considerably different, its meaning was essentially the same: "everything is given" ("*tout est donné*," as Bergson used to say),[14] and it is of secondary importance if this is expressed in theistic, pantheistic, or atheistic language.[15]

(3) Protests against this gloomy theological determinism were not lacking. From the time of Plutarch until the time of the Enlightenment the incompatibility of predestination with the moral attributes of God had been painfully felt. The situation did not change significantly when, with the coming of classical science, theological determinism either merged with, or was replaced by, the determinism of nature. Orthodox Calvinists welcomed this merger, since they regarded the growing evidence for exact laws in nature as confirmation of their beliefs. A number of more liberal theologians and philosophers were delighted that the capricious God of traditional religion was replaced by the rational God of modern science whose knowledge is perfect and whose will is

immutable. We have merely to glance at the development of modern philosophy: Spinoza and his later disciples; post-Kantian philosophy—Fichte, Schelling, Hegel, Schleiermacher, and the British neo-Hegelians; and the fusion of positivism and pantheism in Herbert Spencer. The spectacle is the same. But in more sensitive minds the emotional reaction to the notion of universal necessity was certainly less cheerful, or at least far more ambiguous. Spinoza's *amor Dei intellectualis* is a mixture of sadness and resignation (Spinoza, *Ethica* 5.19: "He who loves God cannot expect that God should love him in return"); and in Nietzsche's hymn on "The Ring of Necessity" there is an underlying note of despair which probably contributed to his final collapse. The most violent protests against necessity (whether divine or not) can be found in the poets and novelists from Byron to Camus. Modern titanism is a revolt against the omnipotent God or God-nature. "Nature omnipotent and blind," to use Bertrand Russell's words,[16] is one of the most persistent themes of modern literature.

But all such protestations were based on emotional and moral grounds. Were any based on rational and empirical grounds? There were very few in the last century. John Stuart Mill, who was still impressed by the argument from design, rightly concluded that the very notion of design implies the limitation of power in the designer. "The evidences, therefore, of natural theology distinctly imply that the author of the cosmos worked under limitations; that he was obliged to adapt himself to conditions independent of his will and to attain his ends by such arrangements as those conditions admitted of."[17] Mill was also pleased that his notion of a limited God did away with the morally unacceptable attribute of omnipotence but did not exclude omniscience. Whether by *omniscience* Mill understood the integral knowledge of the future is not clear in the context of this passage. It was, of course, impossible to expect from the author of *The System of Logic*, altogether immersed in deterministic science, any critical challenge to what was then the main dogma. Charles Renouvier's doctrine of a God limited in power is more interesting. It is unfortunate that not a single book of his was translated into English, although he decisively influenced William James. The central thesis of his philosophy was his criticism of actual infinity which led him to correct Kant's solution of the famous four antinomies. According to Renouvier, only the theses are correct. Their antitheses are wrong and can be disproved, since they are based on the concept of actual infinity which Renouvier regarded as intrinsically contradictory. Thus the world must be finite in both space and time. There is no such thing as infinite indivisibility of space, time, and matter. There are absolute beginnings (*les commencements absolus*) in nature, hence the possibility of spontaneity and freedom by which new causal series are initiated. From this it follows that there is the First Beginning of the whole cosmic causal series (which makes Kant's discussion of the fourth antinomy, as Norman Kemp Smith observed, superfluous).[18] The audacity of Renouvier's finitism is, indeed, striking. It is less so in the present century when physics seriously considers the reality of physical contingency, the finiteness of space, "zero-time" (the Big Bang theory), and the discreteness of both space and time. It required the perspicacity of William James's genius to recognize the significance of Renouvier's anticipations. Reciprocally, it was Renouvier who was the first to publish James's philosophical essays in French in his *Critique philosophique* even before they appeared in American philosophical journals.

William James's rejection of determinism in his famous essay "The Dilemma of Determinism" betrayed the influence of Renouvier and was seemingly motivated by moral reasons. Rigid determinism excludes freedom and responsibility and destroys any distinction between good and evil because it makes even the most hideous crime a necessary part of the whole. In this respect James's response was nothing new. Plutarch, Servetus, and others made this point long before pragmatism. But in reading James's essay carefully, we can discern another motive, quite different from mere ethical revulsion, which I do not hesitate to call rational or metaphysical.

James pointed out that the classical form of strict determinism, when all consequences are explicitly drawn from it, leads to rather strange and counterempirical conclusions. It converts the universe into a static block in which time is converted into a mere illusory appearance and the future is only a hidden present. Hence his term "block universe." Poincaré used the term "huge tautology."[19] In such a universe there is no novelty, no contingency, no creation, no freedom. "Everything is given"— *tout est donné* — in the words of Bergson, who was developing James's ideas in a systematic way.[20] It was also Bergson who pointed out that the metaphysics of the block universe is a natural philosophy of the human intellect which found its most extreme form in Eleatic philosophy.

What remained unsatisfactory in James's essay was that he apparently affirmed the reality of novelty on the human level only. The prestige of classical determinism in 1884 was such that any general doubts about it appeared rather foolish. Even Bergson in his first book, *Time and Free Will*, confined himself to a defense of human freedom only, though he was already emphasizing the close correlation of time and novelty. At that time only Renouvier, Boutroux, and Peirce held a then heretical view that indeterminacy in the physical world existed, even though at the time it was too minute to be detected experimentally. It was a truly bold anticipation of what began to appear in twentieth-century physics following quantum theory. In the words of Hermann Weyl, the world of modern physics is "the open world," the very opposite of a block universe. He concluded his book by saying that "the old classical determinism of Hobbes and Laplace need not oppress us any longer."[21]

Allow me now to return to one very strange implication of classical determinism, whether philosophical, theological, or even scientific. It is the assertion that, properly speaking, there is no such thing as a genuine, not yet existing future, since what we call the future is a hidden present, known only to God or to the Laplacean Mind. This latter term is merely a metaphorical designation for the timeless order of nature. This assertion runs contrary to our immediate awareness of succession, which is the most pervasive feature of our experience, whether sensory or introspective. To this most obvious objection the defenders of the static view respond in the following way: "We do not deny time; we merely regard it as an appearance. The true reality is beyond time and change, but it *appears* to our limited mind in the form of gradual unfolding." This view was upheld from the time of Parmenides to this century by such thinkers as Bradley, McTaggart, and all those who accept "the mind dependence of becoming." I remember one young colleague who wrote a dissertation on Bradley and who was always correcting me rather indignantly, insisting that for Bradley time is not unreal, but only "apparent." It was rather a naive answer, since the magic word *appearance* does not remove the enormous difficulties of the Eleatic and neo-Eleatic view. At its worst, the word *appearance* is a mere cover word for *unreality* — in other words, a mere semantic trick. (In truth, McTaggart spoke quite frankly and unashamedly about the "unreality" of time.) At its best, it could mean only that reality is split into two completely heterogeneous realms: the true reality which is beyond time and change, and the lower reality which is in time. This is the weirdest type of bifurcation of reality, much worse than the dualism of Descartes, since for him both matter and mind were still in time. How can we conceive of two types of reality whose very coexistence is excluded by their mutually incompatible attributes? If we exclude becoming from the objective world we must still retain it in the psychological subjective realm — otherwise our illusion of time could not even arise.

William James formulated this difficulty clearly as early as 1882 in his comment on Hegel:

> Why, if one act of knowledge could from one point take in the total perspective, with all mere possibilities abolished, should there ever have been anything more than that act? Why duplicate it by the tedious unrolling, inch by inch, of the foredone reality? No answer seems possible.[22]

Indeed, a satisfactory answer cannot be given and certainly has not yet been given. The main reason why it is so difficult to give up strict classical determinism with all its implications is that its rejection seemingly implies its complete opposite — a radical, miraculous indeterminism, a transformation of the universe into a chaos of disconnected events, mysteriously appearing and disappearing without any cause.

James anticipated this objection in his criticism of the block universe, referred to above:

> Nevertheless, many persons talk as if the minutest dose of disconnectedness of one part with another, the smallest modicum of independence, the faintest tremor of ambiguity about the future, for example, would ruin everything, and turn this goodly universe into a sort of insane sand-heap or nulliverse, no universe at all.[23]

Hence the panic about the alleged suicide of reason which led a number of philosophers and even some physicists to oppose the revision of determinism in physics. But such fears are completely unfounded since they are based on an elementary misunderstanding. Determinism has not disappeared from physics. It was superseded by statistical determinism on the microphysical level and its classical form remains approximately valid in the world of our dimensions. Microphysical indeterminacies can have enormous effects on our scale, of course. It is being suggested that living organisms are, so to speak, "amplifiers" of microphysical indeterminacies.[24] The main error of those fearing a collapse of rationality or the suicide of reason, however, is their assumption that there is only one type of rational coherence in the universe, that of tautologous implication, the identity of cause and effect (*causa aequat effectum*). This is not true. Even in the dynamic universe successive events do cohere, but their connection is not of a rigid kind which would wipe out any difference between cause and its effect, any difference between the present and the past. The emergent type of causality is, in fact, more rational and more empirical, since it preserves the very essence of the present. This differentiates it from its causal ancestor and prevents a counterempirical merging of all successive phases into a fictitious timeless pattern. Nobody has stressed the causal (though not predetermining!) influence of the past more than modern process philosophers. One need only recall the fundamental importance of memory in Bergson's thought, and that of causal efficacy in Whitehead. Let those who fear the chaotic universe read "Order in a Creative Universe" in Charles Hartshorne's *Beyond Humanism*.[25]

Today, when physics no longer provides a decisive support for classical determinism, there remains only one last argument in its favor: the traditional formal law of the excluded middle, applied to propositions dealing with all future situations. Obviously, if every proposition is timelessly true, no matter whether an occurrence to which it refers is in the past or in the present or in the future, determinism (even fatalism, as Richard Taylor observed) is unavoidable.[26] This is why Aristotle rejected the validity of the law of the excluded middle for propositions referring to future situations. The statement "There will be a sea fight tomorrow" is now neither true nor false, but objectively uncertain, or merely possible. It was the same concern which inspired the Polish logician Lukasiewicz to invent the three-value logic with possibility (symbolized by ½) as an intermediate value between truth (1) and falsity (0). This is a logical counterpart of the basic thesis of process philosophy that in the open universe possibilities exist in excess of actualities into which they are gradually converted. The traditional opposite view, upheld by a number of logicians including Quine, insists that every proposition is tenselessly true or false, whether or not the facts to which it refers are in existence. But this again leads to a shocking bifurcation of reality. On one side are what Quine calls "eternal sentences," a quasi-Platonic realm of propositions, half of them eternally true, another half eternally false.[27] On the other side is the realm of concrete historical occurrences in which the eternally true propositions are *gradually* embodied. We thus have again what James called "duplication by a tedious unrolling, inch by inch, of the foredone reality,"[28] with all the difficulties mentioned before. Quine and all traditional logicians have a new, usually atheistic, edition of the Book of Life in which everything that has happened or will happen is eternally and unchangingly preregistered in a sort of cosmic refrigerator. It is predestination without God.

I conclude on a more theological note. As Whitehead observed, medieval and modern philosophers acquired an unfortunate habit of paying metaphysical compliments to God.[29] They magnified God's knowledge and power by removing any limit to them, and they were only uneasily and uncomfortably aware that they thus virtually eliminated God's moral attributes — love, justice, and mercy. As Servetus rightly observed, the doctrine of predestination converted the human person into a log or a stone, into a mere *it*, a virtually lifeless puppet in the prearranged cosmic play. Even more serious is that God was thus transformed, unwittingly, into a mere *It*, into Infinite Substance, whose capitalized initials were supplied to save human respect and devotion to what was indifferent and foreign to the human mind. The notion of God as Eternal Thou, the essential component of genuine religious, or at least theistic, experience, is stifled by the conceptual machinery which maximizes flatteringly God's power and glory, thus turning God into a huge, impersonal It and committing, in Whitehead's words, "the deeper idolatry of the fashioning of God in the image of the Egyptian, Persian, and Roman imperial rulers. . . . The

Church gave unto God the attributes which belonged exclusively to Caesar" at the expense of the "brief vision of Galilean humility" which "flickered throughout the ages, uncertainly."[30] The notion of despotic divinity, omnipotent and indifferent, remained always unacceptable to morally sensitive and genuinely religious minds, as much to Plutarch as to contemporary American personalists and process philosophers. It remained so even when it was combined with a worship of the concept of Being, which was basically the same idolatry on a more abstract level. It acquired a great prestige by its alliance with the strict determinism of classical science, especially in physics. But today, in the light of profound revolutionary changes in that science, such alliance has lost its prestige. The notion of predestination is without any rational and empirical justification.

NOTES

1. Albert Schweitzer, *The Mystery of the Kingdom of God* (New York: Macmillan, 1950), pp. 141–44.

2. "Ipsa ergo praedestinatorum conscriptio dicitur liber vitae." In art. 3 Thomas refers to the same view as Augustine's in *Civitate Dei* 22.15: "Praescientia Dei, quae non potest falli, liber vitae est."

3. Charles Montague Bakewell, *Source Book in Ancient Philosophy* (New York: Scribner's, 1909), p. 8.

4. Arthur Cushman McGiffert, *Protestant Thought before Kant* (New York: Harper Torchbooks, 1961), p. 68.

5. "Praeterita autem non fuisse contradictionem implicat."

6. All these Calvin quotations are found in H. Bois, "La prédestination d'après Calvin," *Revue de métaphysique et de morale* 22 (1918): 669–715, especially pp. 674–81.

7. Ibid., p. 674.

8. Roland H. Bainton, *Hunted Heretic* (Boston: Beacon Press, 1953), p. 195; Roland H. Bainton, *The Travail of Religious Liberty* (New York: Harper Torchbooks, 1951), p. 91; Jean Schorer, *Jean Calvin et sa dictature d'après des historiens anciens et modernes* (Geneva, 1948), p. 80.

9. Albert Schweitzer, *The Mysticism of Paul the Apostle* (London, 1931), p. 6.

10. "Plutarch's Refutation of the Stoic Theodicy," in Bakewell, *Source Book in Ancient Philosophy*, pp. 278–89.

11. Ethan Allen, *Reason the Only Oracle of Man* (New York: Scholars Press, 1940), p. 88.

12. *Jordani Bruni Nolani opera latine conscripta* (Florence, 1889) 1.4, chap. 14, pp. 32–33.

13. E. Du Bois Reymond "Über die Grenzen des Naturerkennens," in *Wissenschaftliche Vorträge* (Boston, 1896), p. 39.

14. Henri Bergson, *Creative Evolution* (New York: Random House Modern Library edition, 1944), p. 45.

15. Charles Hartshorne correctly observed that the modern doctrine of necessity is a result of a "secret alliance" between theological and naturalistic determinism ("Contingency and the New Era in Metaphysics," *Journal of Philosophy* 29 [1932]: 429). See also a more detailed and documented analysis in my articles "The Doctrine of Necessity Reexamined," *Review of Metaphysics* 5 (1951): 11–44, especially pp. 14–25; and "Toward a Widening of the Notion of Causality," *Diogenes* 28 (1959): 63–90.

16. Bertrand Russell, "Free Man's Worship," in *Mysticism and Logic* (London: George Allen & Unwin, 1925), p. 48.

17. John Stuart Mill, *Three Essays on Religion* (New York: Henry Holt, 1874). See the essay on theism, pp. 167ff.

18. Norman Kemp Smith, *A Commentary on Kant's Critique of Pure Reason* (New York: Macmillan, 1930), pp. 496–98.

19. Henri Poincaré, *Last Essays* (New York: Dover Books, 1963), p. 112.

20. Bergson, *Creative Evolution*, p. 45.

21. Hermann Weyl, *The Open World* (New Haven, Conn.: Yale University Press, 1952), p. 55.

22. William James, "On Some Hegelisms," in *The Will To Believe and Other Essays in Popular Philosophy* (New York: Dover Books, 1956), p. 271.

23. William James, "The Dilemma of Determinism," in *The Will To Believe and Other Essays*, pp. 154–55.

24. See Appendix 2, "Microphysical Indeterminacy and Freedom: Bergson and Peirce," in my book *Bergson and Modern Physics: Reinterpretation and Reevaluation*, Boston Studies in the Philosophy of Science, vol. 7 (Dordrecht, 1971).

25. Charles Hartshorne, *Beyond Humanism* (Chicago: Willett, Clark, & Co., 1937).

26. Richard Taylor, "Fatalism," *Philosophical Review* 72 (1962): 56–66. On this and similar views see the critical comments of Steven Cahn in his book *Fate, Logic, and Time* (New Haven, Conn.: Yale University Press, 1967).

27. Willard Van Orman Quine, *Word and Object* (Cambridge, Mass.: MIT Press, 1960), p. 193.

28. James, "On Some Hegelisms," p. 271.

29. Alfred North Whitehead, *Science and the Modern World* (New York: Macmillan, 1926), p. 258.

30. Alfred North Whitehead, *Process and Reality* (New York: Macmillan, 1930), p. 520.

4

The Tradition of Modernity

JOSEPH PRABHU

MY TOPIC IS THE philosophy of modernization. At the cost of embarrassing vagueness, I will define it as an attempt to understand our global human condition today. I firmly resist the equation of modernization with westernization. That equation has had disastrous results, both theoretically and practically. I wish to question some of the philosophical assumptions underlying such cultural imperialism. I wish to show that traditions of thought and feeling have been contemptuously dismissed and more often trampled upon, at great cost not just to those traditions but also to the aggressors. Imperialism is the outer manifestation of an inner disease.

Once this critical job is accomplished, the constructive task becomes one of distinguishing between humane aspects of Western culture and those that are simply barbarous. Is the price in barbarity that the culture pays for its alleged progress indeed ineluctable? I shall then ask how countries like India might resist the pressure to borrow slavishly from the West and how they might face the challenge of developing models of modernization creatively adapted to their own cultural and historical traditions. I am not speaking merely of a confrontation between East and West. Structures of technology, mass communication, and world trade, and the possibility of world annihilation make this question an essentially global one.

The single most important notion underlying this modern Western consciousness is that of reason itself. In examining the modern Western understanding of reason I wish to focus on Hegel because of his enormous influence in shaping that consciousness. Modern philosophical consciousness has inherited a very ambiguous legacy from him. There are accordingly three parts to my paper: (1) a sketch of the Hegelian concept of reason; (2) a historical argument showing that the very success claimed for the notion resulted in its historical breakdown and repudiation, and that subsequent philosophy and theology have ever since contented themselves with deliberately limited models of reason; and (3) an attempt to demonstrate that whatever its historical justification, such repudiation is normatively mistaken, and that what is needed is not a jettisoning of Hegelian ambitions, but an effort to place them within an understanding of religion different in its emphasis from that of Hegel. Specifically, what I want to argue is that by his divinization of history, Hegel slights the mythic and transcendent elements of human experience and so prepares the way for our current obsession with history narrowly conceived and the related ideas of will, purpose, project, and so forth, an obsession which, I would contend, has had calamitous results. The metaphysical challenge facing us is to develop a notion of reason that, on its own grounds, leads beyond itself to an openness in faith to the promptings of that spirit which is neither nature nor history but the inexhaustible ground of both. But this is not simply a metaphysical challenge; it is a political and religious challenge as well, taken up at the metaphysical level, on the assumption that political and religious life are guided and conditioned by metaphysical notions. We have to find a way to halt the present narcissistic intoxication with our own powers, often exercised without rhyme or reason.

Hegel's central purpose is to work out a theory of freedom that builds on the Kantian notion of autonomy. Politically this requires overcoming the individualistic, ahistorical, formal, and diremptive Kantian notion of individualistic *Moralität* with Hegel's concept of *Sittlichkeit*, the ethical life of an ongoing community. Religiously Hegel feels that his task is to come up with a doctrine of Spirit somewhat different from the orthodox theistic conception of God, leading as the latter does to an unhappy consciousness forever longing for a fulfillment unachievable in this life and to a master-slave relationship between God and human beings obviously destructive of human freedom as Hegel conceives it. It is important to realize that the overcoming of both political and religious estrangement requires a metaphysical construction that can adequately articulate the relations of nature, history, and Spirit. The problem of society is itself a religious problem, which in turn leads to a speculative metaphysics.

About this metaphysics, let me say just a few, necessarily dense words. Hegel's ultimate goal is to restore the unity of thought and being, not as a static timeless Form, but as a process of formation. This process is both eternal and temporal, since it is the same process looked at from different perspectives which are shown to possess an underlying unity as modalities of Spirit. Thus the unity of thought and being is originative as well as original, inasmuch as both are grounded in the absolute, which timelessly alienates itself-as-thought from itself-as-being. Yet these are two sides of the same spiritual reality. Spirit, says Hegel, "remains with itself in its other."[1] This self-othering, however, has to take a temporal form for it to be a genuine other of the eternal self-activity of Spirit. The unity is thus an achieved unity, and the absolute is essentially a result that contains and fulfills its own process. This is Hegel's distinctive logical idea: a process of pure self-instantiation, which instantiates itself in particulars, and through such a process instantiates itself at the same time as self-instantiation. It has affinities with Fichte's absolute ego, purged, however, of its subjectivism inasmuch as it is a process of pure self-relatedness, with nothing underlying it, that is ontologically prior to selfhood, even though it displays characteristics of the Self in operation.

Its deeper affinities lie, however, with Aristotle's notion of *theoria*, whose ontological and theological components are harmonized in the divine self-reflexivity of theory. For Aristotle, both thought and being are grounded in the unity of Infinite Thought and Being, and are thus not merely finite entities but modalities of the Infinite, which particularizes itself in the finite. Thus, finite reality can only be finite if it is a moment of the Infinite. As far as thought is concerned, God is involved in the knowing process, and any knowledge which stops short of God would not be knowledge in the full sense. Reason is therefore inherently religious.

The crucial difference, however, between Aristotle and Hegel is his historicizing of Aristotelian *theoria* and the notion of a self-sufficient, timelessly complete God that it contains. Hegel fills Aristotle's transcendent *archas kai aitias* with the content of Christian eschatology, seen not in terms of a Kantian *Jenseits* unfulfillable in this life, but in terms of a *Diesseits* that bespeaks a real transformation of this life and whose full meaning lies ahead in the historical future. Hegel's strategy in a sense is to play Kant and Aristotle off against each other within an interpretation of Christianity that anchors and stabilizes its eschatological elements by the historicity of the Incarnation, which points to the already achieved and still continuing transfiguration of the finite. At the same time, it is important to him to preserve the relative transcendence of God in the detachment of theory, a move that prevents a pantheistic identification of God and world, and of Absolute Spirit and World Spirit. This understanding of Christianity allows him to avoid the Scylla of Kantian futurism and the Charybdis of Aristotelian archeology.

The blending of Aristotelian, Kantian, and Christian elements makes Hegel's philosophy essentially a philosophy of history, but as the latter has the absolute as its beginning and end, it is transformed at the same time into a philosophy of religion. Hegel describes his theological philosophy of history as a theodicy, a justification of the ways of God, inasmuch as history is the other side of God's being. But it can be distinguished from an orthodox Christian idea of providence, inasmuch as the Absolute Idea does not operate as an external agent of history, but rather in and through the thought and action of historical subjects. There is, however, a logical cumulativeness and teleology in history, which turns upon the dialectic of subject and object, which in turn is grounded in a notion of divine rational subjectivity. The full grasp of their role as instrumentalities of Spirit transcends the consciousness of historical agents; the "cunning of reason," however, is able to harmonize their actions and passions with the self-realization of Spirit.

Thus Hegel must be considered an essentially religious philosopher, but a religious philosopher of a distinctive kind. On the one hand, he is fiercely critical of supernaturalism, deism, fideism, and religious subjectivism, and the watering down of theological doctrines into ethical, psychological, or existential affirmations. It is not surprising, therefore, that Hegel was suspected of being a profoundly irreligious philosopher. But on the other hand, Hegel explicitly says, "As a matter of fact, the content, need, and interest of philosophy represents something which it has in common with religion. The object of religion as well as philosophy is eternal truth in its objectivity, God, and nothing but God and the explication of God."[2] There are many other passages that make the same point. The clue to Hegel's conception of religion lies in the phrase "eternal truth in its objectivity," which indicates that Hegel sees theology as ontology and First Philosophy, in the manner of Aristotle and Proclus, so that his biographer Rosenkranz's designation of his entire work as *"ein perennierendes Definieren Gottes"* and Heidegger's characterization of it as an "onto-theo-logic" are entirely justified.[3] We are also provided with a clue to the ambiguity at the heart of Hegel's philosophy of religion: it claims to be both a critique and a justification of religion at the same time and in being so is a profoundly original philosophical theology of the order of Aquinas. The hierarchical ordering of everything in the universe that Aquinas accomplishes in terms of his metaphysics of being, Hegel accomplishes in terms of a doctrine of Spirit that finds itself in all things. It was Karl Barth, a surprising admirer in view of his own strongly anti-Hegelian position, who among twentieth-century students of Hegel first saw this clearly:

> It is rather that everything that seems to give theology its particular splendor and special dignity appears to be looked after and honored by this philosophy in a way incomparably better than that achieved by the theologians themselves (with the possible exception of Thomas Aquinas). Theology taken care of once and for all, is here not surpassed in the act of this philosophy, but in fact surpasses itself.

Barth then goes on to ask:

> Why did Hegel not become for the Protestant world something similar to what Thomas Aquinas was for Roman Catholicism? . . . It may be that the dawn of the true age of Hegel is still something that will take place in the future.[4]

It is that question which I now wish to explore. Philosophy after Hegel has accepted his conception of the human being as radically temporal and historical, but it has rejected his claim to have completed and fulfilled time in eternity and history in Absolute Knowledge. What is at stake here may be better described by going a bit more deeply into the relations between time, history, and eternity in Hegel's thought.

Hegel's doctrine of time and eternity may be explicated by contrasting it to two conceptions he criticizes. On the one hand there are interpretations of eternity like that of Kojeve, who interprets Absolute Knowledge as implying the abrupt end of history. On the other hand, we have the notion of endlessness, for which Hegel's model was a straight line extending indefinitely. The first, from Hegel's point of view, is guilty of temporalizing the eternal, while the second is an example of what he calls a bad Infinite because of its essential indeterminateness. Hegel's account of the relation of time and eternity is quite different:

> The finite is perishable and temporal, because unlike the Notion it is not in its own self total negativity; true, this negativity is immanent in it as its universal essence, but the finite is not adequate to this essence. . . . The Notion, however, in its freely self-existent identity as I = I, is in and for itself absolute negativity and freedom. Time therefore has no power over the Notion nor is the Notion in time or temporal; on the contrary, it *is* the power over time, which is its negativity only *qua* externality. . . . The Idea, Spirit, is *eternal*. But the notion of eternity must not be grasped negatively as abstraction from time, as existing, as it were, outside of time; nor in the sense which makes eternity come *after* time, for this would turn time into futurity, one of the moments of time.[5]

Eternity then externalizes or negates itself in time, which is therefore this negativity "only *qua* externality." It can be conceived of as a circle enclosing the whole of time. Given that the enclosing and the enclosed are correlative and call each other forth, it makes no sense to talk of eternity outside of time. Eternity is wholly in time and time is wholly in eternity; but eternity is always complete, whereas time must work its way to real completion in the sense of making possible the final and definitive manifestation of eternity in time. This may appear to be contradictory, because if we say that time is a necessary externalization of eternity, which latter is itself in the process of completion, then is not the completion of eternity dependent on that of time? We must distinguish carefully between logical and temporal orders. Such dependence as eternity has on time is part of its internal self-differentiation and therefore timeless from the point of view of eternity. Spirit as eter-

nity is the annulment of time but its perpetuation in and as history. The categories of the *Logic* already contain a temporal moment as their inner side that requires an outer expression. Thus it
would be senseless to talk of becoming, coming to be, and ceasing
to be, without any events or things that actually did so. And yet
Spirit is pure negativity, negating every form that things and events
do take in time. It is clear then that in talking of time and eternity we are talking of a single reality with two inseparable aspects
or points of view. Time is an essential aspect of Spirit's creative self-
consciousness. As total negativity and the power over time, Spirit
as eternity is distinct from time, but Spirit is like Cronos, "who begets all and destroys what he begets."[6] As self-creating, therefore,
Spirit as eternity is time. Human beings are conscious of their temporality and hence rightly intuit the difference between their status and the eternality of Spirit. But given that time is an element
in Spirit's self-consciousness, our temporality is itself part of eternity, without making eternity itself temporal, and the task of philosophy is to rise above the one-sidedness of the merely temporal
and see eternity manifested in it as the eternal present. "The great
thing," says Hegel, "is to apprehend in the show of the temporal
and transient the substance which is immanent, and the eternal
which is present."[7]

With these clarifications we are in a better position to tackle
the paradoxes of Hegel's philosophy of history. When we speak of
God as being constituted in and through history we should distinguish between the eternal and the historical aspects of such
self-differentiation. It is only on the basis of God's eternal self-
differentiation that history is able to move and to fulfill its role as
the other self of God. The eternally complete but also eternally
self-developing freedom in God grounds its necessary outer expression in history and thus empowers progressive freedom in it. Hegel
emphasizes the point that divine eternal history is the basis of
human history:

> The Idea is ever present; Spirit is immortal; with it there is
> no past, no future, but an essential *now*. This necessarily im-
> plies that the present form of Spirit comprehends within it
> all earlier steps. These have indeed unfolded themselves in suc-
> cession independently; but what Spirit is, it has always been

essentially; distinctions are only the development of this essential nature. The life of the ever-present Spirit is a circle of
progressive embodiments, which looked at in one aspect still
exist beside each other, and only as looked at from another
point of view appear as past. The grades which Spirit seems
to have left behind it, it still possesses in the depths of its
present.[8]

The blending of Greek and Christian elements is quite clear.
Hegel takes a Greek idea of eternal perfection but infuses it, via
the notion of Spirit understood as will and freedom, with real
change and development, rather than conceiving it statically in
terms of the eternal return of the same. This is the basis for the
all-important distinctions between nature and Spirit for Hegel, in
that nature presents endless variations of the same, whereas Spirit
as will and freedom implies real development. "In nature the spe-
cies makes no progress; in the realm of the Spirit, however, every
change is progress."[9] He has an essentially Greek view of the relation of Spirit to time, namely, an everlasting present; but he fills
this notion not with the eternal cycle of nature, well ordered and
self-sufficient, but with the real change made in history by the
coming of Christ ("the nature of God, of being pure Spirit, is revealed to man in the Christian religion"),[10] an event whose historical nature is contained eternally in the essential nature of God.

The metaphysics of history had its beginning and end for
Hegel in the absolute. The failure to understand this, or perhaps
the fact that they understood it too well, made the Left Hegelians
convert this metaphysical historicism into a historicism based solely
on the will, for which the future is primary. For Hegel, on the other
hand, it is the eternal present of the Kingdom of God, manifested
in the Christian Incarnation and anchored historically in the truth
of the unity of human and divine natures revealed in Christ, that
is primary. All history is essentially divine history for which "there
is no past, no future, but an essential now," because "it compre-
hends within it all earlier steps"[11] and future ones too. Hegel is
clearly not a historicist in the conventional sense of someone who
equates truth or reality with the purely contingent process of history. He overcomes such historicism by his insistence that human
history is the appearance of divine history, the laws of whose un-

folding are conceptually accessible to human intelligence as an integral element of divine self-consciousness.

It is this claim of having penetrated divine self-consciousness and articulated the very thoughts of God that rightfully shocked Hegel's successors, as indeed it shocks us too. The repressiveness of the Prussian state, whose social role Hegel seemed to glorify on metaphysical grounds, appalled the Left Hegelians and Marx, who now sought to stand Hegel on his head and translate his retrospective historicism into a historical futurism analyzable in purely secular political terms. The doctrine of the completion of world history and in particular of Western Christendom as a civilization provoked Kierkegaard to denounce Hegel's theological view of history and to substitute for it the absurdity of Christianity embraced in faith, seen now as a leap of decision in the present moment. Nietzsche took the dissolution of the Hegelian synthesis to its ultimate conclusion by proclaiming the bankruptcy of reason and by attempting to put the will and the imagination in its place. It is he who saw more clearly than anyone else at the time that history becomes meaningless without theological underpinning, and that humanist or socialist programs of social reform or evolution avoid asking the nagging question about the meaning of human existence. Finally in Heidegger we have the rejection of the Hegelian notion of the self-clarity of Spirit at the end of history and a substitution of such a metaphysical historicism by "historicity," the ever-receding horizon within which history unfolds, which horizon is not itself history. Heidegger radicalized this temporality and banished eternity completely from the horizon of human existence. His project was itself motivated by Husserl's failure to fuse a Platonic conception of the structure of things with the Kantian doctrine of the transcendental ego.[12] Husserl's *"die Sache selbst"* present within subjectivity soon acquired the temporal character of the transcendental ego. Heidegger accepted the radical temporal finiteness of existing human *Dasein*. Repudiating any notion of the overcoming of such finitude in the complete or absolute thought of beings, he opted instead for a notion of truth as *aletheia*, disclosure, and suggested that the proper human response is an attitude of letting things be.

Much of twentieth-century philosophy is fulfilling Nietzsche's claim of the barrenness of reason once its spiritual support has been denuded. The contemporary crisis of reason has been well charted by Gadamer, Habermas, Stanley Rosen, and Richard Rorty. For those whose affiliation is with analytic philosophy, Rorty's book *Philosophy and the Mirror of Nature* will prove sobering. For what the book shows convincingly is that the issues which analytic philosophers have taken so seriously—empiricist theories of perception, the mind-body problem, theories of meaning and reference—are all generated within a set of historical assumptions which, on examination, turn out to be historically relative and questionable. Thus, Rorty says:

> We owe the notion of a "theory of knowledge" based on an understanding of "mental processes" to the seventeenth century and especially to Locke. We owe the notion of "the mind" as a separate entity in which "processes" occur to the same period and especially to Descartes. We owe the notion of philosophy as the tribunal of pure reason, upholding or denying the claims of the rest of the culture, to the eighteenth century, and especially to Kant, but this Kantian notion presupposed general assent to Lockean notions of mental processes and Cartesian notions of mental substance.[13]

But Rorty is concerned not just with tracing the genealogy of these ideas, but with showing that they cannot sustain the claims of a rock-bottom, foundational status made for them. Rorty's own suggestion is a Wittgensteinian one: to free the philosopher-fly from the fly-bottle constituted by certain pictures that hold him or her captive, and to discourage the philosopher-fly, once having attained liberation, from getting right back in again. If Rorty had performed the same deconstructionist job on Wittgenstein that he does on other analytic philosophers he would have seen that the notion of philosophy as therapy is not only parasitic but also historically specific, rising out of the particular unrest of fin-de-siècle Vienna and symptomatic of the very spiritual exhaustion it so poignantly tries to cure. When reason is divorced from the good, as I shall argue reason today is, it leads as Nietzsche said to a situation where everything is permitted—even mass self-destruction.

Reason today is acquiring mastery over nature by relying on human powers alone, powers that in Descartes's time were preeminently represented by the new mathematical physics. The methodological exclusion of the goodness of the discovered mathematical order leads easily into present-day scientism. With this identification, any epistemological impetus to render science itself comprehensible within a framework of possible knowledge and to justify it within that framework is denied. Instead, one has the equation of philosophy with the philosophy of science. Quine unabashedly says that philosophy of science is philosophy enough and reduces science itself to physics. The practical correlate of this scientistic notion of reason is an instrumentalism that manifests itself in every area of practical life: ecologically in an ever more extensive and violent plunder of nature; socio-economically in the drastic reorganization of society and ways of life to meet the demands of efficiency and higher production; ethically in the ignoring of the innate dignity of the person in favor of that which is useful; and finally, politically, in the viewing of citizens as atomistic entities, whose competing claims and demands have to be reconciled with one another and with the demands of higher production, regulated by the state.

The theory and practice of a society go together and have to be seen as a whole. If this unity of theory and practice, with all the tensions implicit in such unity, is granted, then I do not think it is far-fetched to connect the notion of instrumental reason with the most horrifying manifestation of such reason, namely, the escalating nuclear arms race. As soon as one talks of reason in this context one is led to talk of reason leading to its opposite — unreason. What is astonishing about the rhetoric supporting such a race is that the highly technical jargon of throw-weights, delivery systems, megatons, and preemptive deterrence cloaks a puerile view of a world of two powers, one unquestionably good and the other unquestionably bad, locked in permanent war, where the victory of one necessarily implies the destruction of the other. Nor is this a view that emanates just from the Pentagon. The winter 1981 issue of *Daedalus* features intellectuals whose perspective, though couched in more sophisticated prose, is no less infantile.[14] For what is one to make of a defense policy that has spent a trillion dollars in the past ten years, and plans to spend a trillion more in the coming four years and another trillion in the three years after that? The moral dimensions of such militarism are horrifying: each billion dollars spent on the arms race represents food for fifty million of the world's undernourished children for a year. American military spending, prior to the recent increases which treble the per annum level, is greater than the combined incomes of the earth's poorest billion people.[15] This is not to mention other worldwide problems of economic imbalance, the development of the world's poorer nations, pollution, energy, health, education, housing, and so forth, which are left relatively untouched because of the resources being poured into arms production.

The notion of deterrence that is used as a reason for increasing military spending is a farce when each of the superpowers some twenty years ago already possessed enough weapons to destroy one another and large parts of the world many times over. Secondly, the idea that the United States is merely responding to a gigantic Soviet threat overlooks the fact that the increase in the Soviet military budget in the 1970s is itself a response to frequent nuclear intimidation by every American president from Truman to Reagan, with the possible exception of Ford. Daniel Ellsberg has carefully documented instances of such intimidation, from Truman's deployment of B-29s, officially described as "atomic capable" at the start of the Berlin Blockade in June 1948, through the Berlin crisis of 1961 and the Cuban Missile Crisis of 1962, to the bellicose rhetoric of Ronald Reagan.[16]

My purpose in raising this issue is to use it as the most dramatic instance of the consequences of the scientism mentioned earlier. For if reason is now equated with science and science therefore is absolved from the task of self-legitimation and self-justification, then there is nothing to stop scientists from deifying their own constructions. Large-scale technology acquires its own momentum, a momentum that soon engulfs its own creators. It is this logic that leads E. P. Thompson, the social historian, to write:

If the handmill gives you society with the feudal lord, the steam mill society with the industrial capitalist, what are we given by those Satanic mills which are now at work, grounding out the means of human extermination? . . . I know that the category which we need is that of exterminism.[17]

And he goes on to say:

As to "The Bomb," the refinement of nuclear weaponry has been steadily eroding the interval in which any "political option" might be made. The replacement of liquid by solid fuel means that rockets may now stand in their silos instantly ready. . . . This hair-trigger situation . . . has encouraged fantasies that a war might actually be launched with advantage to the aggressor . . . or that a "limited" war might be fought in which only selected targets were taken out. . . . Today's hair-trigger military technology annihilates the very moment of "politics." One exterminist system confronts another and the act will follow the logic of advantage within the parameters of exterminism.[18]

I have come a long way from Hegel and metaphysical historicism. It is time now to review the argument and to conclude where I began—with Hegel himself. I have said that the contemporary crisis of reason is marked by the disjunction of reason from the good or from any notion of value beyond the utilitarian one. But if values are methodologically excluded from the mode of enquiry, we cannot expect them to find their way into the answers. And if intrinsic value is absent from both processes and results, then, even if these processes are carried out successfully by producing the results they are designed to bring about, the question still arises as to the significance of such successes. If there is no rational way of answering that question, we are in a situation of nihilism, where successes are indistinguishable from failures. Some such nihilism, I have been trying to argue, can make sense of what is itself senseless—the nuclear arms race and the serene indifference to the dangers involved in it. This is, of course, not at all to deny that the automatism of nuclear escalation is fueled by the clash of ideologies and by the political and economic formations that underly it.

It is because I believe that the present technological and economic ideology is intrinsically connected with the modern Western form of historical consciousness that the figure of Hegel becomes historically important—because, more than anyone, it is Hegel who ushers in our modern historical consciousness, even though, as I have indicated, he would have been fiercely critical of it. It is true that the historicity of human existence is itself prefigured in the astronomical discoveries of Galileo and Copernicus and the resultant experience of a radical contingency of existence within the natural world, in contrast to the essential human existence within an ordered cosmos characteristic of the ancient and medieval world views. But it is precisely that contingency and its possible nihilist consequences that Hegel attempts to sublate within the notion of a necessity in history grounded in the rational necessity contained in the absolute.

Hegel's deification of history is directly tied up with his deification of reason, and it is this twin deification that constitutes both the glory and the abject failure of his system. It is its glory insofar as it not only achieves a metaphysical ordering of reality but also articulates with unmatched rigor the finality of this world. Reason, the Christian *logos*, according to Hegel's understanding of it, is the preeminent form of divine revelation, so that one is not dependent on the dispensation of a Supreme Being up there for an apprehension of the truth and sacredness of this world. No, the requisite resources for such apprehension lie within us and beyond us too, inasmuch as these resources also permeate the cosmos. The true significance of that absolute commandment to "know thyself" is that in knowing ourselves at the deepest level we get to know the infinite Spirit as our innermost being. Furthermore, it is to Hegel as one of the great theologians of the West that we must turn for artillery against those patently inadequate forms of religion which still represent a failure to face up fully to the complexity and mystery of the world. It is not at all surprising, therefore, that after decades of existentialist and neo-Reformed theology, the tide is turning today toward types of theology which are beginning to take history and politics seriously. These theologies find in Hegel an invaluable resource.

But when all that has been granted and one's debt to Hegel duly acknowledged, there still remains the fact that the divine has not been grasped and comprehended in his thought, leave aside rendered self-conscious. What is worse, there is the welling suspicion that precisely in the attempt to do so the true infinity of Spirit has been grossly misrepresented. Various commentators have remarked on the complete this-worldliness of Hegel's thought and its glaring lack of an otherworldly dimension. While agreeing with them, and while also not wanting to revive any two-world dualism, I would argue in addition that in dissolving the essential tension between the eternal and the historical, a tension that remains in their unity-in-difference, Hegel ends up misrepresenting both the eternal and the historical. The historicizing of the eternal without remainder destroys its status as eternal. If the transcendent and the immanent, the *Sollen* and the *Sein*, are made the same, then transcendence is rendered neither possible nor, for that matter, desirable. And yet the whole basis of transcendence is that of a good and a truth which, while manifested in this world, could not possibly be completely manifested in it. Hegel does acknowledge that the reconciliation his system achieves is far from universal and in fact is confined to the realm of thought, lacking outward universality. But even then Hegel does not doubt that a complete philosophical reconciliation in his terms has been achieved. Indeed, he cannot, for to allow for that possibility is to destroy the very basis of his philosophic construction.

What is palpably missing in the relentless conceptualism of Hegel is the mythic dimension, so important a part of Greek and Indian thought. Philosophy cannot afford to destroy the delicate balance between *mythos* and *logos* that the Greeks maintain, which is why there is no suggestion of an absolute self-consciousness in Plato. It may be argued that Aristotle is more congenial to Hegel in this regard, in that he comes closer to the Hegelian tactic of construing Form as activity, and his *noesis noeseos*, or self-thinking thought, is able to bring about an identity of absolute subject and object in the divine self-reflexivity of theory. But Aristotle's God, in self-thinking, does not also think the world, far less provide logical explanations of it. Rather, at the beginning of his *Metaphysics* Aristotle asserts that myth and wisdom go hand in hand. From the point of view of *logos*, the powers of the mind appear limitless. And indeed they are, but precisely because myth is the ever-receding boundary against which philosophical thinking proceeds. Myth is something that we find ourselves in and that we live, and while that experience drives us to thought, it can never be thought through.[19]

Where does this leave us? Closer perhaps to Hegel's friend and early mentor Hölderlin than to Hegel himself. For while Hölderlin's gods, like Hegel's, only come alive in human subjectivity, and while Hölderlin too attempts to bring together nature and history in the clarity of human consciousness, nature for him remains other and inexhaustible, a siren continually teasing human creativity to express its mystery in song and poetry. Less poetically, it brings us against the limits of philosophy and beyond them into the realms of religion and politics. "When philosophy has gained the truth of which it is capable," says Roberto Unger, "it passes into politics and prayer, politics through which the world is changed, prayer through which men ask God to complete the change of the world by carrying them into his presence and giving them what left to themselves they would always lack."[20] Religion for its part can be confident of its infinite resources only when this infinitude has been pointed to by the necessary experience of fully exploring and running up against the finitude of both philosophy and politics. Otherwise it remains empty and insipid. That, of course, is the challenge facing a truly political theology, a theology both for and of politics, that can face philosophical criticism and at the same time enrich philosophy.

NOTES

1. G. W. F. Hegel, Preface to the *Phenomenology of Spirit*, trans. A. V. Miller (Oxford: Clarendon Press, 1977), p. 14.

2. G. W. F. Hegel, *Lectures on the Philosophy of Religion*, 3 vols., trans. E. B. Speirs and J. B. Sanderson (New York: Humanities Press, 1962), 1: 19.

3. Karl Rosenkranz, *Hegels Leben* (Berlin, 1944), p. 400; Martin Heidegger, "The Onto-Theo-Logical Nature of Metaphysics," in *Essays in Metaphysics: Identity and Difference*, trans. K. F. Leidecker (New York: Harper & Row, 1960), pp. 35–67.

4. Karl Barth, *Protestant Thought from Rousseau to Ritschl*, trans. Brian Cozens (New York: Harper & Row, 1959), p. 280.

5. G. W. F. Hegel, *Encyclopedia of the Philosophical Sciences* (1830) Part 2, *Hegel's Philosophy of Nature*, trans. A. V. Miller (Oxford: Clarendon Press, 1970), para. 258, p. 35.

6. Johannes Hoffmeister, *Dokumente zu Hegels Entwicklung* (Berlin, 1936), p. 364.

7. G. W. F. Hegel, Preface to the *Philosophy of Right*, trans. T. M. Knox (Oxford: Clarendon Press, 1942), p. 10.

8. G. W. F. Hegel, *Philosophy of History*, trans. John Sibree (New York: Dover Press, 1956), p. 79.

9. G. W. F. Hegel, *Reason in History*, trans. R. Hartman (New York: Liberal Arts Press, 1953), p. 68.

10. Hegel, *Lectures on the Philosophy of Religion*, 2:330.

11. Hegel, *Philosophy of History*, p. 79.

12. Stanley Rosen, *Nihilism* (New Haven, Conn.: Yale University Press, 1969), p. 36.

13. Richard Rorty, *Philosophy and the Mirror of Nature* (Princeton, N.J.: Princeton University Press, 1979), pp. 3–4.

14. See the devastating reply by E. P. Thompson, "A Letter to America," in *Protest and Survive*, ed. E. P. Thompson and Dan Smith (New York: Monthly Review Press, 1981), pp. 3–55.

15. These figures are taken from William W. Rankin, *The Nuclear Arms Race: Countdown to Disaster* (Cleveland, Ohio: Forward Movement Publications, 1981), pp. 16–17.

16. Daniel Ellsberg, "Introduction: Call to Mutiny," in *Protest and Survive*, ed. Thompson and Smith, pp. i–xxviii.

17. E. P. Thompson, "The Logic of Exterminism," in *New Left Review* 121 (May/June 1980):7.

18. Ibid., p. 10.

19. I am indebted to Raimundo Panikkar for helping me to appreciate the significance of the mythic. See his *Myth, Faith, and Hermeneutics* (New York: Paulist Press, 1979).

20. Roberto Mangabeira Unger, *Knowledge and Politics* (New York: Free Press, 1975), p. 294.

PART II

Redefining Religion

5

Religious Pluralism: The Metaphysical Challenge

RAIMUNDO PANIKKAR

PLURALISM IS FASHIONABLE. Political pluralism has almost become a democratic dogma. Yet few people are aware of the radical revolution such a pluralistic world view entails if we draw the ultimate consequences. It amounts to giving up one of the pillars on which many a civilization has built its fundamental ideas for at least twenty-five centuries: the harmonious correlation between thinking and being. Truth was the traditional name for this correlation. In pluralism, thinking ceases to be the controller of being. The different religious traditions become expressions of the creativity of being striking ever new adventures into the real. Reality is only intelligible in part and *a posteriori*. Thinking alone does not help us much to deal with reality. We need a kind of cosmotheandric confidence which sets us in harmony with the real without annihilating in us the power to be active participants in the life of reality.

Because religions are the natural place for ultimate issues, this fact emerges more clearly from a cross-cultural and interdisciplinary approach to the problem of religion and truth. Religions offer the locus of ultimate truth and point the way to it. They do not speak about it directly, but a certain primordial apprehension of reality stands at the basis of each religion. When these fundamental insights are spelled out in a universe of discourse, we discover divergent conceptions of reality. Some of these different conceptions are accidental to the main thrust of the religious quest, but some are fundamental. Delete the effective presence of the an-

97

cestors and many American and African religions collapse. Suppress historical consciousness and Christianity loses its bearings. Destroy *karma* and many an Asian religion is crippled.

In a word, there is a constitutive link between a certain conception of reality, which can be expressed intelligibly, and the religion which espouses it. It should be clear from the very outset that we are dealing with the intellectual side of religions, which is where the problem of religious pluralism arises. And it is in this respect that we speak of truth in religions. Religious conflict, therefore, is rooted in each religion's primordial apprehensions.

The demands of rationality leave the following main options open:

1. Only one religion is true. All the others are, at best, approximations.
2. Religions refer ultimately to the same truth although in different manners and approximations. Ultimately they all are equal.
3. All religions are false because of the falsity of their claim. There is no such ultimate destiny.
4. Each religion is true because it is the best for its adherents. Truth is subjective. *"Religion ist Privatsache."*
5. Religions are the product of history and thus both similar and different according to the historical factors that have shaped them.
6. Each religion has unique features and presents mutually incommensurable insights. Each statement of a basic experience is to be evaluated on its proper terrain and merits, because the very nature of truth is pluralistic.

I wish to make a case for the sixth option. We need first to clarify our nomenclature, and then situate the other options. Finally we need to elucidate the metaphysical challenge of religious pluralism.

I. DRAMATIS PERSONAE

By *religion* I mean the set of symbols, myths, and practices people believe gives ultimate meaning to their lives. I stress the believing factor, for religion is never just an objective set of values. Religion is always personal and necessarily includes the belief of the person.

A basic experience (*Grunderfahrung*) or primordial apprehension of reality refers to that mostly spontaneous and often uncritical human attitude which subsequently expresses itself in a set of more or less organically linked symbols, myths, and practices. This basic experience, which does not need to be self-conscious, is at the origin of a particular religion and conditions the ultimate convictions regarding the nature of reality and the meaning of life. Very often this basic experience is that of the founder of a religion with all the accretions of tradition. Sometimes it is just handed down from time immemorial and reinterpreted again and again within a certain mythical continuity. Each religious person assimilates more or less deeply this basic experience and often recreates it. The religious traditions play, obviously, a major role in shaping this personal basic attitude. A typology of these basic experiences would offer a first approach leading to the classical divisions of humankind's religions. It is the diversity and discrepancy of those primordial apprehensions, rendered visible through the intellectual expressions of them, that pose the problem of religious pluralism.

Let us understand by *truth* that quality or property of reality which allows things to enter into a *sui generis* relation with the human mind and which finds its main expression in human language. Truth may entail a correspondence between things and our thinking, or it may be a construction of our mind or of a supreme mind. At any rate, truth implies a certain correlation between our faculties of apprehension and what they apprehend. The question of truth is a question of the intellect and for the intellect. The truth of religion is not its symbols, myths, and practices but the intellectual content of them, its interpretation. We are concerned here with the interpretations given to the basic experiences underlying religions. *A true religion* is an ambiguous phrase. Religions can only be true or false inasmuch as they speak to our mind and our mind reflects upon them. In this sense a true religion has to fulfill these two conditions:

1. It has to deliver the promised goods to its members; in other words, it needs to be truthful to its own tenets. This

does not mean that the dwelling-place of the ancestors, or nirvana, for instance, has to be somewhere, or that the person who commits a mortal sin goes to a physical place called hell. It means, however, that those who follow the Commandments or the *Dharma* or observe the Four Noble Truths will reach the end or fulfillment of life that the particular religious tradition describes — independently of the many possible cosmological and anthropological interpretations of the same tenets. A true religion must serve its purpose for those who believe in it; it must achieve existential truth, honest consistency.

2. It has to present a view of reality in which the basic experience is expressed in an intelligible corpus that can sustain intelligent criticism from the outside without falling into substantial contradictions. This does not mean that God must exist in the crude or literal way in which an outsider may think. It means, however, that world views which accept the reality of gods, for example, can present themselves in the arena of human critique and meet the questions put from the outside so as to be able to present a picture which is consistent if not convincing for everybody. A true religion must achieve essential truth, authentic coherence.

The plurality of religions does not need to tackle the problem of religious truth. It acknowledges simply the fact that there are many religions. Let them crusade one against the other, if they so wish. But religious pluralism cannot bracket the question of truth. It has to take a stance among allegedly contradictory religious intellectual affirmations. Thus, the problem. Pluralism is not a supersystem. It accepts the fact that the human condition does not possess an all-encompassing view of reality.

There is a parallel with linguistic, cultural, and philosophical pluralism. These pluralisms do not defend a *lingua universalis*, a superculture, a metaphilosophy. Linguistic pluralism will not assume that one existing language is more adequate to human beings than another. It will not defend *a priori* the idea that all human intuitions molded in one particular language are necessarily translatable into other linguistic worlds. Each language is unique and any translation will have to agree first on the equivalent human experience within its own linguistic world. Cultural pluralism admits different forms of being a cultivated person and thus will not impose one culture above another. The assumption, for instance, that modern technology is a universal value beneficent for everybody is at loggerheads with cultural pluralism. Philosophical pluralism recognizes as valid and yet incompatible different forms of philosophizing and, in the last instance, of philosophies.

Only after the acceptance of these three pluralisms will we be prepared to discuss and eventually accept the legitimacy of religious pluralism. This latter, in fact, presupposes the other three. Religious pluralism recognizes the authenticity, validity, and truth of different religions once their mutual incompatibility has been established on solid rational grounds.

Religious pluralism would not present a major difficulty were it not for the intellectual dimension of religion. Symbols, myths, and practices do not have any claim to universality. They do not conflict with their peers because they, unlike the universe of logical discourse, do not claim any other truth than their proper authenticity. I will concentrate on this intellectual side of religion precisely to situate the limits of the intellect and to discuss the challenge presented by religious pluralism. By *metaphysics* I understand that discipline which accepts both a human capacity for thinking the supraempirical and the reality of the supraempirical itself. It is also ontology or just the power of thinking 'being'. I am not assuming here any particular philosophical stance.

II. THE INADEQUACY OF THE MONISTIC ANSWERS

I call monistic all approaches to the problem of religious pluralism in which truth is said to be one: either One for all or one for every single individual. The method is monistic because it recognizes only one single yardstick to measure the merits or demerits of all religions as if this yardstick were recognized by all and were so neutral as to lie outside any religious tradition. The first five options mentioned earlier (see page 98 above) fall in this category.

1. Only one religion is true.

That, obviously, is my religion. There is something very telling in such a conviction. We should not dismiss it lightly because of the danger of fanaticism and the factual abuses of such a belief. We are now making a theoretical or a philosophical analysis, and not just reflecting on the sad experience of history. It is an extremely coherent and rational position. If I believe I am participant in the truth, and I see and hear that other people have what I cannot but call wrong opinions, I will have to say so. "Amicus mihi Plato, sed magis amica veritas" ("Plato is my friend, but I love truth more"). This does not mean that I am intolerant; rather it can make me compassionate. It does not need to breed haughtiness; it may equally foster a sense of dignity and responsibility. Furthermore, precisely because I believe in the truth of my religion I will discover my own religiousness wherever I find parcels of truth. It will spur me to interiorization and also to converting people to the liberating truth — as I see it.

And yet this position is unconvincing even on theoretical grounds. It assumes that, if not I personally, at least the community of my religion has such an access to the universal truth as to have the right to exclude anybody who does not think or behave according to the lights that we have received. Truth is only my truth, or at least our truth. Even assuming that an omniscient God has spoken to us, we cannot eliminate the human factor of our limited understanding and the divine freedom to speak to others, even if we understand God to have promised not to do such a thing. God might have spoken once and been heard in different ways and in different times. It violates, further, the common human experience of the diversity of races, peoples, cultures, and ways of thinking, and tends to reduce everything to manageable parameters. It is a closed position.

There is a more subtle variation of this same position. It affirms: "Some religions are true and some others are false." There is a rationale behind such a position. We may find degraded forms of religion. We would call them wrong, harmful, not only as regards accidentals but in their central tenets. Religions of hatred, racism, exploitation, and dominance should be considered wrong religions. They could be called false because they contradict the very accepted purpose of religion, the salvation or fullness of humankind, in whatever sense we may understand this salvation or fullness. I will come to this later on, because we are dealing here not with the affirmation that there may be wrong religions but with the statement that some religions are true and some are false.

This distinction is generally used for the purpose of distinguishing two groups of religions: our group, the true one; and the other group of false religions. Some scholars agree that the high religions or great religions or world religions form a group of true religions, while the so-called primitive religions and sometimes also animism or polytheism form a group of false religions. Islam and Christianity in Africa are allied against fetishisms of all sorts. Hindu India has a certain condescension toward the tribals, which are considered false religions by many adherents of the high-caste religions.

Yet who sets the criteria for such judgments? All too often a political decision puts on philosophical garb. Where are we to put the dividing line between true and false religions? We may fairly assume that the religions we brand as false consider themselves to be true. The criterion for judging the truth or falsity of a religion is intrinsic to that religion. Otherwise we are assuming *a priori* a kind of universally accepted standard, which is certainly not the case. We may assume that the logical laws of contradiction and identity are universal, but religions deal with human life, which is not a logical unfolding. Humanity has reason and we may agree in calling the human being a rational animal, but humankind is more than pure reason and human life more than rationality. Pluralism elevates other dimensions of reality to the same rank as rationality.

2. *All religions are ultimately true.*

All say the same thing at the ultimate level. This is an opposite position to the previous one. It has its partial justification. It represents a very understandable reaction against the intolerance, shortsightedness, and sheer ignorance of other people's religiousness. If one goes deep enough into one's own tradition one discovers how far one is from the goal and how relative are all our ways of thinking, speaking, behaving. Truth is one, but we poor mortals see it in many ways. And if we investigate all the religious traditions of humankind we shall discover the same patterns, the same thrust toward the infinite, and, ultimately, the same ineffable, mystical experience. Only with sympathy and understanding can we approach the vast field of human ultimate beliefs and then we shall easily discover how alike they are. Religions are different paths to the same and unique goal. It may be legitimate to defend a transcendent unity of religions, but it should be made very clear that this unity also transcends reason.

This position is weak in that it does not take sufficiently into account that the paths belong also to the goal. It seems to accept a Kantian 'thing-in-itself' transcendent and an aloofness which has nothing to do with our approaches. It wants to make mystics of us all, and it tries to reduce religions to what may perhaps be their quintessence but which is certainly not their total nature. If we take religions seriously we have to listen to what they themselves say, and most of them zealously guard their identity by differentiation. They would not agree that they are just the same. There is an inherent nominalist attitude in this option which is directly contrary to many religious traditions. Names are sacred; words are not interchangeable; not even languages are accidental. Human expressions cannot be isolated and they are more than mere labels. Nominalism is a useful scientific tool but does not do justice to religious phenomena. If religions do not say the same, they are not the same. If we insist that all religions are equal in spite of the divergency of their doctrines, we are minimizing the role of reason or putting religions on a suprarational level outside the jurisdiction of reason. In the first case, we are saying that it does not matter whether we affirm God or *ātman* or the reality of the world or the unreality of evil. We are saying that rational discrepancies are unimportant. Ultimately we despise reason, which puts up barriers and raises rational questions. In the second case, we are defending the view that the truth of religion is so esoteric and deep that there can be no public talk about it. We bar the entrance to reason and further rational enquiry.

3. *All religions are equally false.*

This is also an understandable overstatement due to the well-known facts of the scandal of traditional religions in the history of humanity. The inertia of tradition is sometimes so strong, the resistance to adaptation so weighty, and the religious hubris so patent, that those who would carefully put arguments in favor of this thesis would certainly not lack data.

Yet the dark side of religious history is not its only side. When religions can be so bad and so good, it may very well be that they represent a very deep-seated ingredient of human nature. Further, this position seems to contradict itself theoretically, for the very statement about the falsity of all religions is a religious statement and thus is also false. If the statement were true it would constitute the foundation for a true religion, namely that set of symbols and practices that has eliminated all the religious superstitions.

A more refined formulation would state that all religions are equally inadequate because they try to command injunctions and formulate ideas which are beyond the reach of any human agency. Most religions would answer that they are well aware of this fact and that they do not claim such a perfection. Again, the defenders of this position may retort that no religion delivers the liberation it promises and no religious doctrine is without contradictions. To this it may be responded that for many people religion seems to satisfy this ultimate ideal and give them not only peace and solace but also that fullness in which they believe. Religions are human facts, and the fact remains that many insiders of so many religions seem not to see or not to mind the alleged doctrinal contradictions. In other words, they are not convinced of falsehood and in that sense the affirmation that religions are false is based only on the criteria of the public prosecutor.

Further, as we have already hinted, this criticism of religion purifies religion but does not destroy it. It may say that all those transcendent goals are nonexistent and that there is no ultimate meaning in life. Yet this discourse is already a religious one defending the true religion as that which helps us lead a this-worldly and empirical day-to-day life. Under this assumption, this would then be the true religion: that which finally performs what traditional religions aimed at fulfilling but in a mistaken direction.

4. Religion is a private affair.

Religions are so highly unique and personal that any comparison is out of the question. Each one is the best for its members. After all, truth is what I make out of it. A disincarnated truth is not a truth at all, but only an abstraction. This position avoids many of the pitfalls of the previous ones. It takes religions seriously, and persons as well. It vouches for respect and tolerance. It contains a healthy confidence in the other who sees things in a different manner than I do. It makes rational an agreement to disagree.

But it is also unsatisfactory. It falls into a subjectivism from which there is no issue: you see things one way and I see them another way. It makes dialogue impossible and robs us of any criteria for passing judgments. We may not even agree on what is good and bad, for our moral vision is also dependent on our intellectual convictions. What is good and bad cannot be isolated from what is true and false. It is a position leading to solipsism and ultimately suffocation. There is, besides, the flagrant phenomenological and historical contradiction to that thesis. Religions are the least private human phenomena that we know. Cultures, wars, politics, and human relations of all sorts are influenced by the religious convictions of people. On a less metaphysical plane this position converts religion into the tool of a single individual. I pick the best religion for me and may even concoct my own, a sort of spiritual cocktail. The individual chooses religion as a consumer in a supermarket chooses a favorite flavor of yogurt. It allows a proliferation of religions, producing a religious inflation in some cultures. Anyone can be founder of a new religion.

This position should not be confused with the affirmation that religion has to be personal. This confusion should be avoided on at least two accounts: (a) from the side of the person, and (b) from the side of the religion.

a. The more personal a religion is, the less individualistic it is. A person implies a relationship, a knot in a net of relations. A person is the simultaneous conjugation of all personal pronouns. There is no *I* without a *Thou* and all the rest.

b. The more personal a religion, the more it really is a religion — that is, the more it draws from the well of tradition and the more it influences others and is influenced by others.

5. *Religions are historical constructs.*

This amounts to saying that religions all have a common historical origin, that they are historically related, and that their respective truths have to be understood historically because ultimately truth is historical. There are many merits in this position. It helps us explain the interactions and mutual influences of religion. It gives us an understanding of the similarities and differences, and opens our minds to understand religious variety in a world context.

Yet there are many unanswered questions in this approach and it cannot cope with all the divergencies. The historical fact of religion is certainly true, but religions are more than historical facts, ultimately because humankind is more than history. Why has a historical fact like the burial of the dead had so many different interpretations? To reply "Because the contexts were different" only shifts the question to the context. Further, there are religions which do not accept the myth of history as the field on which they unfold their basic experience. To trace the historical sources of Krishna worship, for instance, is totally irrelevant to the believing *Vaiṣṇava*; the point is not whether we all come from a common experience, but the fact that my Krishna experience today is what counts and is certainly not to be equated with any other. We do not exchange lovers. History plays an undeniable role, but some elements cannot be reduced to history.

Even assuming that we had succeeded in drawing a genealogical tree of all religions, the fact would remain that this tree produces not only apples but also oranges and many other fruits — some sweet, some sour, and not all equally edible. The variety of religious practices could perhaps be explained as expressions of a common urge, but doctrines have a special claim to universality and truth that makes contradictory statements unacceptable.

This main point leads us to the sixth hypothesis, which includes many of the valid points of the previous ones. It fills a gap left by the others and attempts to overcome a monistic methodology without falling into a chaotic atomization of methods.

III. THE NONDUALISTIC HYPOTHESIS

Religions differ. There is no doubt about it. We see it and they themselves affirm it. Some differ less than others and we may even find structural areas where they coalesce. All deal with the sacred; all recognize a certain presence of transcendence; all have rituals and myths. But humankind is not a skeleton. As medicine is not anatomy, so religion is not a formal structure. It all depends on the flesh and life we put into those structures.

Furthermore, religions have doctrines. One should not identify a religion with its doctrinal aspect, but one should not minimize it either. Though no great thinker of a religion will identify the existential path of that religion with its intellectual formation and interpretation, most religions have an intellectual side. The intellectual scheme of a religion's founders, doctors, and masters — that is, its orthodoxy — reflects the basic experience of that religion's representative people. These fundamental convictions face the adherent of a religion toward the mystery of truth. They are the formulated dogmas of that religion. Each religious tradition offers this intellectual context out of which the particular thinker will carve his or her own text. Not only are these texts different, they are often mutually contradictory. There are a number of mutually exclusive views of reality among diverse traditions and also in the interior of each tradition. This diversity of human opinions regarding ultimate matters is as universal as any other human phenomenon.

Efforts toward harmony are always welcome as an indispensable first step. They dispel misunderstandings, supplement different views, complement sparse ideas, criticize otherwise unnoticed inconsistencies. What was once a stumbling block becomes a common and accepted doctrine. There are interpenetrations, mutual influences, and even mutual fecundations. But we are finally left with several well-elaborated, complex, and yet mutually irreconcilable views of reality.

Philosophers, theologians, and religionists have tried to bring religious differences to a deeper unity, but these efforts have made what they say meaningful for only one party in the discussion. We can call African religions polytheistic as long as the Africans themselves do not read our books. We can call the Buddhists anonymous Christians as long as they do not call Christians anonymous Buddhists. We may call atheists believers in the nothingness of the absolute as long as atheists do not hear what we are saying. There is an innate political impulse to reduce everything to our categories of understanding, stretching them as much as possible, but there are certain limits to it. Any language has to be accepted by both parties concerned and we cannot transgress the mutually accepted meaning of the words. The traditions of the respective partners are on their shoulders and they cannot stretch the meaning of words beyond a given coefficient of flexibility. The hard fact remains that for the present we disagree and do not see any way out. To retort that we have different contexts and perspectives helps certainly to dispel false and superficial incompatibilities, but the disagreement is also shifted to the perspective and the justification of the shift. The great intellectuals of humankind were not so naive as to reduce all divergencies to our passions, weaknesses, or lack of information.

Nāgārjuna's efforts at overcoming a plurality of doctrines are well known and not unique. The Cartesian scandal regarding the plurality of mutually contradicting Christian theologies is repeated time and again down the centuries. And yet philosophies, theologies, and religious discrepancies thrive after all the dialectical, rational, and mystical methods and philosophers' stones. Almost every independent thinker in the history of human thought wants, if not to start afresh, at least to make a breakthrough that will convince the listeners of the insufficiency of the intellectual answers prior to this particular contribution. Are we going to say that all our predecessors were wrong?

I am not propounding a skeptical or agnostic attitude, which contradicts itself the moment it is formulated: if we cannot be sure of anything, then we cannot be sure even of our uncertainty! Nor am I defending complementarity and perspectivism, useful as these methods are to overcome misunderstandings and hurried condemnations. In fact, I am prepared to believe that most of the discrepancies among religions are complementary and supplementary views coming from a multiperspectival approach. The best thinkers of the world have been well aware that the context determines our perspective and that a problem can be seen from many angles. Yet when all is said and done there still remain irreducible aspects that force us to say that we are right and they are wrong.

I am also unsatisfied with an eschatological consolation that here on earth, since we are not *jīvan-muktas, comprehensores*, realized beings,we only know as if we were looking through a dark glass or were enmeshed in the *avidyā* of fragmentary knowledge. Even if this may be the case, we still struggle with each other because we take to heart what we see, understand, and believe. At the end all may be well and we may all agree and see the whole truth; meanwhile, however, treating our human divergencies lightly would amount to a sin against human dignity.

Though ecumenism has its place, what I am now emphasizing is that the ideal is not the total unity of ultimately one religion or one truth. The real world is one of variety and complexity which does not exclude harmony. Uniformity is not the ideal; monism is wrong. Pluralism penetrates into the very heart of the ultimate reality.

The basic problem is this: humans differ fundamentally. The marketplace of world religions is where these discrepancies appear most acutely and fundamentally because they are ultimate. It is no wonder that the most serious wars of human history have been religious wars, not excluding the last World War. I am talking at the ultimate level of discourse, once all the other resources at our disposal have been exhausted. I am talking about the divergencies between a Śaṅkara and a Rāmānuja, an Aquinas and a Scotus, and, *a fortiori*, between an Averroes and an Abhinavagupta, a Luther and a Dōgen, a Marx and an Aurobindo, a Newman and a Maimonides — sociology of knowledge notwithstanding.

One may say that those are not religious differences. I disagree; they are. Śaṅkara's *Dharma* is different from Rāmānuja's in spite of the label *Hindu*. Saint Thomas's basic insights about analogy, essence, and existence are the basis of a religious attitude different from that of Scotus, even if we put them under the umbrella of Christianity.

Either we consider this state of affairs an anomaly, a result of original sin, alienation, our irritating limitations, and the like, or we see this human condition as reflecting the very nature of the real without idealizations of any kind. The traditional answer is inclined to the former hypothesis, for reasons of moral and political character. One has to account for human shortcomings and, in the monotheistic tradition, God cannot be made responsible for the evil in the world. But the theoretical underpinning of such a belief is the widespread notion that ultimately reality has to be intelligible; that there is a total correspondence between thinking and being because God or the absolute reality is pure mind, sheer Spirit, intelligibility itself. The traditional answer was bent on say-

ing that God knows everything, that the Church shares in this privilege, that the Emperor embodies the whole, that the *kevala-jñānin*
has all the answers, that the master knows better, and the like. It
is only we poor mortals, ordinary believers, citizens, or peasants,
who do not have such insight; in itself reality is assumed to be conceptually transparent.

But one result of what I call the cosmotheandric experience
is that reality does not need to be totally intelligible in itself. This
basic experience discovers a threefold character of *cosmos, anthro-
pos,* and *theos;* of matter, consciousness, and freedom as three in-
tertwined constitutive dimensions of the real. If we take religious
pluralism seriously we cannot avoid asserting that truth itself is
pluralistic — at least for the time being, which is our being in time,
and on which we need to rely for our very thinking.

To be sure, not all religions raise claims incompatible with
others. Many religions consider the religious behavior of the neighbor, even if contrary to the customs of the group, as something de-
manding religious reverence and approval. Yet even within the fold
of one single tradition there are fundamental convictions which
appear incompatible with others. A Vedāntin, for instance, will
respect a *murtipūjaka* and even agree that at a certain level of religious consciousness image worship is the most conducive activity for liberation, but will defend a superior stage where such worship is not necessary and is even harmful. It is the Vedāntin, of
course, who decides what is the superior stage.

A case for pluralism can be made by analyzing the common
phrase that "we agree to disagree." What does it mean? On *what*
do we really agree? Let us assume that bombing, torture, chemical warfare, and the like are at stake in our intellectual discussion
about the existence of God. Without pluralism, the other is either
mentally weak or morally bad. In either case we have to take action and not just tolerate the other. The conflict can only be han-
dled reasonably if we assume that the other is also a source of understanding and that dreadful consequences will not follow: an
atheist may still go to heaven; a monotheist may still have a non-
alienated and full human existence; a militarist may still be the
best means for peace. Real tolerance, and not just coping with
the other, can only be justified if pluralism is the factual structure
of reality.

Reality is not reducible to one single principle. The single principle could only be an intelligible principle. But reality is not mind alone, or *cit*, or consciousness, or spirit. Reality is also *sat* and *ānanda*, also matter and freedom, joy, and being. *T'ai chi*, the Great Ultimate, is not the sum of *yin* and *yang*. Reality is not transparent to itself. It does not allow for a perfect reflection. Reality is also spontaneity, an ever new creation, an expanding energy. God's thought is divine and as such equal to God, but God is not just thought.

Are there then many truths? No. A plurality of truths (of the same thing and under the same aspect) is contradictory. Truth is pluralistic, we said. This amounts to saying that being itself is pluralistic, that reality is irreducible to a monolithic unity, irreducible to pure transparency, irreducible to intellect or Spirit. There is a nonontological dimension of reality (freedom, nonbeing, silence, and so forth) and also an opaque one (matter, energy, world, and so forth), besides the proper human dimension (consciousness, mind). Monism does not correspond to truth and thus to the nature of reality. And yet dualism is not acceptable either. The very notion of dualism at this ultimate level supersedes itself (*hebt sich selbst auf*). We cannot speak intelligibly of dualism without assuming a deeper underlying unity which enables us to speak of *two* principles. If they are two, they are two more or less homogeneous units. There is a bridge between the two. What we have called pluralism is better named Trinity or *Advaita*. This is neither monism nor dualism. The word *pluralism* is of course ambiguous. It does not mean here a kind of atomism or plurality of ultimate elements of the universe. At this level I prefer the expression *nondualism*, which is what underlies most of the traditional wisdoms of the world.

Before we explain a little more this inherent polarity of reality, we must meet a formidable difficulty: the problem of falsehood. Can there be a false religion? Does pluralism allow us to handle such cases? Have we no tools to condemn a racist religion, for instance, or a religiosity of hatred? We shall say that it is a wrong and a bad religion, but religion it is, and we shall have to reckon with it. Those people are not just cranky people. Evil is not a mere mistake, an error of vision or perspective. It is a hatred, an aberration, an incomprehensibility. Evil is by definition impervious to human comprehension. This does not mean that everything unintelligible is evil, as the gnostics are inclined to think. But it implies that there may be people grasped by the dark side of reality who put evil forward. It is the very pluralism of the real that gives to evil all its tragic seriousness.

Pluralism has a better answer than the already known and defeated answers of monism and dualism. These two latter systems are able to give excellent theoretical justifications, but they fail to discover a way to maintain dissent and still somehow embrace the dissenting party. No alternative is left besides the elimination of the wrong party. It has to be defeated because ultimately error is sin, evil. Pluralism, on the other hand, is neither individualistic subjectivism nor impersonal objectivism. With the former we could condemn nothing. With the latter we could condemn anything we disagree with. The nondualistic approach accepts the relativity of truth but not sheer relativism. This is to say, truth is constituted by the total relationship of things, because things *are* insofar as they are in relation to one another. But this relation is not a private relation between a subject and an object. It is a universal relationship so that it is not for any private individual or group to exhaust any relationship. Truth is relational, thus relational to me, but never private. There is no such thing as private truth. On the other hand, truth is not an immutable or absolute quality totally objectifiable in concepts or propositions independently of time, space, culture, and people. Each person, we said, is a source of self-understanding and of understanding, a knowing subject and not only a known object.

How, then, shall we discriminate between true and false religion? When this constitutive relativity of truth is hampered by isolating it from this total relationship we fall into error. When a particular religion isolates itself from the rest of the world and does not accept relation, dialogue, or intercourse; when it becomes a sect refusing communication and communion with the wider world, then this kind of totalitarianism condemns itself by the very fact of implicitly condemning others.

I am not defending the view that truth is with the majority or that it all should be publicized in the marketplace without any right to privacy or secrecy or esoterism. I am not denying the right of any religion to challenge the rest of the world. On the contrary,

I am submitting that error entails isolation and breaking of relations. As long as there is dialogue, struggle, discussion, and disagreement we have conflicting opinions, different and even contradictory views; but all this appertains to the very polarity of
reality. In this view we also relativize error. From my vantage point
my opponent is wrong, but not absolutely wrong unless the group
or person in question breaks loose from (*ab-solutus*) the rest of us.

Pluralism can only be consistent without falling into a self-
defeating irrationalism if we release being from the strictures of
thinking. Being must ultimately be free from already established
logical rules. It is true that thinking is bound to being, to what is.
Thinking detects the reality of being and has to be loyal to it.
Thinking follows being and tells us what being is. Thinking can,
as it were, catch up to the new adventures of being. Thinking penetrates deeper into the mysteries of being. But it also does something
else. Thinking dis-covers, unveils, what 'being' is doing, what 'being' is being, without curtailing it with what until now thinking
has thought. For the relation between thinking and being is not
a closed one. Being or reality transcends thinking. It can expand,
jump, surprise itself. Freedom is the divine aspect of being. Being
speaks to us; this is a fundamental religious experience consecrated
by many a tradition. And to hear 'being' is more than to think it.

Authentic religions are manifestations, expressions of being.
They harbor those basic experiences which represent the very life
of reality. They are like the explosion of those nova constellations
in the astronomical universe. Out of nowhere, with no logical relation to what is there, the ultimate religious intuitions are jumps
in the being of 'being'. Deductive thinking is here of no avail. We
are dealing with spontaneity, with a 'being' that is still being and
has not simply been.

Religious pluralism liberates us from the servitude of 'being'
to what *was*. It prevents us from deducing what is and even what
shall be and what must be from what we already know. It opens
a free future which no deductive thinking power can ever fathom.
Being expresses itself in different ways; it thinks also in different
manners. Religions reveal to us different facts of truth because truth
itself is multifaceted. We are unable to bring different basic experiences of human beings into one single thought system because
reality is that mystery which transcends not only our thinking but

thinking as such. The variety of the ultimate human traditions is thus like the many colors of nature. We should be not monochromatically obsessed, but loving gardeners of all that grows on valleys, slopes, and peaks of that reality of which we are the human partners.

6

Is a Hermeneutics of Religion Possible?

DAVID TRACY

I. THE PLURALITY AND AMBIGUITY OF RELIGION

DEFINING RELIGION MEANS facing the fact that any definition represents a particular perspective; and that religion is peculiarly elusive, because it is so pluralistic and cognitively and ethically ambiguous. What the best Western definitions actually achieve is not the nature or essence of religion, but specific characteristics of the religions *as* religious. Characteristics like the numinous, the sense and taste for the infinite, the feeling of absolute dependence, ultimate concern, the dialectic of the sacred and the profane will inevitably represent a particular perspective and therefore be partial. Yet precisely through their partiality they disclose the inevitable pluralism and ambiguity of religion, as well as its richness.

Such at least is my hypothesis. Allow me to test it with Kant's understanding of limit in religion.

Kant explains *limit* as that which can be thought but not known.[1] In the West we think of God as the religious limit, and the Absolute as the philosophical limit. I suggest the more flexible category of 'the whole' to find some way to include non-Western religions as well. To think 'the whole' even if we cannot know the whole, moreover, discloses a second use of limit. This second use is best described as a disclosure of the limits to ordinary experience, language, and reason disclosed by the thought category of 'the whole'.

Nor is this kind of experience and language absent in common human experience and language itself. As I have argued at length elsewhere,[2] it is a correct use of language to speak of a

116

religious-as-limit dimension *to* ordinary experience and language. This religious dimension is disclosed in the limit-experiences of human existence. Those experiences include not only the positive limit-experiences of fundamental trust, joy, peace, love, but the profoundly negative human limit-experiences of anxiety, guilt, death, bereavement, alienation, and oppression. Moreover, religious-as-limit-to is present in a more reflective, less existential form in the limit-questions of scientific, moral, and aesthetic inquiry. These limit-experiences and limit-questions can disclose the reality of a genuinely religious dimension to ordinary experience and language, but they do not constitute *a religion*. Rather, like the limit-concept of the whole, these limit-questions and limit-experiences disclose a religious dimension to common human experience and language. They show the limits to the ordinary and, when reflected upon in the context of the whole, disclose a limit-to dimension of ultimacy.

On the basis of such limit-questions and limit-experiences, one may also be willing to risk an interpretation of the classic religious expressions. Paul Ricoeur observes that this involves risk. To risk what? An interpretation. An interpretation of what? The religious classics. Why? Because in the religious classics one may find the whole disclosed, what Jews and Christians call revelation. This revelation is the self-manifestation of the whole by the power of the whole as witnessed to in the classic religious expressions.

The risk is inevitably great. For religion is an ambiguous phenomenon in both human thought and history. Religion is cognitively ambiguous. Its cognitive ambiguity may well yield positive fruit for thought and life, but it may also yield such negative intellectual fruits as irrationality, obscurantism, and mystification.

And the cognitive ambiguity of religion is more than matched by its moral ambiguity. Religions release frightening, even demonic realities — as the tragedy at Jonestown disclosed anew. Yet this cognitive and ethical ambiguity of religion should be sufficient evidence that religion is intrinsically pluralistic and ambiguous. The turn to interpretation theory might help us see this often overlooked fact with greater clarity.

One key to interpretation, after all, is that interpretation is a primary phenomenon. We do not first experience and then interpret. Rather our experience is always already an interpretation. And insofar as we hope to interpret that experience rightly we will turn to the paradigmatic expressions of experience, especially language. To understand at all we must interpret. To understand anything we should first interpret its classic expressions. In the case of religion, this means that William James was correct that we should first interpret what he called the extreme cases, the saints and mystics, or what I am here calling the classic religious expressions.

By this turn to the interpretation of classic religious expressions as expressions, some of the difficulties of earlier interpretations of religion are resolved. One need not appeal, for example, to the Romantic ideal of some kind of religious virtuoso who is thereby able to interpret the expressions of the religious geniuses. Nor need one appeal, as Christian theologians often do, to the confusing claim that we can only interpret a religion by believing in it. Nor need we reject the expressions of religious experience as if expressions were wholly secondary phenomena.

All expression is primary. The subject matter of any text comes to us as a formed subject matter whose world of meaning results from composition, genre, and style. No classic expression, moreover, is likely to yield an easy, definitive single reading. Rather we are likely to find in the interpretations of the religious classics just what we find in the interpretations of all the classics: an inevitable pluralism of readings. This pluralism need not be chaotic, insofar as we can develop criteria of relative adequacy for better and less accurate readings. In interpreting the religious classics, we are also likely to find that a distinguishing characteristic of a religious use of any form of discourse, any genre, is a limit-use of that form.

Consider, for example, the now familiar contemporary discussion of the interpretation of the parables of Jesus in the New Testament. Unlike their historical-critical predecessors in exegesis, recent hermeneutical exegetes insist that genre is a productive, not merely a taxonomic, device. As productive, the genre produces the referent of the text by finding a proper form to express it. Moreover, as a religious use of this particular genre of parable, the form itself is radicalized, even transgressed and taken to its own limits. One can witness this transgression in the parables of Jesus: for example, in the extraordinary actions of the characters and in the dénouement of these otherwise very ordinary, realistic stories. The limit-qualifiers employed express the model and metaphor of what the reign of God is like. It is like what happens in the story. The specificity of religious language is disclosed not only in the limit-concept of the whole and the limit-questions and limit-experiences manifested in the religious dimension of existence; that same kind of specificity is also manifested in the explicitly religious use of any form of expression. The limit-character is shown not simply by its pointing back to the limit-concept that can be thought but not known, but by pointing ahead to the limit-referent of these concrete expressions. That referent as limit-referent may be the whole or God now manifest in and through these explicitly religious expressions. The expressions, as forms of discourse transgressed and brought to their limits, manifest their own clues to what kind of manifestation these peculiarly religious texts disclose.

In principle religion will prove both cognitively and ethically ambiguous and pluralistic, ever in need of new and relatively adequate interpretations of the expressions in the religious classics. We are left, therefore, where we began — with the religious classics always in need of new interpretation. The interpretations will be at best relatively adequate and always pluralistic. Yet if guided by the rubrics of contemporary interpretation theory, it may yet be possible to show how and why some claim to relative adequacy for particular readings can be made. But for this claim we must turn to a discipline which I here tentatively name a hermeneutics of religion.

II. A HERMENEUTICS OF RELIGION AND THE CONFLICT OF INTERPRETATIONS

The plurality and ambiguity of the religious phenomenon has given rise not only to a pluralism of readings of any classic religious text but also to a pluralism of methods of inquiry into religion. Indeed the phrase *religious studies* designates no agreed-upon method but serves as an umbrella term for a wide variety of disciplines and approaches to the phenomenon of religion.

In general terms, religious studies designates any study of religion as a phenomenon. There are clearly several ways to conduct this study. Three such ways deserve closer attention. The first is any analysis of how religion functions in a particular individual, society, or culture. That analysis will ordinarily be conducted by the use of some approved method within another discipline: psychology of religion, sociology of religion, or cultural anthropology of religion. There is, to be sure, enough strife over methods within each of these disciplines to ensure that any one functional study of religion, for example, sociology of religion, will itself yield a pluralism and often a conflict of readings of the phenomenon. Indeed the same kind of internal strife will also affect both the other two major approaches to religion.

The second is the claim to an autonomous discipline for the study of religion which employs an explicit analysis of the phenomenon of religion such as the holy. This discipline will sometimes be called history of religions or *Religionswissenschaft* or the scientific study of religion. This central mediating discipline, above all, most needs reformulation, I suggest, into a hermeneutics of religion. Thereby, we might be able to clarify the necessity of this discipline for mediating between both earlier functional analyses and later normative or substantive analyses. As hermeneutical, this mediating discipline might also disallow its own understandable temptations to become either purely historical-critical or even covertly functional or theological.

The third candidate for the study of religion is philosophical and theological studies. These latter studies are often called normative. This description is somewhat misleading insofar as it seems to suggest a *de jure* rule or norm imposed upon the phenomenon. Yet the term *normative* can be accurate insofar as it notes that philosophical and theological studies of religion, by the very nature of the disciplines, ordinarily do not confine themselves to descriptions of religion, whether functional or substantive. More exactly, philosophy and theology will ordinarily raise the question of the truth-status of the interpreted religious phenomenon. The conflict over what constitutes truth in religious questions is usually a major and notoriously complex concern of both philosophical and theological analyses of religion.

Theology, for example, is normative in the *de facto* — not the *de jure* — sense that it attempts to develop mutually critical correlations between the meaning and truth of an interpretation of a particular religious tradition and an interpretation of the contemporary situation. Because of its concern to develop criteria of public accountability for the meaning and truth of religions, theology can be further described as constituted by three major subdisciplines: fundamental, systematic, and practical theology. These latter subdisciplines are distinguished along a spectrum from concern for the relatively abstract to concern for the relatively concrete. Each subdiscipline attempts to develop public criteria for establishing the truth-character of the correlations established between the two interpretations. But let us also note that, besides its own responsibilities to publicness, theology is also dependent upon interpretations of religion as an autonomous phenomenon. It is this latter factor, I shall suggest, which unites theology to all other studies of religion and demands, within theology itself, the incorporation of the results of that mediating discipline which I have called a hermeneutics of religion.

Although there remains some functional utility to such traditional distinctions as those between normative and descriptive studies of religion or between functional and substantive studies, I have come to believe that these traditional distinctions now serve only a limited value. Whatever the scholar's own position on the autonomy or nonautonomy of religion, every student of religion presumably has some heuristic or developed notion of what religion is, and therefore already possesses some interpretation of religion to guide her or his research in religious studies. Indeed, it is difficult to see how any purely descriptive or purely functional analysis could proceed at all without some theory about which phenomena will count or not count as religious.

My own suggestions concerning methods in religious studies are, first of all, that theological and philosophical studies of religion must render their notions of religion explicit insofar as they claim to study critically the claims to meaning and truth of a particular religion.

Functional studies of religion, on the other hand, may — but need not — render explicit the claims to truth in the religions under study. Yet even here, scholars will need to use certain heuristic notions of what religion is as a phenomenon in order to proceed at all. These notions, in principle, could and should be rendered explicit in order to understand what counts and does not count as religion in these functional analyses.

And, finally, an autonomous mediating discipline of religious studies is crucially needed by all other scholars in religious studies.

That mediating discipline is needed by functional studies to guide any heuristic notions of religion actually operative in the study itself. The discipline is needed by theological and philosophical studies to guide the particular expressions and understandings of religion in this particular religious tradition. I have come to believe that the best way to describe this central mediating discipline is to rename it a hermeneutics of religion.

All I can hope to do at the moment, however, is to outline the basic character of this mediating discipline. Insofar as a hermeneutics of religion could provide interpretations that were not dependent upon Romantic notions of the interpreter as virtuoso nor on Romantic notions of empathy and divination of the mind of the author, this discipline could avoid some of the Romantic hermeneutical principles of traditional *Religionswissenschaft* while reformulating the need for that now largely dormant discipline. This discipline could incorporate the results of historical-critical methods and such explanatory formalist methods as semiotics and structuralism without utterly historicizing or formalizing the interpretation. It could also provide one communal way around the present impasse of formalist vs. historicist methods or the earlier impasse in history of religions of phenomenological vs. historical-empirical methods. Insofar as this discipline would not allow the imposition of *de jure* demands or norms upon the interpretation of the phenomenon, it would be able to distance itself from both the over-claims of any methodologism and any residual temptation to covertly theological positions in hermeneutics of religion.

But such "insofars," I realize, must remain at present not even a promise but only a hope. That hope has some grounding insofar as one's claims for interpretation are geared to the *de facto* (not *de jure*) process of interpretation. Yet it must remain only a hope until such time as a careful and detailed analysis of how this emergent discipline might break the series of impasses cited above. In the meantime, I must be content to elaborate only the basic warrants for that hope by describing the broad outlines of what such a mediating discipline would look like.

The first choice any prospective interpreter of religion makes is the choice concerning what phenomenon to interpret. In keeping with my reformulation of the Jamesian strategy suggested above, let us agree to choose first the classic religious expressions.

The prospective interpreter may believe either that religion is one of the great creative forces of the human spirit or that it is a deadly confusion. Yet whatever one's predilections on religion, the interpreter must be sure that the phenomenon to be interpreted is a genuinely religious one. The surest way to assure that is to choose for interpretation one of the religious classics of a particular religion. By choosing a recognized religious classic the interpreter will make two gains: first, the phenomenon, whatever else it is, will be religious; second, the phenomenon as a classic religious expression will lend itself to an interpretation theory that is designed to deal with expressions of experience and not directly with claims to purely unexpressed experiences.

With the choice of a single religious classic the interpretation will begin. Then the three steps in interpretation could be employed. The interpreter is likely to note that the religious classic will provoke some fundamental existential question for the human spirit as well as some particular response to that question as expressed in the particular classic religious text. As soon as any provocation is recognized by the interpreter, the second step of the interpretation process occurs. Not only are we provoked by the classic as by an other; we are also alerted by that otherness to a recognition of our own preunderstanding. The very otherness, even alienness, of the religious classic heightens the interpreter's consciousness of her or his own preunderstanding of religion. The effects of our cultural tradition on religion along with the effects of our own participation in a particular religious community now become more conscious to us. This history of effects does not (contra Hegel) become fully conscious but does become more conscious than prior to the provocation by the religious classic itself.

This initial interaction of the claim to attention provoked by the religious text and the preunderstanding (including the prejudgments) of the interpreter becomes a genuine interpretation when this initial interaction takes the more specific form of a conversation. Then the interpreter is willing to enter into the to-and-fro movement of the questions and responses of this classic text. When those religious questions become our own questions, then, as interpreters, we enter into a conversation with the now common subject matter of both text and interpreter. As in the interpretation of any other classic, this does not mean that the interpreter must

give up her or his own powers of critical reflection on these now
common questions. Nor does it mean that we will abandon a recognition of our own historicity. Indeed the exact opposite is the case
for, as Gadamer correctly and provocatively insists, "to understand
at all we must understand differently (than the original author)."[3]
It does mean, however, that if interpreters are to interpret the religious phenomenon as religious, they cannot simply impose their
prior value judgments upon it, by claiming autonomy and neutral-
ity, or by asserting that these questions are unintelligible and not
open to any understanding and therefore not open to interpretation. These *de jure* moves crash against the fact that once the text
has elicited its kind of question and forced the interpreter to consider a response to that question, the process of interpretation as
conversation has already begun.

The responses of the interpreter may range from mild interest to a full shock of either repugnance or recognition. In every case
along the whole spectrum of possible responses, as long as any claim
to attention is allowed at all, the conversation guided by the now
common questions on the common subject matter continues.
Neither interpreter nor text but the common subject matter takes
over in genuine conversation.

Interpretation as authentic conversation will not occur, however, if the prospective interpreter will not allow any provocation
from the religious text because the interpreter already knows that
this conversation is hopeless. Nor will a conversation occur if one
decides that so autonomous is the text that the interpreter cannot
consider her or his own critical responses as part of the conversation which is the interpretation. Nor will interpretation as conversation occur if the interpreter decides that the real meaning of the
text by definition cannot be found through the text itself but must
be found behind the text—in the mind of the author, the socio-
historical conditions of the text, or the response of the original audience to the text.

And yet, as this last textual factor indicates, there is also need
for two major correctives of the conversation model in order to assure that the full arc of contemporary interpretation occurs. Since
we are interpreting expressions when interpreting the religious classics, we are interpreting a structured whole which expresses its
claim to our attention through composition, genre, and style. The

text produces its world of meaning in front of the text as a possible way of being in the world. Thereby does the text produce a genuine possibility for the imagination. That possibility first comes to us simply as a claim to attention. As that claim provokes our attention and preunderstanding to the point where a conversation on a now common subject matter occurs, the interpreter will also recognize that the subject matter is always already a formed subject matter. The subject matter comes as an expression. As expression the interpreter finds the need to employ explanatory methods to develop her or his initial understanding and to check, correct, or even confront that initial understanding by the use of explanatory methods. All such methods — whether semiotic, structuralist, or literary-critical formalist — may serve as developments, checks, correctives, and challenges to the initial understanding. On this hermeneutic model, these methods serve these functions best by showing how the claim to attention provoked by the text is in fact produced as a world of meaning, a referent, in front of the text through work of the text itself.

On this reading, therefore, there is no reason to hold that a hermeneutics of religion should disallow such semiotic explanations of the religious classics as Louis Marin's analysis of the parables or such structuralist analyses as Claude Levi-Strauss's analysis of mythic structures. It is true that a hermeneutics of religion of the kind described above will not agree that these interpretations are fully adequate. Yet it will not only agree, but insist, that such interpretations are legitimate moments of explanation in the fuller process of interpretation. Any explanatory method that helps to show how the text produces its sense and referent is entirely appropriate to a hermeneutics of religion. As Schleiermacher's insistence on grammatical methods shows, as Gadamer's own recognition of the roles of structure and form demonstrates, as Joachim Wach's attention to classic religious expressions indicates, there is no reason in principle for the hermeneutical tradition to disallow the use of explanatory methods to develop, check, correct, and challenge one's initial interpretation. Creativity in interpretation is not opposed to explanation and method. The very pluralism intrinsic to the religious phenomenon itself, moreover, should encourage the use of the plurality of explanatory methods within the fuller process of interpretation. These methods may also serve to show how the explicitly religious use of any form — any genre or style — is a limit-use that produces the referent of the religious classic as a religious-as-limit mode of being in the world.

A second corrective should also be operative in contemporary hermeneutics of religion. Insofar as there is not only a plurality but also a cognitive ambiguity in every classic religious text and insofar as every classic religious text and tradition includes in its history of effects a moral ambiguity that *can* become a repressed systematic distortion, there is also need for the development and use of various hermeneutics of suspicion with their attendant critical theories upon the religious classics.

All the great hermeneutics of suspicion (Marx, Freud, Nietzsche) remain relevant methods of interpretation. Each develops a critical theory to inform its hermeneutics of suspicion. The critical theories are employed to spot and emancipate the repressed, unconscious distortions that are also operative in the classic religious texts and in their history of effects through the classic religious traditions. A hermeneutics of suspicion is demanded by the nature of the religious phenomenon itself.

It is sometimes claimed that the various hermeneutics of suspicion are simply taken from the secular classics and then used by interpreters of the religious classics to interpret religion. Yet as contemporary political, liberation, and feminist theologians correctly insist, these methods of suspicion are entirely appropriate to employ on inner-religious grounds. The reason for this, I believe, is clearly demonstrated in the Jewish and Christian traditions. For both, major strands of these traditions — generically the prophetic and the mystical — include explicitly religious hermeneutics of suspicion that demand constant self-reformation and self-suspicion by the tradition on the tradition's own religious grounds.

Bultmann is correct, on hermeneutical grounds, to insist that the prophetic-eschatological strand of Christianity demands demythologizing. At the heart of any prophetic tradition is a profound hermeneutics of suspicion in regard to all religious expressions as possibly idolatrous. At the heart of every prophetic tradition, therefore, is a demand for any critical theory that helps to uncover repressed illusions — including the repressed illusions of sexism, racism, classism, and so forth, that are also operative in the Jewish and Christian religious classics.

Nor is it the case that the mystical strands of the religious traditions are lacking in their own form of a hermeneutics of suspicion. For the great developments of spirituality in all the traditions, including the Jewish and Christian, were developed to find not mere errors but systematic unconscious illusions. The very use of the word *discernment* in the Christian traditions of spirituality, like the use of the word *enlightenment* in Buddhist traditions and the development of kabbalistic traditions for deconstructing texts in Jewish mysticism, is a clue that the mystical traditions also include their own hermeneutics of suspicion to be applied, above all, to such religious experiences as ecstasy and vision. In short, in both the mystical and the prophetic strands of the religious traditions, explicitly religious hermeneutics of suspicion already exist. As operative, these methods of interpretation of the pluralistic and ambiguous phenomenon of religion empower an internal religious hermeneutics of suspicion while also encouraging the incorporation of any other external hermeneutics of suspicion. As a pluralistic and ambiguous phenomenon, religion does not merely allow hermeneutics of both retrieval and suspicion: it demands both.

CONCLUSION:
A HERMENEUTICS OF RELIGION AS POSSIBILITY

All I have attempted here is to suggest why there is need for a mediating discipline named a hermeneutics of religion in contemporary religious studies and what the basic outline of such a discipline might be. If that outline can be developed, then real benefits could accrue for all. Among those benefits, I believe, would be the following: first, there would exist an explicitly hermeneutical mediating discipline that would develop interpretations of religion in the direction of a responsible pluralism faithful to the internal pluralism and ambiguity of the religious phenomenon itself. A pluralism of readings would not be free-floating but would hold itself responsible to the use of the kind of criteria suggested above at every stage of the process of interpretation. That pluralism of readings, above all, must hold itself responsible to a consensus in the whole community of inquirers in religious studies. No member of that community, for example, would have to depend simply upon the great virtuosi of religious interpretation. Rather each inquirer would enter into conversation with all the classic interpreters of religion on now communal and public grounds.

Second, a hermeneutics of religion could, as a discipline, genuinely mediate its interpretations as heuristic models worth employing by both functional studies of religion — like psychology of religion and sociology of religion — and theology. All these further disciplines, of course, would be entirely free to provide further tests, correctives, and challenges of the interpreted religious phenomenon in keeping with the demands and criteria of their own discipline. But the fact of a single mediating discipline known by all students of religion would at least assure that the pluralistic conversation would prove again a genuinely communal one aimed at and, in principle, expressive of some developing consensus on interpreting religion. Then there could be, in principle, at least enough consensus within the entire community of inquiry to spot fruitful disagreements and agreements and to correct the tendencies of both functional and normative approaches to impose their disciplinary standards upon all interpretations of religion.

Third, within my own discipline of Christian theology, the use of a hermeneutics of religion could serve as one communal constant in the further tasks of theological reflection. Insofar as theology develops mutually critical correlations between meaning and truth in a particular religious tradition and in the contemporary situation, a hermeneutics of religion would both prove a valuable communal tool and relate theology more internally to the other disciplines in religious studies. Finally, such an insistence within Christian theology upon the need for a hermeneutics of religion might aid the recognition of the intrinsic plurality and ambiguity of the Christian religion itself. That inner-Christian theological recognition of its own plurality and ambiguity might, in turn, free Christian theologians from the bond of any residual exclusivism and open Christian theology, at the very beginning of its reflections, to the reality of all the religions. The Christian theological habit of raising those questions only after the systematic task has been done has imprisoned many Christian theologies (including my own) in a relatively external relationship to the other religions as well as to the other disciplines in religious studies.

I cannot claim, of course, that I have provided sufficient warrants in this proposal to ground my hope for that emerging discipline. Nevertheless there are sufficient warrants to raise anew the question of whether a mediating discipline for all religious studies is now available again through the use of contemporary interpretation theory. Such, at least, is my basic hope and some of the reasons for the hope that lies in me.

NOTES

1. Immanuel Kant, *Critique of Pure Reason*, trans. Norman Kemp Smith (London: Macmillan, 1929), p. 273.

2. David Tracy, *Blessed Rage for Order* (New York: Seabury Press, 1975), pp. 105–36.

3. Hans-Georg Gadamer, *Wahrheit und Methode* (Tübingen: J. C. B. Mohr, 1960), p. 292.

7

Art and Religion

ELIOT DEUTSCH

"RELIGION AND ART STAND beside each other like two friendly souls whose inner relationship, if they suspect it, is still unknown to them."[1]

I. THE CREATION OF A RELIGION-WORK

A *religion-work*, as distinct from a *religious work* (of art or whatever), is a specific rite, hymn, dance whose primary function is to lead the participant in it to a distinctive religious state of being, as this state may be defined in a particular religious tradition. In the religion-work, in contrast to an artwork, aesthetic contemplation is by intention secondary to this primary function of "leading-to." The religion-work is thus always allied to magic: relationships and encounters that bring about a control over, or transformation of, self or others are demanded and expected of the work.

Who creates a religion-work? Not an individual. Try to imagine a particular person deciding to create a ritual the way an individual artist may decide to set up an easel and begin painting. Religion-works are group expressions that have arisen organically — in the context of cult needs. They express a collective will, not an individual genius.

The participant in a religion-work is thus part and parcel of the creative process which brings it into being. Without the participant the ritual is a lifeless, empty form. The participant, though, it must be understood, is not just another individual *qua* subjective individual, as though he or she were performing a private ritual. A ritual may be performed in private, but it demands always a collective context or group identity. Without the cult we don't have a ritual; we have an obsessional neurosis.

The participant in a religion-work feels that the spiritual power or god to which the work is dedicated is present in the work, but in such a paradoxical way that the work itself generates the presence. When the participation-creation of the work is completed, as with primitive religious consciousness generally, the felt power withdraws and is there only latently. In contrast to the artist's exciting sense of *discovery,* as Eliade and others have convincingly shown, the creator-participant in the religion-work has an awesome awareness of *recovery.* Artists feel that they are bringing something new into being; participants in a religion-work that they are reenacting a timeless possibility.

The religion-work, like the artwork, is thus a kind of play. Creativity is play (is sport, *līlā* in Sanskrit), and in the religion-work this creativity calls for a special role-playing or acting, one which, from the standpoint of the participant-creator, must be entirely unself-conscious. The role-playing must be a complete stepping out (*ekstasis* in Greek) from one's ordinary functional life; one must literally become the role during the time of the play. And this is perhaps why so few of us today are capable any longer of being full participant-creators of religion-works. We are fearful of losing ourselves in the intense self-giving that is required. We are afraid that with the abandonment of self-control we may encounter the demonic.

In art the play must be entirely natural to the artist; that is to say, it must be a spontaneous, albeit highly disciplined, expression of one's being. In religion the play is a cosmic offering, with the player being utterly forgetful of his or her own being.

II. GOODNESS AND ART

It is often thought today that there is an inherent and perhaps irreconcilable conflict between art and morality or between aesthetic and ethico-religious consciousness. This conflict arises, it seems, from the recognition that on the one hand art and morality (religion) are kindred forms of spiritual life and on the other that there are sharp differences between them and that, accordingly, they make opposing claims upon us. Sidney Zink sums up the sharp differences and opposing claims in these compact terms:

> Morality insists upon the interconnectedness of experiences; art insists upon the self-containedness of each particular experience. The moral man scrutinizes the given action for its relations to other actions; the aesthetic man absorbs himself in the immediate experience. Morality insists upon the inviolability of the man, art upon the inviolability of the experience. Morality recognizes the fact of dimensionality in life; art stresses the fact of qualitativeness. The first would make life consistent; the second would make it intense. Morality speaks in the interest of the whole, art in the interest of the part.[2]

Historically, of course, at other times and in other places, this way of characterizing art and morality would have been unintelligible. The dominant presupposition from Hellenism to the Renaissance was simply that art was subservient to the demands of morality, as theologically defined and understood. Art was a vehicle for teaching and illustrating the faith and did not enjoy an independent life of its own.

Today, on the other hand, art has established its autonomy. Most aestheticians and critics today would even go so far as to say that the only goodness in art is of a strictly aesthetic kind. A work of art that is aesthetically right is simply good by virtue of this rightness — without moral remainder. We allow intrusions from the ethical into art only insofar as they can be taken over and entirely assimilated by purely aesthetic considerations.

Plato and Tolstoy were perhaps the most articulate and historically important opponents of any view which upholds the radical autonomy of art. According to Plato (*Ion, Phaedrus, Republic, Laws*), works of art appeal to the passional elements of the soul and, by the pleasure they afford, divert the soul's attention from rational contemplation, its proper end. Recognizing the efficacy of art to excite and stimulate, Plato would, in an ideal republic, ban artworks and artists who were intent on this excitement. Only that which was conducive to fostering harmony and order in the soul would be tolerated.

Tolstoy in his famous essay *What Is Art?* wages the most thorough and sustained attack on a formalist view of art and its related art-is-autonomous standpoint. He insists that art does not have properly to do with pleasure so much as it has to do with the communication of feeling. And when the work of art is right it has to do with communicating those feelings which are intimately related to the basic religious perception of the society; the perception for modern Western society having to do, so Tolstoy believes, with the universal kinship of all humanity. Working from an expression theory of art Tolstoy argues that artists have certain vivid feelings which are embodied in their works and which are then evoked in others. For the sake of the universal society the cognitive dimensions of art must be intelligible to the vast majority of humankind; it is the ordinary person in fact who discerns most clearly the natural accord between the feelings embodied in the artwork and genuine religiosity.

Now Plato's puritanism and Tolstoy's religious socialism are quite unacceptable. Plato neglects completely the revelatory powers of art and wrongly assumes that aesthetic satisfaction is of the same nature as sense pleasure. Tolstoy fails to understand the difference between art as expressing various religious feelings and art as the suffusing of a structured content with a feeling tone; and he fails to appreciate the distinction between complexities in art which are appropriate and sheer unintelligibility.

Placing art under morality or excluding the moral from art are not the only ways by which the alleged conflict between art and morality can be adjudicated. Kant, with his notions that "the beautiful is the symbol of the morally good" and that "the mind is made conscious of a certain ennoblement and elevation above the mere sensibility to pleasure received through sense,"[3] tries to give some content, however thin, to the idea of a perfect accord obtaining between the ethical and the aesthetic — in other words, to the idea that there is no essential conflict between them. Croce also takes a step in that direction when he writes:

> The basis of all poetry [art] is human personality, and, since human personality finds its completion in morality, the basis of all poetry is the moral consciousness. Of course this does not mean that the artist must be a profound thinker or an acute critic; nor that he must be a pattern of virtue or a hero;

but he must have a share in the world of thought and action which will enable him, either in his own person or by sympathy with others, to live the whole drama of human life.[4]

But the artist's having "a share in the world of thought and action" and the spectator's mind being "ennobled by a shared higher-than-just-sense experience" are clearly insufficient to resolve the problem — which is to locate the moral dimension of art within the framework of art's required autonomy. The resolution of the problem, I think, is this: creativity, and thus art, by its nature is celebrative and calls for a loving consciousness.

Creativity always manifests concern, and thus by its very nature art is a celebration of selfhood and the world — if not in their actualities at least in their real potentialities. A Goya *Disasters of War*, a Grünewald *Crucifixion*, a Picasso *Guernica* are affirmative, for they point to and take their judgmental stand from a concern for human dignity and worth. If artists were overcome by dejection, by despair and agony, they could not create. They might be able to shout and scream, as others might do, although more likely they would sink into apathy and hopelessness; in any case "being overcome" is not conducive to creativity and indeed is incompatible with it.

Recognizing the immense cruelty often exhibited by fellow human beings as well as the capacity for cruelty in oneself; seeing gross stupidity, selfishness, and perversity which seem always to intrude into human affairs; being aware of that nothingness, the obliteration, that appears finally to render all human achievements futile, the artist, nevertheless, as artist, possesses that loving consciousness which acknowledges an intrinsic value to self and other. Without that acknowledgment the artist would not be able to recognize the possibility of creating worth and value in the truth and beauty that is to be there in the work of art. Art cannot help being celebrative.

This moral dimension of art has nothing to do, then, with the motive of the artist; it has to do only with that special lovingness which informs imagination and intuition and which is at the heart of artistic creativity. This love, this concern, this celebration resounds in the work and demands our openness to it.

Hence, at this level of spirituality there is no conflict between art and morality, as here the ethico-religious is taken up as one with the aesthetic: with love, the aesthetic — while maintaining its full integrity — is inseparable from the ethical. The artist may or may not be moral by conventional societal standards; the work may or may not have beneficial moral effects upon others; but the work of art is necessarily good by virtue of the celebrative power made evident in its structural content.

III. RELIGION AND THE ARTWORK

Both art and religion may be revelatory of being. Each, in its way, may present something of the spiritual life for response and experience; each may articulate intuitions of spiritual being. What makes a work of art religious? Many works of art are said to be religious because of their subject matter, because of what they are about. The subject matter of an artwork, if taken as a content of it, must, then, be distinguished from the meaning, or the proper content, of the work. Albert Hofstadter draws the distinction nicely in this way:

> It is helpful to distinguish between content in the sense of material or subject matter included in the artistically constructed figure and content in the sense of the particular meaning of the work itself, for the expression of which the materials and subject matters are brought into it. A landscape painter includes a rock, a pond, and trees in his paintings. They are materials, subject matters, introduced into the artistic composition for the sake of making the figure. The figure as a whole is the total composition itself — the landscape, as such, is the meaning that belongs to it as just that total artistic composition.[5]

The subject matter of an artwork is what the elements in the work may be said to refer to or what the work as a whole may, if it is appropriate, be about. The meaning, the content in the fullest sense, of the artwork is the formed unity of the particular work itself as it embodies and conveys a unique concrete meaning or intuition of being. The artwork, I maintain, is religious when that concrete intuition is of spiritual being. Religious art is not simply art that has religion as its subject matter. The representation of the Crucifixion, of a meditating Buddha, or the inclusion of clearly identifiable religious symbols of whatever tradition by itself constitutes what some people call religious art, but it is only religious art at its most transparent, purely nominal, and aesthetically uninteresting level.

It is here, of course, that the battle between art and religion over the obligation of art to conform to theology has often been fought. And the conflict is not just a historical curiosity. As sophisticated and prominent a modern thinker as Jacques Maritain can still write that

> Sacred [religious] art is in a state of absolute dependence upon theological wisdom. There is manifested in the figures it sets before our eyes something far above all our human art, divine Truth itself, the treasure of light purchased for us by the blood of Christ. For this reason chiefly, because the sovereign interests of the Faith are at stake in the matter, the Church exercises its authority and magistracy over sacred art.[6]

But art is sacred, I would argue, only insofar as it is revelatory of spiritual being; only insofar, that is, as it radiates with an intuition of spiritual being. Maritain confounds a whole type of artwork with religion proper and refuses thereby to acknowledge the emergence of the artwork as an autonomous form of spiritual life. Hofstadter writes:

> Religion interprets reality by means of symbols and rituals that depend only in part upon their expressive appearances to communicate their meanings. The consecrated wafer does not need to look like the body of God. Its religious potency and meaning depend more on representational connections in the mind, often quite independent of the symbol, than on its actual aspect. . . .
>
> What art does is to articulate an image which exists as the object of intuition and which gives to intuition an immediate grasp of meaning.[7]

The artwork which is entirely dependent for its meaning upon its subject matter tends to be didactic and of little aesthetic interest. The religious dimension of art rests, then, precisely on that articulation of "an image which exists as the object of intuition," when that intuition is of spiritual being.

Turning now to the other side of the artwork and religion kinship, the aesthetic dimension of religion is often taken to consist in a spectator's disinterested appreciation of a religious ceremony as an aesthetic object — as if the religion-work, in formal terms, were a kind of artwork. Now it is of course possible to adopt this kind of aesthetic attitude to anything whatever, and it is also true that religion-works frequently contain formal qualities that lend themselves to aesthetic appreciation quite readily, but it should also be clear enough that one who is seeking aesthetic qualities per se is better advised to look for them in their primary place with their full expressive potentiality, namely in works of art. One would be well advised to look for the aesthetic dimension of the religion-work at a somewhat deeper level of experience. That level, I believe, is the one which involves us once again in symbol and meaning.

Hofstadter separated religion from art by placing the former in the domain of conventional symbolic values. But this is too strong a separation, for if it were so, one would respond to a religion-work not religiously, but only cognitively — with, to be sure, the various emotive factors which accompany any cognitive concern. The conventional symbolism is, I agree, dominant in religion, but it is effective religiously only insofar as it is allied, at one end, with the magic power associated with the primitive and, at the other end, with the spiritual meaning of art itself.

I have argued elsewhere that there is a primitive stage where art and religion are indistinct: what we have at this stage are art-religion works which engender and express a kind of magical power.[8] The value of the religion-work, once the separation between an artwork and a religion-work occurs, lies precisely in the degree to which this power-engendering is still present, engendered not by symbolic meanings as such but by ritual patterns and movements, gestures and sounds, invested with magical potency.

At the other end, the religion-work is participated in religiously because of the degree to which its conventional symbolic meanings are made alive by the presence of spiritual being as articulated in the work. The conventional symbolism — with the symbols being commensurate with the theology of the particular tradition — is the subject matter of the work and also its dominant content; but the work itself, at this end of the spectrum, is for a participant and spectator a religion-work and not just a bare conveyor of symbols. With genuine religion-works the conventional symbolism is always partially transcended and an essential spirituality is made manifest.

IV. RELIGIOUS AND AESTHETIC EXPERIENCE

In philosophy of religion as well as in aesthetics the notion of *experience* has, until very recently, come to dominate discussion. Among philosophers of religion, religious experience, at least since William James's *Varieties of Religious Experience,* has generally replaced such topics as proofs for the existence of God; and among philosophers of art aesthetic experience has been analyzed far more extensively than, say, the traditional concept of beauty.

Religious experience, of course, is immensely varied. Three major forms are usually distinguished: the mystical, the theistic, and, for want of a better term, the primitive.

To begin with the third: primitive religious consciousness, which is often associated with the religion of peoples in primitive societies,[9] sees regularity in experience but not lawlike or nomic structures. It sees events, as it tends to see itself, as belonging to a group, and not as instances or exemplifications of universal principles. Hence the interplay of magic and religion in primitive religious consciousness.

But it is not that primitive religious consciousness sees things as *having* souls or spirits; it sees things as *being* souls or spirits. Primitive religious consciousness is fundamentally that mode of perception that utterly confounds the spiritual and the material — at the level of the empirical. Everything seen is equally materially and spiritually real to it.

And so with aesthetic consciousness, in its way. Not only is the aesthetic allied to the primitive in its involvement with spiritual power, the aesthetic also sees things in their startling particularity and as they are potentially numinous. Withdrawing interest from those functional or practical aspects of things and concentrating attention entirely on what is presented, aesthetic consciousness notices especially those qualities which reveal the singularity and power of things.

The kinship between aesthetic and religious consciousness is likewise exhibited, and perhaps even more intimately, with theistic experience — the experience of human beings in relation to a personal divinity, who is usually taken to be a supreme creator god. (Polytheism may here be collapsed with monotheism, for in experiential terms the polytheist, it is often pointed out, is in fact more of a henotheist who tends to ascribe ultimacy to no more than one god at a time and to relate to him or her accordingly.)

At one extreme of theistic experience we have the experience of unity; of deep communion between self and God, a communion which is ecstatic and overwhelming. Theistic experience is here bordering on the mystical, but with the presence still of both subject and object it comes within the relational order. The unity of self and God in this the most intense loving relation is of two spirits. Lost as the self might be in the intensity of its loving wonderment it nevertheless is there in the full integrity of its own being.

The theistic experience, however, in its most common and basic form is one of encounter. As Rudolf Otto described it, the experience involves a special complex state of consciousness, one that "is perfectly *sui generis* and irreducible to any other."[10] Otto called this special state of consciousness the numinous; it is that which is directed to a *mysterium tremendum*. The *tremendum*, for Otto, involves such elements as "awefulness," "overpoweringness," and urgency; the *mysterium*, wholly-otherness with its sense of fascination. What emerges from Otto's phenomenology of theistic experience is the presence within the experience of conflicting tensions, of attractions and repulsions, of opposing feelings such as that of great power and also helplessness. Nearness and estrangement become the two poles within which the experience vibrates.

At the other extreme of theistic experience we have what we may call the "magical pietistic"— the black mass, the orgiastic tantric. Theism is here allied with the primitive in its emphasis upon magical presence and fear-inspired worship.

Throughout these different kinds of theistic religious experience there is that turning of self over to the Other for the sake of completion; there is loving, faithful consciousness, a faith that is not just invoked in the experience but which is part of an integral process. It is a common mistake, I think, to assume that an experience just happens to begin at some specifiable point in

X's career and that X then undergoes something which he or she then can subsequently reflect upon as "my experience." This kind of assumption leads one to neglect the fact that most interesting and profound experiences are processes of relationship which are integral to, and extend throughout, the development of one's personhood.

The faithful attitude which is at once formative of and expressive of the person makes possible then the self-surrender or giving of self-will that theistic experience requires. The self-surrender, though, is not passive in character; rather, as Otto and others like Tillich have shown, it involves an active integration of emotive, cognitive, and conative dimensions: it involves the whole person. The experience itself then becomes an intensification of these capacities of self, and the experiencer has the sense of enhanced power. Emotionally this is expressed in the joy that is felt and also, often, in the accompanying anguish and feeling of helplessness; conatively in the feeling of liberation and freedom from the constraints otherwise operating in self-will; cognitively in the awareness of a new valuational ground for one's ideas and beliefs.

From this enhancement there follows that self-transformation which, in its most intense form in religion, is a conversion of self or a new birth. The experience process culminates in a reshaping and remaking of the experiencer.

Many of these features or moments of experience are characteristic of the aesthetic as well as of the religious. To experience a work of art one must be open to it so that it may fully be for one. Unlike in religious experience, however, a distance is required between self and object to enable the self to suspend many of the practical interests and needs of everyday life. The semblance quality of the artwork must always be maintained in the self-giving process of the apprehension of the work's form and meaning.

In the experience of an artwork there is also that enhancement of self, that exciting joy, liberation, and self- and world-discovery.[11] And most importantly there is that peacefulness — what traditional Indian aesthetics call *śāntarasa* — that comes from a loving participation in the artwork.[12] Aesthetic experience is loving experience; an accepting, celebrating, affirming relation with an object whose formed content controls the response of the experiencer and for which the experiencer, in his or her own way, seeks completion.

Theists may assert God's need for them as well as their need for God, and transfiguration through the relationship; aesthetic experiencers also find themselves to be new beings when they are truly with that artwork whose excellence may rightfully call for rejoicing.

The mention of *śāntarasa* — the quality of serenity, harmony, fulfillment that is said, in later Indian aesthetics, to be the essence of the aesthetic — brings us to the mystical.

By radically separating the concept from the thing and by stressing the distance between the human and the divine, most of us today have lost not only the sense of divine power experienced by the primitive and the yearning for completion felt so intensely by the devout theist, but their profound sense of wonder as well. It is the mystical which, it seems to me, regains and retains what is best in the primitive and theistic; and the mystical is expressed most clearly in art.

Śāntarasa is the realization of spiritual silence which arises, at the most essential level of aesthetic experience, from the involvement with the radiant splendor of the artwork. Religion and art here assuredly achieve their highest kinship, for the aesthetic here points the way to Reality and to divinity. Experiencers, as well as creators, of the artwork at this level apprehend in and through the work their own being as it is in its wholeness and integrity. The apprehension of the essential in art, the *śāntarasa*, is at once an experience of the artwork and a realization of the self. A harmony prevails in which the self knows itself in relation to Reality.

The mystic, however, in the last analysis, unlike the experiencer of the essential in art, dispenses with all symbols in favor of direct unity or identity with what others believe the symbol merely points to. The mystic doesn't, finally, require an artwork; but then he or she apprehends Reality itself, where nothing at all is required.

These reflections on art and religion are admittedly somewhat disjointed, but I think a certain disjointedness appropriate because of the immense richness and complexity in the relationship between those forms of spiritual life which "stand beside each other" but "whose inner relationship is still unknown to them."[13]

The artist and the saint cannot do each other's work. Art and religion, while allied spiritual activities, are not the same thing.

The religion-work, whose primary function is one of leading

the participant in it to distinctive religious states of being, calls precisely for a participation which goes to define the very character of the work. The religion-work involves a sense of recovery rather than aesthetic discovery, the reenacting of a timeless possibility rather than the bringing of something new into being; the religion-work is a collective expression rather than the product of an individual effort.

But the aesthetic and the religious can nevertheless be seen in close harmony by way of the ethical, for when the goodness appropriate to art is located within the framework of art's required autonomy we see that creativity, by its nature, is celebrative and calls for a loving consciousness.

Art and religion may each then present the spiritual life for response and experience. But what makes an artwork religious is not its subject matter but its content, as this represents an intuition of spiritual being. Conventional religion cannot rightfully make any demands upon art, for the sacredness of art is to be found only in its capacity to be revelatory of spiritual being. On the other side of the art/religion kinship the aesthetic dimension of religion is found not in an aesthetic appreciation of the formal qualities of religion-works per se. Rather, a religion-work is grounded, at one end, in a primitive power which is intrinsic to the work and, at the other end, in what art itself seeks, namely, its being a form that articulates a meaning for intuition when an essential spirituality is made manifest.

The experiences of art and religion likewise disclose similarities and differences, with each contributing to the understanding of the other. Primitive religious experience, with its emphasis upon singular, efficacious happenings, is allied with the aesthetic insofar as the aesthetic also concentrates on particularity and sees things as potentially numinous.

Theistic religious experience is also closely allied with the aesthetic in its interest in self-surrender, emotional fulfillment, and loving consciousness. Both the religious and the aesthetic are formative of and expressive of a process of person-development and lead, when successful, to an enhancement of self and discovery of world. Both often vibrate with the tensions and suffering associated with the intensity of the search and subsequent realization or failure. Both kinds of experience can also point the way to an essential level of spirituality where an enduring harmony is achieved.

The mystical is just that level of essential spirituality where religion and art most closely meet, interrelate, and separate. The aesthetic experience here enables the experiencer to apprehend his or her own being, through the artwork, in its wholeness and integrity. The self is enabled to know itself in relation to Reality. Religious mystics, on the other hand, are able to dispense with artworks entirely. They advance in that abysmal aloneness to the realization of Reality itself.

NOTES

1. Friedrich Schleiermacher, *On Religion, Speeches to Its Cultured Despisers*, trans. John Oman (London: Kegan Paul, Trench, Trubner, 1893), p. 11.

2. Sidney Zink, "The Moral Effect of Art," *Ethics* 60 (1950): 261–74.

3. Immanuel Kant, *Critique of Judgment*, trans. J. H. Bernard (New York: Hafner Press, 1951), p. 59.

4. *Encyclopaedia Britannica*, 14th ed., s.v. "Aesthetics."

5. Albert Hofstadter, *Agony and Epitaph* (New York: George Braziller, 1971), p. 66.

6. Jacques Maritain, *Art and Scholasticism: With Other Essays* trans. J. F. Scanlan (New York: Scribner's, 1954), p. 111.

7. Hofstadter, *Agony and Epitaph*, p. 58.

8. Cf. "On the Concept of Art," *The Journal of Chinese Philosophy* 3 (1976): 373–97.

9. Many historians of religion, in order to avoid the pejorative use of *primitive* to mean savage or barbaric, proffer the neutral definition of primitive religion as just the religion of people in primitive societies. For example, in *Man's Religions*, 3rd ed. (New York: Macmillan, 1963), p. 3, John B. Noss defines primitive religion in terms of "those smaller, less informed, and more isolated societies whose technology is not as highly developed as in civilized societies and whose religious systems are regarded by all in the group, without exception, as indispensable to social harmony and satisfactory adaptation to the immediate environment." Edwin A. Burtt, *Man Seeks the Divine* (New York: Harper & Brothers, 1957), p. 35, also defines primitive religion in much the same way. For purposes of philosophical understanding, however, primitive religion — or religious

consciousness — can perhaps best be taken as an ideal type or model of a certain kind of experience; one that is closest to the origins of religion and yet may be present at any historical period or stage.

10. Rudolf Otto, *The Idea of the Holy*, trans. John W. Harvey (New York: Oxford University Press, 1958), p. 7.

11. The community of art and religion on the experience side is also exhibited in the oftentimes similar negative states of alienation and despair, spiritual dryness, and loss of confidence, in those "dark nights" which bewilder both the artist and the spiritual aspirant. These negative states may be deemphasized, however, in looking for the kinship between art and religion (they are often overemphasized), as they don't seem to constitute the essential linkage between the two.

12. The concept of *śāntarasa* was most fully developed in the thought of Abhinavagupta, a Kashmiri thinker of the tenth century. See my *Studies in Comparative Aesthetics* (Honolulu: University Press of Hawaii, 1975), chap. 1.

13. Schleiermacher, *On Religion*, p. 11.

8

Buddhism, Christianity, and the Critique of Ideology

NINIAN SMART

IT IS IMPORTANT THAT we who study religion not only do so with integrity but also make our voices heard in the wider world. Religious studies is basically mixed in style: at one level it is concerned with trying to describe, present, and explain. But at another level it should not hold back from reflections based upon the knowledge and insights supplied by that first mode — by what may be called the scientific study of religion. I use the phrase but it is important to realize that science here includes structured empathy and that warm dispassion which is necessitated by the subject of our enquiries: human facts and the focuses of those facts. In brief, religious studies also includes reflections about our world. Such reflections can enter the open mainstream of debate about the world's affairs, dominated so often by political scientists, sociologists, and economists. Religious studies has no quarrel with these disciplines. They are indeed part of the fabric of religious studies anyway, for the departmentalizations of academic life need to allow for the overlaps which are brought forth by the seamless web of what we study.

But this very seamlessness means that even the category 'religion' itself is open to question. In the real world human beings find themselves with conflicting world views and values, some of which are traditionally and conventionally to be called religious and others which are secular ideologies. It would be better in my opinion if we considered our field to be not so much religious studies as world-view analysis and evaluation. The mental and

symbolic sides of human beings, the world views which help to
direct and channel feelings and institutions and actions, are as
much worthy of systematic study as the economic aspect; but in
the academy and in the thinking of citizens world-view study is
actually broken up. If it is the world view of smaller societies we
want to understand, we go to the anthropologist. For some purposes we turn to the philosopher and the historian of ideas. If it
is the secular ideologies we are thinking about, we go to the political scientist and the sociologist. For traditional faiths we go to
religious studies. It is a pity that such a breakup of the wider field
occurs. It helps to conceal the power of ideas. It also incorporates
an ideological distinction between religion and ideology (a religious
distinction too) which helps to distort the true seamlessness of the
human world. So it is important that we study religions and
ideologies together, and that we reflect upon them together. That
is why in this essay I wish to think about the relations between two
of the great religions and three of the great ideological components
of recent history. But before coming to my main thesis,[1] which can
be summed up as saying that Christianity and Buddhism can in
a complementary manner offer a critique of the secular ideologies,
I wish briefly to survey the world scene in order to show how the
argument I am going to offer relates to our present condition.

First we may note that we have now entered on the era of
what I call the global city. It is a city, not a village, because there
are differing ethnic quarters in our world, and ghettos, and a very
plural and turbulent mélange of forces. All the ideologies and religions, in brief all the major world views, are in interaction and
contact, just as the economies of the differing parts of the world
are in contact and mutual interpenetration.

Second, certain defined areas of the global city can be discerned. There is the West, formed much by Christianity but also
by other forces, and this may be called the trans-Christian West.
It is mainly social democracies, but includes societies such as the
United States that do not necessarily welcome that designation.
Then there are the various Marxist countries, from East Germany
to North Korea. Then there is the Islamic Belt stretching from West
Africa through the Middle East almost to the shores of Australia,
with scarcely an interruption. Then there are the countries of Old
Asia unconquered by Marxisms, from India through Theravādin

countries to countries like Taiwan and South Korea on the periphery of China, to Japan. These Old Asian countries reflect values drawn from the Hindu, Confucian, and Buddhist traditions, among others, but the most important in many ways is Buddhism. Then there are the countries of black Africa and other areas such as the South Pacific with many smaller societies, mainly Christian but concerned with shaping identities in the face of global, especially Western, forces. Then there is Latin America from Oxnard to Patagonia with its blend of pre-Columbian and Hispanic values, now fermenting greatly in many places in order to establish new dignities for the poor.

These last two cultural areas are of special importance in the ongoing quest for global justice. If in the past there was a division in the West of an acute kind between rich and poor, that is now reflected differently: the northern countries are relatively rich; and Latin America, Africa, and elsewhere represent the new global proletariat. But though it is important for us to bear this problem in our minds, my main argument concerns the relationship of the Old Asian bloc, the Western bloc, and the Marxisms.

It is in this context that, without wishing to undervalue Judaism, Hinduism, Confucianism, and other religious traditions of East and West, I wish to pick out Christianity and Buddhism as the two most significant. They have both for good or ill been very strong missionary religions. Only one other faith, Islam, matches such missionary endeavor. And in this context I am not going to dwell on the relations of Islam to the other blocs, partly because it has strong incompatibilities with the two main traditional religions I am concerned with and thus represents a more intractable problem if we are trying to shape the future of the global city. Partly too it is that my experience is more with these other two.

As for the so-called secular ideologies, I think it is reasonable to think of Western values as having been much shaped by utilitarianism, which sometimes takes the form of scientific humanism. But all countries have also been, indeed by definition, deeply affected by the growth of nationalism, which has something of the properties of religion and which treats the nation as deserving its own state, which then becomes the community of ultimate concern to citizens. It is typically in the name of the nation-state that systematic modernization and education have been undertaken.

Finally, among the major ideological forces of our time there is
Marxism, or rather Marxisms. Marxism has reinforced the idea of
the nation-state, because it concentrates power, supplies a notion
of "the people" that almost inevitably refers to the nation, and
serves as a strong instrument in a number of struggles of national
liberation.

Now a certain paradox, or rather set of paradoxes, is to be
found in regard to the secular ideologies. First, there is the paradox of happiness. Utilitarianism and the welfare ethic suppose that
we have an idea of what human happiness consists in, yet the more
we focus on this idea, the more open to essential debate it seems
to be. The paradox of nationalism is that its logic leads both to ag-
grandizement and to a kind of federal respect for other national
groups. The problem of the Marxisms is that the vaunted liberation of the ordinary man and woman takes the form of strong
conformism.

Indeed we may note that the old church-state alliance under
the rubric of *cuius regio eius religio* is now most obviously to be
found in Marxism, where citizens are expected to accept the official ideology. If secularization means the separation of church
and state then it is *least* evident in Eastern bloc countries, insofar
as Party is the new church. The fact that we artificially separate
religion from secular ideology sometimes obscures this thought
from us. If we call those societies in which ideological or world-
view conformity is expected *monistic* ones, then the countries of
the Marxisms are the most effectively monistic in the present world.

Now if we look at both religious and secular world views as
on a par with one another we can see that some of the world is
witnessing religious-secular syncretization. Thus typically we find
forms of Christianity which syncretize with utilitarian humanism, others which syncretize with nationalism, others again with
both, while Latin American liberation theology involves a certain
blend of Christianity and Marxism. Similarly, one may see such
cross-syncretisms in Buddhism. Nevertheless, the religions do hold
in principle to the notion of the transcendent, of a religious ultimate which lies beyond this world. And this, I shall argue, provides a vantage point from which we may criticize the secular notions of happiness, nationalism, and so on.

But can Buddhism and Christianity, for instance, truly be allies in this? Do they not notoriously differ in presupposition and practice? Indeed they do, and I regard Therāvāda Buddhism in particular as a test case of most Western theories of religion. There is no real creator in the Therāvāda, no Yahweh numinous out of the storm and at the still day of the creation of the world. There is no final resting place in heaven in the company of God, but rather an ultimate liberation in which all individuality has been shed. There is no story of the Fall or of a redemption, though there is an alternative story of the preaching of Shamma. Even if in the Greater Vehicle there comes to be numerous echoes of Christian faith, and even if in Christian mysticism, especially in Pseudo-Dionysius and other exponents of negative theology, there are many echoes of Buddhist emptiness, there are still great conflicts and divergences.

Nevertheless, there is a case for seeing a kind of harmony between the two: not a unity, but a complementarity. Before I come to this let me make an obvious but often neglected point about religious truth.

It is clear that we live in a religiously plural world. It is clear also that in nonreligious matters epistemology has become greatly undogmatic. Imagination, experimentation, falsification, testing, criticism, probing: these are the methods of the scientific mind. Yesterday's orthodoxies are today overthrown. We know the fate of Lord Kelvin, and how suddenly the not-so-long-ago despised theory of continental drift is now official doctrine. We recognize in the scientific and intellectual world the need for the critical mind and the death of dogmatism. The same necessarily applies to religion. Even the theory that religion is different and depends therefore on transcendental revelation and divine certainty is itself open to debate and so is uncertain. Every religion or world view has to come to terms with other world views and theorize about them, recognizing them as alternatives. It is not surprising that in such a disturbingly uncertain world there are conservative backlashes. But the general temper of the contemporary epistemological scene is pluralistic, revisionary, experimental.

Inevitably the days of dogmatism in religion are over. This is reinforced by social facts in the open societies of the West: if I do not like the pronouncements of a pope or guru I migrate to another community or none at all. Even joining a collectivity such as the Roman Catholic Church is an individual act. I can sacrifice my individual freedom if I wish to, but it is I that do it.

In such a world as this every position must come under the scrutiny of criticism. This is where my faith may indeed learn from others. In such a situation it matters not that Buddhism and Christianity are so different and do not, cannot, constitute a unity. They can serve as mutual critics and can thus learn from one another.

Moreover there is a certain congruity in some of their aspects. Thus Christianity focuses on a Christ who was self-emptying and met death upon the Cross: he was the reverse of a self-aggrandizer. This is a myth of emptiness. Buddhism has instead a philosophy and contemplative path of emptiness. In the one there is a mystic expression of emptying; in the other, a dialectical and metaphysical expression thereof. Similarly the self-sacrificing *bodhisattva* has affinities with Christ, compassion relates to Christian love, and in both traditions the loss of self has positive meaning.

Moreover, they can serve as correctives to one another. Buddhism stands as a corrective to the ever-recurring anthropomorphism and violence of the Christian tradition which have resulted in part from its strange frenetic dynamism, and in part from its injection of the numinous into its ongoing history. Christianity can supply Buddhism with a greater sense of history, inevitable in an emerging world-consciousness, and powerful ideals of social transformation.

Moreover both have fingers pointing to the transcendent, a religious ultimate lying beyond this world. It is one of the functions of traditional doctrine to preserve this sense of the beyond, and Buddhism recognizes very clearly the provisional character of the means by which we do the pointing. This is in accord with that creative epistemological pluralism and uncertainty to which I referred earlier. So, though we may wish to abandon older dogmatisms and doctrinal confidences, we can rightly insist upon the need for us to allude to that transcendent ultimate which forms the final basis of the faith. Our tree has its roots in heaven, not in the sky.

For this reason both the Christian and the Buddhist are amphibious creatures, voyaging through life in two elements, in the element of earth and in the transparent water of the other world. For the Christian and the Buddhist ultimate happiness may be reflected in everyday life but yet lies beyond it. Thus the silent tran-

scendent, so differingly portrayed in the two religions, serves as a
vantage point for the creative criticism of this world and so too of
the secular ideologies. Thus I can see an emerging alliance between
the two faiths which will help to bond together in creative interplay the cultures of Asia and the West.

I have not stressed as I might have done the extraordinary
degree to which Christianity has paved the way in religious self-
criticism. One cannot think of another faith which has been so very
critical of its very origins, of its deposit of faith, of its way of life.
This is part of the glory of the Protestant element within the Christian dynamic. Christianity's self-criticism is the complementary
echo of the Buddhist idea of skill in means, which supplies a way
of conceiving how the forms of religion should not get congealed
and mistaken for what they represent and seek for. Christianity
in this self-criticism has been syncretizing with the open and plural
society of the modern West. It is as if the radicals of the Reformation and the questioners of the Enlightenment were made for one
another. At any rate we have the grounds of an alliance in the post-
Christian West between religion and scientific enquiry. It is also
the basis for a loose congruity between faith and the pluralism of
the open society. It is as if secular society, running out of this-
worldly critiques of itself, turned to faith to see a higher and different critique. For the self-criticism and skill in means of the two
great religious traditions I am treating are not just concerned with
revision, but with *revision in the light of eternity.*

We have here on the Christian side the elements of what may
be called an interrogative theology, a critical theology which uses
the mysterious Eucharist to challenge the assumptions of our world
— to challenge shallow conceptions of happiness or suffering, to
challenge the insane demands of the nation-state, to challenge the
collectivities of social conformism. It is not that utilitarianism, nationalism, and the Marxisms are altogether bad; if they had been
they would not have commanded so much loyalty and power. But
their aims are all, from the point of view of the transcendental critique, provisional. Thus we may try to multiply wealth and to dis-
tribute it as widely as possible: this alleviates much of human misery and increases opportunities of enjoyment. But beyond that lies
the question of what ultimate happiness can consist in. The removal
of deprivation clears away rocks in the path of that quest, and crea-

tion of enjoyments may supply some necessary ingredients in the
full life. But neither is by itself an ultimate aim.

Again, it is true that we are not lone individuals. Our personhood is a product both of individuality and of what is precipi-
tated in us by society. In revering a fellow human being I need
too to revere what she or he holds dear, and much of that will be
summed up in the values of the group to which she or he belongs.
Thus in revering the Greek I must pay tribute to her or his Greek-
ness. In the modern world it is increasingly the people or nation,
usually given its autonomy in a nation-state, that is the group of
ultimate concern. And in giving people a sense of identity and in
nurturing and protecting them the nation-state has its virtues. But
it must come under the critique and challenge of the universal religions. The Christian interrogation and challenge demands to
know whether the nation really can rightly be the ultimate focus
of loyalty.

The demand that states should respect human rights is a noble one. But on what do such rights rest? They are not something
merely conferred by the constitutions of the states, for then once
again the state becomes supreme. From the Christian perspective,
such rights flow from the manner in which each person derives his
or her stamp and image from above.

Both Buddhism and Christianity, in mounting a challenge
from the beyond—from so to say the noumenal glory which lies
the other side of the world as presented to us—are necessarily disruptive of social conformism as conceived in the varieties of institutionalized Marxism. For here even more acutely there is created
a presumption of the human being governed by the collectivity
which fits neither the Christian nor the Buddhist image of the eternal outreach of the individual.

In brief, the major ideologies of the contemporary world come
under a transcendental challenge.

In a sense what I am arguing for is a kind of critical federalism at two levels. First, at the level of human groups, it is a con-
venient and in many ways meaningful arrangement to form the
world into ethnic or national autonomous groups. But insofar as
these recognize one another as legitimate, the federal mentality
has already arrived, and loosely there begins to emerge a pattern
of regional federalisms, which may in due course come to be a

world federalism. But beyond that level, there is a federal approach to the human spirit: that the differing faiths need to recognize each other's rights, and insofar as they do so they enter into a peaceful struggle of values in which they function as mutual critics. This is the relationship of Buddhism and Christianity for which I have been arguing.

Yet here and in other parts of my argument a paradox occurs. After all there are forms of religion which do not recognize fully, or at all, the rights of others, as we well know also from human history. There are forms of ideology which do not share the pluralism of my approach.

Here two comments are in order. First, epistemologically and in the light of the study of religions and world views, those religious forms which have fanatic certitude are unsound. I believe that the spirit of modern science, of humanistic enquiry, and of critical education is not truly compatible with monistic orthodoxies. This is where truth itself is subversive of the official Marxisms and threatening to conservative restatements of traditions of every kind. This is where, frankly, I find Islam as having greater difficulty coming to terms with open modernity than many other religious traditions.

The second comment is that the pluralist can allow those with monistic inclinations to express themselves, provided they do not threaten the overthrow of the pluralist society. I like to think of the Marxist and the fundamentalist as fellow travelers; as long as the liberal ethos dominates, then we can use the challenging insight of these others.

Let me be clear, however, about the concept of 'the liberal' here. It will readily be apparent that political liberalism has often taken oppressive forms. For one thing, the pluralist societies of the North have also been chauvinist and have made often cruel inroads into the cultures and economies of the South. The old-fashioned liberal has often been smugly culture-bound.

It is one of the presuppositions of both Christianity and Buddhism that faith is for all people, for the whole world. That is, every policy and outlook must be judged not only because it is good for us, but because it is good for all people — or indeed all living beings, for Buddhism points dramatically to even wider considerations of welfare. We must inevitably be concerned with the dignity of all groups in the global city.

Ultimately this federalism of the spirit must have its attraction to the multiethnic South. We are all of us culturally threatened in one way or another, but the threat is most especially to those smaller cultural groups of Africa, Oceania, and elsewhere for whom the impact of Western modernity has been so powerful. The major problem on our psychic agenda is that of fashioning a newly conceived identity. And that implicitly involves *identities*. Zulus and Cook Islanders can hardly think of dominating the world; but they can try to create a world which is safe for their varied values.

Thus there is a certain natural alliance between the values of critical Buddhism and Christianity on the one hand and of the multitudinous South on the other. It is an alliance between some of the deeper values of four of our blocs: the trans-Christian West, Old Asia, Latin America, and the other South. Because this triangle of forces is found most particularly in the areas around and in the Pacific Ocean I like to think of the new outlook as the Pacific Mind. The gentle pun is not without meaning either. For both Buddhism and Christianity see war from the side of eternity, and thus can only tolerate violence, if at all, as a means to a greater peace. Thus for me the great blue waters of the Pacific Ocean are a symbol of a new triangle of East and West and South.

I have presented these conclusions as reflections out of the study of religion. What I present is only loosely based upon the scientific study of religion and is more closely related to the scientific study of world views, which is the wider task for today. Let me add some thoughts which arise out of our methods in that study, for they are also relevant to the wider reflection.

First, in looking to world-view analysis as a discipline we are echoing the logic of politics and economics. In these areas we isolate an aspect of human behavior and institutions (economic behavior and institutions, for example) and then use various approaches to illumine them — intrinsic economic or political theory, sociology, history, and so forth. The study of religion is limited like that and so is, more broadly, what I have called world-view analysis. Here we isolate the beliefs and symbol systems of human beings and use various approaches (history, anthropology, sociology, and so on) to illumine them. Then we can raise questions about the relationships between aspects. Thus we can ask to what degree certain symbol systems are reflections of the economic milieu in which they find themselves. We can ask this the other way round: to what extent is an economic system in part shaped by the symbol system and the world view of the people operating it? This is the classical question of Max Weber and arises today with renewed relevance in development economics.

I regard the fact that we pay so little attention in our society to world-view analysis and descriptive religious studies as a scandalous secret claim that these things are not important — that economic studies are much more important than the study of values and beliefs. The fact that we invest so little in world-view analysis is itself an implicit materialism in the bad sense. It is quite common in Western universities for there to be no department of religious studies, but impossible for there to be no department of economics. So the first main comment about our field is that in affirming it we are affirming, to put it crudely, the causative effect of symbol systems in human affairs. We need not overstress this. Often religion and ideology are determined from outside. It would be contrary to my epistemological ethos to deny the force of some projection theories of religion. But even so, there is a way in which world views have their own dynamic and power. It is important to reaffirm this in the face of a technocratic materialism which cripples our thinking in the modern West, even in material matters, such as relations with Iran and Japan.

The second main observation I would make drawing upon the methodological stance of our field is this. It is important in the human sciences to take account of consciousness. Human intentionality is one of the forces which affect the world. We are not here dealing with unconscious molecules and insentient rocks. In physics and geology we can screen out thoughts of empathy, but not in the human sciences. Part of what we have to do is understand the feelings and ideas, the "placement," of the people, whose actions and reactions we are considering. This involves what I call structured empathy. In order to understand the Iranian revolution part of what we need to do is to get inside in an informed manner the minds of Shi'a Muslims who have been affected by threats to their faith and society by modern changes. This structured empathy is what is referred to in my favorite Native American proverb: "Never judge a man until you have walked a mile in his moccasins." So our task is, in brief, moccasin-walking. Now this stance, though important in itself as a methodological tool, also affects attitudes. It leads to a greater capacity of understanding, which may lead one toward new forms of pluralism and toleration. As an educational process it is, in my view, vital to the training of the imagination. There is scarcely anything nobler than trying to enter imaginatively into the thought worlds and feelings of others. Even if it can only be done somewhat imperfectly, it is still worth undertaking. It is an imaginative capacity deeply neglected in our schools and educational systems. But it is something which we in religious studies can proudly present as one of our major methodological concerns.

It is a way of becoming conscious too of our own presuppositions. It clarifies our own cultural values and at the same time lets us take wings beyond them. It is a means of becoming true citizens of the world.

It often occurs to me that such *epoché* and moccasin-walking is helped by some of the attitudes and techniques of Buddhism. Actually what we need is a strange blend of Buddhist and Christian values: on the one hand the stilling of feelings that get in the way of empathy, and on the other the re-creation of others' feelings — it involves a stilling and yet also a generation of feeling. But the relevance of the religions to this is quite incidental. The method has validity in its own right, and we need to ask always: what methods can be used to enhance such structured empathy? It is a vital first step in world-view analysis.

In brief our field is resistant both to those who secretly despise symbol systems (having their own unconscious technocratic symbol system in which material forces are the major symbol) and to those who try in the human sciences simply to screen out our consciousness — whether out of methodological behaviorism or because of a too fanatic structuralism or for whatever reason. We must believe that minds and symbols are important.

What I have tried to do then is to present a global world view — or rather a fragment of a global world view — as a result of reflecting about the analysis and description of world views. For reflection about religion generates its own thoughts at a higher logical level, and it is some of these that I have been trying to pursue.

My position can thus be summed up as follows: No world view can be certain. Dogma is to be replaced by criticism and interrogation from the beyond—a kind of cross-questioning. I have looked at two of the great missionary faiths and have seen them as mutual critics. The one supplies a view of history, a social dynamic, and a transcendent way of understanding the sanctity of persons. The other supplies a check on violence and anthropomorphism, and a new vision of selflessness. They jointly can act as critics of the secular ideologies, giving an eternal twist to the notion of true happiness and to the analysis of suffering, posing questions to the state and fashioning a new federalism of the spirit. At the same time the values of the study of religion and world-view analysis reinforce a new, transcendental pluralism.

When, in California, I look upon the Pacific, I cannot help thinking of the Buddhist East at the far side of the waters, or of the identity problems of Japanese and Cook Islanders; nor can I fail to think of white Australia and the values of the West. In thinking of a new Pacific Mind I also, of course, think about our churning identities in the West. Perhaps such a Pacific Mind can pose a question mark to all those intolerant cultural forces which animate our political and economic life.

NOTES

1. Ninian Smart, *Beyond Ideology: Religion and the Future of Western Civilization* (San Francisco: Harper & Row, 1981). These Gifford Lectures expound on my present thesis.

PART III

The Quest for Common Ground

9

The Meaning of Pluralism for Christian Self-Understanding

JOHN B. COBB, JR.

THE FACT THAT THERE is a plurality of other religious movements in the world besides Christianity has always been obvious to Christians. That some of these have some positive value has rarely been disputed. What is new is the idea that a plurality of religious movements each deserves respect in its own terms and that Christians should not make claims for their doctrines of a sort that they do not accept as equally legitimate for others to make about theirs.

For persons who are not committed to any one community or tradition to view all such movements as on the same level is far from new. This attitude characterized the court of Frederick II in Sicily with respect to Jews, Christians, and Muslims. Moltmann contrasts this "skeptical tolerance" with what he calls the "productive tolerance" of Lessing.[1] But both these forms of tolerance stand outside Christian theology.

Ernst Troeltsch is the great thinker who forced the issue of religious pluralism upon the attention of theologians. He gave enormous scholarly and intellectual effort to justifying the claim of Christianity to absoluteness, and he finally acknowledged that he had failed. He accepted pluralism. But for him the acceptance of pluralism was connected with the abandonment of the theological vocation.

The task of this paper is to wrestle with the theological legacy of Troeltsch. How is one to understand the Christian faith in light of the challenge to its claim to absoluteness constituted by Troeltsch's life work? To what extent can it acknowledge the pluralism of religious movements?

161

Section I will deal with the history of the actual response. I suggest that it has taken three basic forms: kerygmatic theology, history of salvation theology, and liberal theistic theology. I will describe these briefly. In Section II I will engage in critical evaluation of the three positions. In Section III I will present my own constructive ideas.

I. EXPOSITION

(1) The dominant Protestant response to the challenge of pluralism has been kerygmatic theology. Karl Barth stands as its uncontested leader. Through Hendrik Kraemer its implications for the relation of Christianity to other religious traditions won control of the ecumenical movement. This theology still determines the official formulations of the World Council of Churches.

Kerygmatic theology defines itself against apologetic theology. One main form of apologetic theology had been to display the universal character of religion and then to show that religion comes to its fruition and fulfillment in Christianity. This was the program of Ernst Troeltsch, the program which he finally abandoned.

Against this program Barth argued that the interest of Christian theology should not be in religion. Religion is a human phenomenon which may indeed be studied as any human phenomenon is studied. But theology witnesses to what God has done in Jesus Christ. This is not a human phenomenon. It cannot be studied by historians or sociologists. It cannot be argued for or proved. It can only be attested by those who have been led by God to believe. Christians are those who have been called by God to witness to God's saving act.

Barth does not deny that Christians also produce a religion. But this is their sin rather than an expression of faith. They attempt to act so as to attain salvation. Religion is this effort of human beings to save themselves or to gain salvation from God. Faith knows that this is wrong, since God has already done all that needs to be done. Faith frees us from religion and for the world.

The implication for other religious movements was clear. Since they lacked faith in Jesus Christ they could be nothing other than efforts to save themselves. In this they were no better and no worse than Christians who did the same thing. Christianity as a religion is on exactly the same plane as all other religions. In this sense Barth was a religious pluralist.

The negative evaluation of religions that follows from Barth's position is not a negative evaluation of human beings who participate in one or another religious tradition. God became human for the salvation of all human beings. God's work in Christ has reconciled all. Ignorance of this work may limit some of its effects, but it does not block the reconciliation. God has already, once-for-all, reconciled all humanity to God. The Christian approaches the participant in another religion, not as one who because of erroneous religious affiliation is in need of salvation, but as one who has already been saved by God.

The net effect of this view is not so much to condemn religions as to ignore them. The real drama is between God and individual persons. The structures of religious life can be neglected.

Although the World Council of Churches never committed itself to Barth's tendency to universalism, its approach since Tambaram has largely reflected other aspects of his theology. It does not understand Christianity as one religion alongside others which must establish its superiority as a religion. Nor does it understand Christianity as the fulfillment of the religious quest. On the contrary, faith is directed to Jesus Christ, in whom God acted without regard for religion, for the salvation of all people.

This theology comes to expression as the World Council seeks to relate practically to other communities of belief. One way is by proclaiming the gospel, and this is continuously affirmed in World Council pronouncements. But there is also need for Christians to work together with others in God's world. To this end it is important to overcome mutual suspicions and misunderstandings, and for this purpose it has instituted a subunit on Dialogue with People of Living Faiths and Ideologies.

The title of this subunit is informative. First, the dialogue is to be with people, not with religious communities and their representatives. Second, the avoidance of the word *religions* is significant. We do not talk with people by virtue of their religion. The term *faith*, while problematic in many ways, avoids a positive appraisal of religion. Third, no distinction is made between people who think of themselves as religious believers and those who are committed to other types of movements. Marxism is on the same plane as Hinduism.

The central purpose of dialogue in the World Council view is not exchange of ideas about the meaning of life, ultimate reality, or salvation. The central purpose is to build human community among people who for whatever reason are fragmented into conflicting groups. If sharing deep commitments, even religious ones, is conducive to building human community, that is permitted. But insofar as World Council-sponsored dialogue has in fact become interreligious dialogue, that is in tension with its mandate.

Recently the most influential current proponent of kerygmatic theology, Jürgen Moltmann, has spoken out against the pejorative implications of kerygmatic theology for other world religions. He has pointed out that these religions were not what Barth had in view, that there is much in them that is valuable, and that Christians should enter into dialogue with them with the expectation of learning and being changed in the process. In all this he goes beyond what the World Council has thus far been willing to say. Moltmann believes that precisely because "Christ has come and was sacrificed for the reconciliation of the whole world,"[2] Christians should have unlimited interest in other religions and what can be learned from them. Hence he advocates from the perspective of kerygmatic theology a full-scale interreligious dialogue.

This does not change, however, the secondary character of religion in relation to Christian concerns. He writes:

> For Christianity the dialogue with the world religions is part of the wider framework of the liberation of the whole creation for the coming kingdom. It belongs within the same context as the conversation with Israel and the political and social passion for a freer, juster, and more habitable world. Christianity's dialogistic profile ought to be turned to the future of the liberating and redeeming kingdom in the potentialities and powers of the world religions. That is a profile which Christianity can only acquire in dialogue with others.[3]

(2) The movement of the Roman Catholic church into dialogue has been based on a very different response to the challenge of pluralism: history of salvation theology. Instead of accepting the pluralism of religions and locating what is supremely important

outside of the religious frame, Vatican II and most Catholic theologians since then have understood that God works for salvation in and through the religious life and the religious communities of human beings. Salvation is, for Catholics, a religious matter. The evaluation of the plurality of religions is the evaluation of their success and value in the history of salvation.

Karl Rahner is the single most influential Catholic theologian of this century. His position is that God works salvifically everywhere. People can be saved whether or not they are related to the Catholic church or consciously accept Jesus Christ. People saved in this way he calls anonymous Christians. The religions of the world are used by God in this salvific work. Thus they are positive vehicles of salvation. But they are not on a par with the Christian church. Once the Christian church is fully established in a community there is no longer any need for other religions there. Their function in the history of salvation is superseded by that of the Christian church. But this does not mean that these other religious communities do not continue to contain anonymous Christians.

Hans Küng has not been satisfied with this view. It seems to him still too arrogant. God saves Hindus as Hindus, not as anonymous Christians. Also, each religion continues to function in God's providence until the end. Their roles are not superseded by Christianity. In this view, the mission of the church is service to these other religions.

Küng's position is still quite controversial, but it is not far removed from significant tendencies in the church's leadership. Pope Paul VI called for a dialogue about salvation with other religions, implying that they have real knowledge of salvation. In preparing for dialogue with Muslims the Vatican Secretariat appeared to assume that Islam has a more than temporary role in the economy of salvation and that the role of Christians is to help Muslims fulfill that role.

Official Catholic theology is thus willing to go a long way in expressing respect for other religions and their role in the divine economy of salvation. But like the official position of the World Council of Churches it avoids explicitly indicating that the church has anything to learn from other religious traditions. The position seems to be that the church is already in possession of all needed

knowledge. The dialogue is part of its mission for the sake of the
world. It is not out of its own poverty that it seeks wisdom from
others.

Many Catholic scholars have protested this lingering arro-
gance in the church's attitude and the one-sidedness of the dialogues
that must ensue if only the other religion is to learn. But the most
successful opening up of the history of salvation approach to Christian learning from others is by the Protestant Wolfhart Pannenberg.

Like the Catholic theologians Pannenberg sees the history of
salvation as largely identical with the history of religions.[4] He sees
that religions have always competed with one another in terms of
the convincing power of their gods. All have an inner tendency toward universality, and they fail or succeed in new situations according to their ability to become appropriately inclusive. Thus
no religions in fact remain the same. Successful religions are successful by virtue of their ability to assimilate what is of value in
others.

There is a tension between these historical facts about all religions and the tendency of religions to find their norms in past
manifestations of deity. Since they define themselves in terms of
faithfulness to their deity and define the deity by past manifestations, they claim to be unchanging when in fact they are changing. This often inhibits needed growth.

The great exception in Pannenberg's view is Israel. Israel knew
God as the God of promise; hence it looked to the future as the
locus of God's full manifestation. It could affirm the new historical occurrence as the revelation of the God whom it already knew.
Nevertheless, in Israel this openness to the new was severely checked
by commitments to past forms of God's appearance. It is only in
Jesus that this bondage to the past is radically broken. For the Christian God is the God of the future. Hence in principle the Christian is completely open to learning from other religions more about
this yet to be fully manifested God. In the process Christian beliefs can be transformed. It is precisely this ability of Christianity
to be changed by others, Pannenberg holds, which constitutes its
superiority and its ability finally to supersede all others.

(3) Other thinkers, more at the periphery of theology, have
objected that even the most open of these positions still falls short
of genuine acceptance of pluralism. Moltmann can be completely

pluralistic about religions, including Christianity, but only because of his Christian conviction that the whole world has been reconciled to God in Christ. This belief itself is not subject to revision through dialogue with those who do not agree. Pannenberg is ready to submit everything fully to historical examination and in this important sense reserves nothing from the dialogue. But his claim that Christianity is destined to supersede all other religions establishes, on the basis of historical study, the absoluteness which pluralism opposes. Of course, if it is true, then it must be admitted. But many prefer to enter the dialogue without such advance assumptions of superiority of one's own tradition, even when that superiority is measured by its greater ability to be changed through dialogue.

This group of thinkers prefers to see dialogue as an exchange among people engaged in a common quest who seek to learn from one another without raising the question of the relative merits of the positions they bring into the dialogue. The participants recognize that they have been formed in diverse communities and that what they can contribute is informed by their experience in those communities. But ideally they make no special claims for the authority of what they say. Among Catholics Hans Küng and Paul Knitter favor this approach. Among Protestants Wilfred Cantwell Smith and John Hick exemplify it. I am calling their position liberal theism.

Since it is assumed in this approach that the dialogue partners are sharing in a common quest, the nature of that quest requires definition. It is ordinarily understood that all have experienced God and are seeking to know God and live appropriately to that knowledge. Theism is the common assumption. Religions are understood to express the human relationship to God, and it is for the sake of understanding God and God's relationship to the world that people from varied religious traditions engage in dialogue.

There are, of course, differences among the advocates. Wilfred Cantwell Smith prefers to avoid the term *religions*.[5] He sees that this term reifies existing communities of believers, whereas in fact there is a fluid history of the religious life of humanity in which communities and movements take ever-changing form. Dialogue should be among human beings whose religious life incidentally owes more to one or another temporary and provisional community or strand within the whole. It is the faith of human beings which is the basis of sharing. This faith is one reality wherever it is found. There is diversity in the forms and expressions of this one faith. There is no diversity of faiths. The task today is to develop a world theology based on the faith and experience of the whole of the human race rather than confessional theologies expressive of the experience of limited communities. Hence Christian theology should give way to world theology. The world theology developed by those who come to this task from Christianity will bear the marks of their Christian experience. But the ultimate purpose is to achieve full inclusiveness, not to preserve the accent of one tradition or another.

Although much of this is acceptable to John Hick, he has given chief attention to clarifying how one ultimate reality can be experienced so diversely.[6] He calls this ultimate reality *God* but cautions that this term must be freed of its particularistic connotations in order to serve as the name of that which has been known in such divergent ways in the different religions. He recognizes that this one reality has been experienced both as personal and as impersonal and that in different experiences different aspects of the one reality may be involved. But the reality in question is the ground of all existence. It is the noumenal cause of all our phenomenal religious experience. Hence no one experience or culturally informed strand of experiences will exhaust it, and all the religious traditions can contribute to more adequate understanding.

II. CRITIQUE

(1) I find something to agree with in all three of these positions, and partly for that reason I cannot accept any of them. The kerygmatic theology rightly shows that what God aims at in the world is far broader than religion. Moltmann is correct that the interreligious dialogue and all our concerns about religious pluralism are a "part of the wider framework of the liberation of the whole creation for the coming kingdom."[7] Religions, like other human movements, may contribute to that liberation. They may also hinder it. Christians have the same reason to engage in dialogue with Marxists as they do with Buddhists. The category of

religion is not determinative of who we are as Christians or who our dialogue partners should be. The question is instead from whom we can learn most that will help us work for the liberation of the whole creation and whom it is most worthwhile for us to try to influence.

But kerygmatic theology has underestimated the importance of historical and cultural traditions, most of which have strong religious elements. The emphasis on dealing with human beings as human beings does not do justice to the profound differences among human beings as they are formed in these diverse contexts. We cannot understand human beings and work with them except as we see them as participants in such communities. This is facilitated when without embarrassment we engage in dialogue with representatives of these communities who can help us to understand not only themselves as individuals but many fellow participants in those communities. Also we should not hesitate to speak, as far as we can, for Christianity as a whole or for the segments of Christianity which we can effectively represent. In short, interreligious dialogue has an importance that the kerygmatic theologians are only barely beginning to acknowledge.

(2) The history of salvation approach has led the Catholic church to full appreciation of the importance of this dialogue. Also, while kerygmatic theology sees history only in terms of the one event of Jesus Christ and the secular movement for the realization of God's purposes in the world, those who follow the history of salvation approach can examine the complex ways in which God has accomplished salvific changes in human society throughout global history. This is much more adequate. The religions, their actual interaction, and their real historical effects can be examined. Strategies for Christian action can be shaped in terms of responsible judgments about the diverse religious movements, their past and present contributions to the whole work of salvation.

The idea of the Christian mission as service to other religions takes on far more seriousness and critical force when viewed in this context than when something similar is said from the kerygmatic point of view. All of this is admirable.

In Catholic formulations thus far the openness to historical inquiry is checked with regard to the Catholic church itself by some dogmatic commitments. But this is not necessary to the history of salvation approach itself. It is quite possible, as Pannenberg shows, to appeal only to historical evidence and let the chips fall where they may—with respect to Christianity as much as to any other religion. And more clearly than any others in this school, Pannenberg shows that the eschatological thrust inherent in the history of salvation approach frees us for complete openness to others. We do not need to defend any past or present form of Christianity in faithfulness to Christ. On the contrary, faithfulness calls for openness, so that the truth may be served and incorporated.

I not only appreciate what has been done in the perspective of the history of salvation but also identify myself with this approach. However, I disagree with particular ideas that seem to be common to all of the major practitioners. For them the history of salvation is bound up with the history of religions. I see no reason for us to suppose that this is the case, or at least I see no reason to assume it. It is as easy to see salvific functions in secularization as in religion. If religion is defined, as is so often the case, as having to do with God, then we must raise the question as to whether Buddhism is a religion and, if not, whether that separates it from the history of salvation. I would prefer to assume that Buddhism has played and is playing an important salvific role along with Marxism and the movement for the liberation of women. To what extent these are religious does not seem to me to be of central importance. I assume that few important human movements are wholly lacking in religious elements, but many of them are not well named as religions, and many do not think of themselves as theistic. It is important that inquiry into the history of salvation take seriously the history of religion, but it is even more important that its subject matter be history as a whole and that the role of religion within saving history be a topic for investigation. In short, I favor a secularized history of salvation as the context for dealing with the religious pluralism of our time.

(3) I agree with the liberal theists in most of their criticisms of the existing forms of both kerygmatic and history of salvation theologies. They are right that some kind of Christian absolute appears in all the major formulations and that this inhibits total openness to other traditions and their claims. This is least true when, as with Pannenberg, the absolute is argued for from public evidence and is itself subject to testing. But I agree with the

liberal theists that even in Pannenberg's case the quest for an absolute as a basis for understanding reflects the long tradition of Christian imperialism and triumphalism rather than the pluralistic spirit.

I agree also with the need for moving toward a world theology which Smith holds before us. An adequate theology for our time must be one which deals with the totality of the evidence, and the diverse religious experiences of the world are an important part of that evidence. But I find his proposal unsatisfactory on several accounts.

First, like the history of salvation theologians, he associates theology in too limited a way with religious experience or what he calls faith. Clarification of our knowledge of God is as dependent upon the social and natural sciences as upon the diverse expressions of faith. His world theology is built on too narrow a base. Second, while he recognizes that his own move to world theology expresses the influence of Christianity, he does not seem to recognize or celebrate how deep the urge in that direction is within Christianity or how specific are the reasons for it. That the world theology to which he points has a Christian character is for him more a limitation than an affirmation of faith. I would reverse this. I see the goal as, precisely, a *Christian* world theology. I would rejoice if there could also develop a Buddhist, a Hindu, a Muslim, a Jewish, and an animist "world theology." But I would expect these to be quite different one from the other. Perhaps some day they would converge. But the desire for them to do so soon shows lack of appreciation of pluralism. Third, his seeking a basis for mutual appreciation of people in the universality of faith impresses me as too provincial. He knows of course that faith is not a central term in all traditions, and that employing it does suggest the sort of favoring of the Christian tradition which he otherwise deplores. He counters that he is abstracting the idea of faith from its specifically Christian character and interpreting it in light of the diversity of religious experience. But I remain convinced that focusing on faith distorts the approach to the truly pluralistic situation. Instead of beginning with the assumption that we can identify what is common to all, it would be better to listen as speakers from each strand of human historical life tell us what they have found most important and how they describe it. I am convinced that in many instances, Zen Buddhism being a notable example, what is central would not be described as faith.

I am not asking merely for a more careful account of what is common to all religious people. My point is that we should give up the use of any language that first separates religion from other phenomena and then tries to identify what is normatively characteristic of all religion. Let us allow Buddhists to be Buddhists, whether that makes them religious or not. Let us allow Confucianists to be Confucianists, whether that makes them religious or not. Let us allow Marxists to be Marxists, whether that makes them religious or not. And let us allow Christians to be Christians, whether that makes us religious or not. Quite apart from any such categories as religion or faith, there is plenty of reason to see that these proper names point to diverse ways of living and experiencing that are important for both the past and the future of the world. Hence, we should take them all seriously, as far as possible in their own terms, and allow each to challenge our beliefs and assumptions. That is a better way to a world theology than the effort to determine what is common to all.

Much the same objection applies to Hick's effort to find a common focus in God. The choice of the term *God*, despite all disclaimers, has the same effect as Smith's choice of *faith*. It suggests lack of attentiveness to what Buddhists are trying to tell us. But shifting terminology to the transcendent or the absolute does not help. The problem is the quest for what is common. Truly to accept pluralism is to abandon that quest. If our liberal theists really wish to be open, they should simply be open. The openness is inhibited by the need to state in advance what we have in common. When commonalities emerge, they should be celebrated. But we should not assume that because we find something in common with one dialogue partner — Islam, for example — we should expect to find that in common with another dialogue partner — Buddhism, for example, or Marxism. Also, when differences emerge we should celebrate them too. Indeed, it is the most radical differences that stimulate the most fundamental reconsideration. It is the insistence of Zen Buddhists, for example, on going beyond faith and theism that makes conversation with them so stimulating for those who find faith and theism to be of ultimate importance.

III. PROPOSAL

In this concluding section I want to offer an overview of the meaning of pluralism for my own Christian self-understanding.

My starting point is with Pannenberg in the conviction that Christianity is one historical movement alongside others. There is nothing about Christianity that justifies our considering it exempt from thoroughgoing historical-critical investigation. Our beliefs about it can only be shaped by such investigation. Nothing historical is absolute; so any tendency to absolutize any feature of Christianity is idolatry.

As a participant in that movement I understand its goal to be, in Dorothee Sölle's words, "the indivisible salvation of the whole world."[8] She understands that chiefly in political terms, and that dimension is extremely important. But salvation must include the whole of the created order, as Moltmann knows, and not only the human sphere. In addition, the salvation of the human involves dimensions that are not usually considered political. It involves the attainment of a unified and adequate understanding of reality, and it involves a mode of experience and action that is appropriate to that understanding.

I see other movements alongside Christianity, and I find it important to evaluate them. Some I judge evil or trivial. Others seem to be carriers of some good but apparently have nothing to offer that cannot be better offered in existing Christianity. Still others contribute to the indivisible salvation of the whole world in ways that Christianity as now constituted does not and cannot. These are of great interest. It is the recognition that there are such movements that constitutes me, in the first instance, as a pluralist.

These movements also vary greatly in value and importance. The contributions of some may be highly specialized and limited. Others offer entire ways of life and thought. Some of these are extremely different from Christianity and yet appear — to the Christian — to be of great value and importance.

If being a Christian meant maintaining Christianity in its now established form, then the results of the recognition of these parallel movements would be relativism. One would either cease to be a Christian or else accept Christianity as one possible way of organizing life among others — and leave it at that. Relativism is very difficult to reconcile with Christian faith, which calls for whole-hearted commitment. If other movements seek other ends than the Christian end, and yet have equal validity with Christianity, then how can one give whole-hearted commitment to the Christian goal? To do so would be idolatrous. But to give partial commitment to the goal would be lukewarmness. Idolatry and lukewarmness are the Scylla and Charybdis of contemporary Christianity.

But there is an alternative to relativism. If Christianity is a living movement, then it does not ask commitment to any form which it has taken in the past. It asks commitment to the task of enabling it to respond rightly in the ever-changing situation. In relation to other movements of the sort we are considering, that means learning from them. To believe that Christianity should be constantly changing and growing does not lead to relativism. The fullness of Christianity lies in the ever-receding future. One can be a wholehearted participant in the present movement as long as one believes that the particular limitations to which one is now sensitive can be overcome.

Let me put the matter strongly. If being a Christian means unqualified affirmation of any form Christianity has ever taken, I cannot be a Christian. But in fact such an affirmation would not be Christian at all. It would be idolatrous and faithless. It would be absolutizing the relative and refusing to attend to the call of the living Christ. But to give complete devotion to the living Christ — as Christ calls us in each moment to be transformed by the new possibilities given by God for that moment — that is not idolatrous or faithless. That is what Christianity is all about.

In faithfulness to Christ I must be open to others. When I recognize in those others something of worth and importance that I have not derived from my own tradition, I must be ready to learn even if that threatens my present beliefs. I cannot predetermine what the content of that learning will be or preestablish categories within which to appropriate it. I cannot predetermine how radical the effects of that learning will be. I cannot predetermine that there are some beliefs or habits of mind which I will safeguard at all costs. I cannot even know that, when I have learned what I have to learn here and been transformed by it, I will still see faithfulness to Christ as my calling. I cannot predetermine that I will be a Chris-

tian at all. That is what I mean by full openness. In faithfulness to
Christ I must be prepared to give up even faithfulness to Christ.
If that is where I am led, to remain a Christian would be to become
an idolater in the name of Christ. That would be blasphemy.

Openness to truth concretely entails openness to the particular truth embodied in another tradition. Such openness leads to
the assimilation of that truth. Sometimes Christianity can appropriate what another tradition offers in such a way that that
movement no longer has any reason to retain separate identity. Its
function in the history of salvation is complete. It is in principle
superseded. It may turn out some day that everything in Marxism
that is of importance in the history of salvation can be appropri-
ated within Christianity. If so, then Marxism would be in principle superseded by an enriched Christianity.

Pannenberg envisions that ultimately Christianity will supersede all other religions. But that expectation does not seem to take
the depth of the diversity among the religions with sufficient seriousness, or to recognize them as complex wholes which lose something of their importance for the history of salvation when they
are reduced to contributions which Christians can incorporate. As
a Christian I am challenged to learn as much as I can, and to appropriate as richly as I can, from these other traditions, allowing
myself thereby to be transformed. I must leave to the future the
question of whether there are limits such that each religious tradition will maintain a separate contribution to the history of salvation until the end. The pluralistic attitude leaves those questions
open. It does not thereby relativize Christianity in a way that reduces commitment to Christ.

My own scenario differs from Pannenberg's at this point. I
believe that Christians are in the process of being transformed by
other religious traditions. I will take Mahāyāna Buddhism as my
example. I believe that in faithfulness to Christ Christianity will
be Buddhized and that we can already discern some of what is involved. The Buddhization of Christianity will transform Christianity in the direction of a greater and deeper truth, a new and
better quality of life, and a fuller ability to serve Christ in the political sphere as well. One need not be halfhearted in participating in this process in faithfulness to Christ.

If Buddhism remains static while Christianity allows itself to be Buddhized, then a scenario such as that proposed by Pannenberg makes sense. In the long run there would be no reason for Buddhists to remain Buddhists if their wisdom had been given a larger scope in an enriched Christianity. But it is unlikely that Buddhism will remain unchanged. While Christianity is Buddhized, Buddhism can be Christianized. Pannenberg may be correct that other religions including Buddhism have more tendency to find their norms in the past and to be unable to identify their fundamental principle in the process of transformation. But Buddhism has shown marvelous powers of transformation in China, Korea, Japan, and now the United States. Perhaps one feature of Christianizing Buddhism will be to enable it to recognize and affirm its historicity more fully than in the past. In any case, a self-transforming Christianized Buddhism appears to be a real possibility. If so, a Buddhized Christianity will confront a Christianized Buddhism. The plurality of movements that constitute the history of salvation will thus remain, though their number may be reduced.

My central thesis here is that for Christianity to be, and to remain to the end, one among others does not involve its relativization in the destructive sense in which this is now felt by so many. It does relativize every form taken by Christianity in time. It does not relativize the process of creative transformation by which it lives and which it knows as Christ.

At another level and in another sense, however, that too must be recognized as one principle by which one community lives alongside other principles by which other communities live. This is a fundamental theological problem for the Christian. As a Christian I believe that Christ is the way, the truth, and the life and that no one comes to know God except through Christ. Does that mean after all that I am rejecting pluralism? I do not think so.

I believe that what Christians understand by "the way, the truth, and the life" is bound up with creative transformation. I believe also that what Christians understand by *God* can be known only in this way. But for the most part this has not been the interest of Buddhists. Buddhists are concerned to gain freedom from suffering by realizing the reality which they already are, their Buddha-nature. They tell us that this can be done only by giving up all attachment, even the attachment to the realization of Buddha-nature. This is a quite different goal from coming to know the

Christian God. I believe that they understand what they are doing and how to do it. If we want to realize our true nature in this sense, we must study their methods.

Gautama found freedom from suffering through radically overcoming all attachment. He thereby attained nirvana. Jesus incarnated the Word of God. These statements do not conflict with each other. I believe they are both true. Believing that Gautama attained nirvana and uniquely showed others how to do so does not conflict with believing that Jesus uniquely incarnated the Word and shows us the Christian God. Both statements are universal claims of vast importance in the history of salvation. The truth of one does not reduce the truth of the other. That there are others besides Jesus whose achievements are of universal importance does not reduce the universal importance of Jesus. It does not count against making radical and exclusive claims for either nirvana or the Word. It means only that we must state very carefully the relation of Jesus, the Word, and Christ. For my part I mean by *Christ* the effective presence of the Word in the world, a presence uniquely realized in Jesus. My exclusive claims for Christ need not conflict with exclusive Buddhist claims for the realization of Buddhahood of which Gautama is the paradigm instance. General comments to the effect either that Jesus is the only Savior or that there are a plurality of saviors do not help. We must always say, saved from what to what. Christians need not give up our exclusivist claims, but we should be very careful to state what it is that is exclusive and to examine our claims in relation to all others. We should strive to share what has been exclusive to Christianity as we appropriate what has been exclusive to other traditions. That is what a Christianized Buddhism and a Buddhized Christianity are all about.

This essay is written from within the Christian commitment. All the judgments I have made are Christian judgments. From the point of view of some people that approach is already rendered obsolete by the pluralism of our situation. They believe that the task now is to stand outside of all the positive religions and to understand them objectively as scholars. Speaking as a Christian I can say that I am glad that some have done this. Historical, psychological, sociological, and phenomenological studies of religion have benefited all of us. But from the Christian point of view, more is lost than gained by shifting from identification with the Christian community to identification with the academic one. Prizing objectivity and learning is fine. But the academic community as such has no larger context of commitment within which to use these rather minor values. Accordingly it has lost the ability to discern importance and to define the university in terms of any humane purpose. To stand outside of all religious communities in order to appraise them impartially has modest value except as it has an effect within the communities. In any case that stance is not truly pluralistic. It has opted for one commitment against the commitments of the communities it evaluates, and it usually does not appreciate the way in which its own commitments are relativized by theirs. It too easily becomes absolutist in its attack on the tendencies to absolutism of those it studies.

From a Christian point of view the values that are present in the academic community are easily assumed within the Christian one. We, too, prize fairness and openness in the quest for truth and understanding. Indeed, in the modern West, these values were derived largely from Christianity in the first place. In the relation of Christianity to the academic community I see no basic problem with supersession. But of course for that to come about the tendencies to idolatry which now beset Christianity will have to be overcome.

It has taken Christians a long time to recognize that there are other movements in the world that are bearers of authentic contributions to salvation that differ from our own. Indeed, even now the resistance to that acknowledgment is very strong. Many Christians fear that their faith will be undercut by such an admission. They want to believe that all that is needed for the indivisible salvation of the whole world is found in the past and specifically in the past of our own tradition. This is understandable, but it is also sin. It is not an expression of faith but of defensiveness, which is faithlessness.

What is most striking, however, is not the timorousness of Christians as we work out the meaning of pluralism for Christian self-understanding. What is more striking is the relative speed with which leading thinkers and leading institutions are moving toward an adequate statement. Both the World Council of Churches and the Vatican have come a long way in recent years. In comparison with the distance traveled, the further distance that is needed is relatively short. All that is required is an act of total trust in the living Christ.

NOTES

1. Jürgen Moltmann, *The Church in the Power of the Spirit*, trans. Margaret Kohl (London: SCM Press, 1977), p. 155.

2. Ibid., p. 153.

3. Ibid., p. 163.

4. See Wolfhart Pannenberg, "Toward a Theology of the History of Religions," in *Basic Questions in Theology*, 2 vols., trans. George Kehm (Philadelphia: Fortress Press, 1970–71), 2:65–118.

5. See Wilfred Cantwell Smith, *Toward a World Theology* (Philadelphia: Westminster Press, 1981).

6. See especially John Hick, "Towards a Philosophy of Religious Pluralism," *Neue Zeitschrift für Systematische Theologie* 22 (1980):131–49.

7. Moltmann, *Church in the Power of the Spirit*, p. 163.

8. Dorothee Sölle, *Political Theology*, trans. John Shelley (Philadelphia: Fortress Press, 1971), p. 60.

10

Thoughts on the Gnosis of Saint John

J. N. FINDLAY

THE BACKGROUND AND PURPOSE of this paper require some explanation. It is not the product of a New Testament scholar, and thus it is neither able to weigh and balance theories as to date, origin, and doctrinal background of the text attributed to Saint John, nor to assess the identification of its author with the beloved disciple elsewhere mentioned or with the author of the Apocalypse, nor to consider his relationship to Gnostics or Stoics or Essenes or other influences in the contemporary Jewish or Christian ambience. It is only the effort of one who recognizes in Saint John's Gospel, if read with an appropriate hermeneutic, a supreme mystico-religious document which can provide guidance at every turn of the spiritual life, but which, if read in another manner, becomes only the expression of a hard-line particularism, which is not less unacceptable in that it acclaims a particular standing in a special relation to another particular on which we all depend for our existence and for all our properties.

Conceive of God, or the supreme object of worship, as a particular among particulars, and as much other than ourselves as other things and persons are other, and religious reverence becomes a repugnant form of heteronomous idolatry, wrought up, moreover, with the blind acceptance of a large number of historic and cosmic myths. But conceive of God as being something beyond category-differences, and which as much transcends particularity as it transcends any form of abstract universality, and which incorporates in strict identity all those values of truth, love, beauty, justice, and so forth, which are all simply universality in action, and which, moreover, as much transcends personality and personal

180

relationships as it also may have in them its supreme expression, and religion and worship at once acquire a perfect sense and reference. And it further becomes possible to give visionary body to that sense by conceiving of a Kingdom in which all personal relationships will be perfected, and by putting at the center of that Kingdom something which still bears the features of the historic person in whom the gospel of the Kingdom was first promulgated and lived. It is in the light of such a hermeneutic that Saint John's Gospel can truly illuminate the spirit, instead of flooding it with mere doctrinal bombast. Whether such an interpretation be spurned as Gnostic or Alexandrian or Hegelian or simply old-fashioned New England "transcendental," it remains one that gives the "good news" of Christianity some purchase on the contemporary mind and which ensures that its glorious myths, rites, and disciplines will not become mere "fragments of a faith forgotten."[1] In what follows I shall throughout base myself on the text of the King James Bible, not because I am unacquainted with the Greek, but because I believe that this text reveals, at every turn, direct inspiration by the holy spirit of beauty and truth, and that it is moreover written in a language which, with its unique combination of the plain Anglo-Saxon monosyllable with the Latin polysyllable, is by far the finest of all human languages.

I shall not comment extensively on the first chapter of the Gospel according to Saint John. It teaches a doctrine of a Logos or Word which is not so much a transcendently existent thing or person, set over against other existent things and persons, but a connective function between two terms, one a uniquely central, independent item called God, and the other a numerous set of dependent items categorizable as things and persons. The Word is, on the other hand, *with* God, and so accorded a nuance of difference from the central term that it is *with*, but at the same time, so intimately a function of that central term, that it can be simply said to *be* the latter, and it is not a function merely extrinsic to the absolute center of things, since that center has this function *primordially*, whether it actually exercises it or not. Everything whatever that in any way differs from the unique Divine Center must have been made by it, will depend on it wholly for its being — and if, in addition, it is human and thinking — for all its conscious illumination, and for all that springs from this. But though this source of light may be all-illuminating, the human gaze is for some reason turned away from it toward the things that it illuminates: the darkness, John tells us, fails to comprehend it. There was, however, another man called John whose task it was to turn human eyes toward the source of their conscious illumination, or at least to make them aware of its universal presence and action. This second John was not himself one with this universal light or its source, but in some fashion reflected it, or bore witness to it. There was, however, another actual man whose relation to the supreme source of light was too close to be characterized as that of a reflection or a witness: he more absolutely *was* the light in question, and so stood to it much as a son stands to a father. He was, however, despite such a close identification, made of flesh and blood as we are, and in him the invisible, intangible source of all conscious light became visible and tangible, and lived among us as a man and a friend. The light that he brought to us was nonetheless not wholly strange, since it had lighted every person that came into the world. And the advanced identification designated by the word *son* was, moreover, one in which all might come to share, provided only that they believed on his name, or identified themselves with his identification. All these assertions must be understood as obeying a logic which will not suffer itself to be crucified on the crux of the excluded middle, nor to bow to canons of identity and diversity, or of affirmation and denial, which are wholly in order when one considers the relations of one finite, particular thing to another but not when one is considering their relations to something which is as much other than everything as it is also totally present in all of them and which permits, further, of all degrees of close affiliation or remote divergence from them severally. Such a convergence of divergent aspects can, on an all-sided examination, be shown to be as little illogical as the convergence of longitudes at the earth's poles can be shown to be ungeographical. And the difficult discourse of Plato in the *Parmenides*, or of Plotinus in the *Enneads*, or of Hegel throughout his dialectic, shows that such a logic can become wholly perspicuous to those who have learned to distinguish all its different strands of meaning, however much it may scare exact thinkers out of their skins. We shall not, however, attempt to persuade exact thinkers to adopt such a logic of interpenetrating aspects. We shall only argue that one cannot hope to understand John's Gospel if one cannot make sense of such a logic.

The first chapter of the Gospel then turns to witness John's disclaimer of being the anointed, incarnate Word himself: he is at most one who will prepare his way. And it begins its account of that way with the recognition of Christ by the Baptist as being the Lamb of God, the sacrificial point of union between an alienated and sinful world and the light and healing that will remove its alienation and sinfulness. In thus beginning his account of Christ's life with this recognition, John reveals an austere unwillingness to endorse the beautiful nativity stories which the other evangelists find so suitable. While not unwilling to incorporate miraculous stories in his Gospel, and while adding to them several of his own, he is unwilling to make the Star, the Magi, and so on, part of his Incarnation, since they arguably fail to make plain the two-way nature of an Incarnation: that it is not merely the descent of the Word into fleshly personification, but also the reaching up of the fleshly human person to the Word which can never have been far from his inmost mind and heart. This reaching up, and the concurrent coming down, must have taken place, stage by stage, in the growing up of the young man in Galilee, among his simple parents and brothers and sisters, and with whatever assistance of Essenes and other inspirers, and with whatever overcoming of personal temptations that may have been a part of it. Without such a reaching up (perhaps only an inverse of a concurrent reaching down) the Logos would not truly have been made human, but would merely have been a mechanism of divine control installed in a human body. John does not, however, think it is his task to sketch the human education which led up to the sonship of Jesus, however well he may have known it. His interest lies solely in its consummation.

In the subsequent narrative we witness a selection of stories and sayings, many of which had already grown up in the complex, little studied way in which religious stories actually do grow up, and others which are John's own creation. They all reflect John's theology of Incarnation and represent what John thought an incarnate Logos would do or say, rather than merely what he remembered Jesus to have done or said. This does not mean that John the Evangelist may not have been John the beloved disciple and that his theology did not grow out of the actual deeds and utterances of his Master. It only means that the theology of John has worked loose from whatever deeds and utterances first inspired it, and has been built up into a new set of deeds and utterances which were needed to complete its expression. What John reports was in great part not done or said at any time, but it expressed the identification with deity which Jesus had experienced, and which by Jesus had been communicated to John. Jesus was the God-transfigured man, and John was the man transfigured by his acceptance of the sonship which had transfigured Jesus. The miraculous descent of the Dove at the time of the baptism is further, in John's narrative, merely a descent *reported* by the Baptist, by which John testifies to its inward and mystical character: it was an inner transformation of the soul of Jesus, not an authentication of his mission from some cloudy, upper source.

We need not dwell on the calling of the disciples except to note its blurring of detail, the ritualistic fashion in which those called at once recognize the Messiahship of the man calling them. However they may have been gathered together, and whatever intuitive criteria led to their selection, they cannot have been chosen in the manner that the chapter describes. But, from the point of view of the Evangelist, their calling had an eternal significance and is best described in the language of eternity. And in the final eschatological verse — "Hereafter ye shall see heaven open and the angels of God ascending and descending upon the Son of Man"— John speaks of the final apotheosis of Jesus in the same language of eternity, without the cataclysmic naturalism of the other evangelists. If John also wrote the Apocalypse, he there relegated that final apotheosis to a poetic millennium, a span of ten centuries that must then have seemed infinitely far away.

In chapters 2 to 5 we then have a number of miraculous stories built, no doubt, upon Christ's actual impact upon certain individuals but used by John to express the ineffable reaching down from the Divine Center of those forces that can transform peripheral humanity. The marriage at Cana, an ordinary union of ordinary Jewish people, becomes a symbol of the transfiguration of all earthly forms of togetherness by a bond which is none other than the convergence of all peripherally dispersed lines of things and persons at their central point of unity. The cleansing of the tem-

ple, arrogant and unhelpful if a piece of history, perhaps symbol-
izes the vanishing of all considerations of profit and loss in the life
which transcends personal advantage. And the identification of the
temple with the divine Son's body which, if destroyed, will be raised
again, is simply a recognition of the timeless nature of the Word's
descent into flesh, which is also an ascent of flesh into the spirit:
once performed, it is a path everlastingly open. And the threat of
condemnation to those who deny the Son of Man's unity with the
Word is not to be taken as a narrow, sectarian rejection, but as an
assertion of the necessary withering of one's inner life if one keeps
it closed to the beauty, understanding, and love which is always
being poured down. Such a refusal requires no external condemnation: to be closed up in this manner is to be self-condemned.
Nothing moreover suggests that such a closure is irreversible.

A similar purport attaches to the discourse with Nicodemus,
where a spiritual rebirth or ascent is equated with a concurrent
spiritual descent, which, on either acceptation, is not to be understood as an ordinary motion of the psyche, but rather as a wind
which "bloweth where it listeth." And the conversation with the
Samaritan woman at Jacob's well, perhaps based on an actual case
of clairvoyance, dwells on the thirst of the soul for the point of unity
upon which all its aspirations converge, and on the slaking of that
thirst from a source which at first seems wholly beyond it, but
which can come to be wholly within it, "a well of water springing up into everlasting life." The worship of the Father in spirit and
in truth can be nothing beyond the reaching up of the finite, peripheral spirit to its central point of unity, a reaching up which
does not eliminate distance, but puts this spirit into a relation of
perpetual, loving *rapport* with that center. Such a complete *rapport* with the center Jesus, as Messiah, believes himself to have
achieved, and seeks to share with all who will, together with him,
make the great turn toward the center. The identification of the
Son with the Father is not, however, in Johannine theology, an identification after the fashion of the formal logicians, but one achieved
and sustained with effort. "My Father worketh hitherto, and I work
. . . the Son can do nothing of himself but what he seeth the Father do . . . for the Father loveth the Son, and sheweth him all
things that he himself doth" (5:17, 19, 20). The identification may
further be so perfect that any approximation to it, or defection

from it, will be judged only in relation to it: "The Father judgeth no man, but hath committed all judgment unto the Son" (v. 22). But nonetheless the Son "can of himself do nothing" (v. 30), and the justice of his judgment is due solely to its conformity with the Father's will. It will be because people have been untrue to that inner light which illuminates them as it does every one, and to the will which is the active side of that illumination, that they can be judged by the anointed one in whom conformity to that illumination, and to that will, have been made perfect. A like message is relayed, in terms of hunger rather than of thirst, by the miracle of the loaves and fishes, perhaps based on an actual, charismatic distribution of food. A distribution of heavenly bread here takes the place of the Samaritan woman's well of water. The self-referring words of Jesus could not, however, on the actual occasion, have been uttered, for they would only have been misunderstood. They express the theology of identification which John reads into all the actual deeds and words of Jesus. Jesus can only have spoken of the heavenly bread that he hoped to give to all, not, incomprehensibly, and to his auditors blasphemously, identified himself with that bread. Only John could have understood such an identification, could have interpreted it rightly. But even so, a blasphemous interpretation, one uniquely connecting a particular with another particular, was by many put upon his words, and must have helped to build up the great ground swell of disapproval which terminated in the Crucifixion.

We shall not comment in detail on the discourses reported by John in chapter 8, where the Pharisees are not persuaded by an address in which the speaker uniquely connects himself with his Creator. Had Jesus simply *been* God in some ordinary-language or formal-logical manner, or simply been sent by God, whatever that may have meant, it would still have been wrong to offend the minds of these learned, pious, enquiring men in such a harsh manner. It seems plain, for instance, that Jesus can never have said to the Pharisees: "Before Abraham was, I am." What only can have happened is that the unearthly authority of his manner irresistibly suggested some claim to a directness of relation with the divine source, which, on *their* view, was totally external and transcendent. They could not have conceived of that profound fusion of a human with a divine nature that Jesus had experienced. John alone would have understood the sense and truth of the utterance he reports, and it is even conceivable that, in some ineffable moment of self-disclosure, the incarnate Word may have uttered these very words to him, perhaps with a divine touch of humor at the violation of grammatical proprieties. It is, however, plain that such a deeply secret, mystical utterance would not have been made to the Pharisees. They were not by any means whited sepulchres, but to hear such talk might very well have made them so.

Chapter 10 also contains a series of assertions that could not, with either propriety or probability, have been made to the Pharisees, whom it could only have confounded in error. They assert a claim to pastoral uniqueness and a condemnation of previous claimants as thieves and robbers. This claim seems to accord with the claim elsewhere made in the Gospel that no one comes to the Father but through Christ. This message is, however, mitigated by the statement in 10:16 that there are other sheep who are not of this fold, but who will be gathered together by the Divine Shepherd and assembled in the final fold. And it is further mitigated in 10:34–36 by the justification of the divine identification in a scriptural text which gives the name of *gods* to all to whom the divine Word has come. The identification which Christ had experienced was in fact an identification with a Word which had at all times been the illumination of people, and which could at all times impart sonship to those who accepted its illumination, even if they belonged to other folds and knew nothing of the Jesus who had experienced this identification in Judea. And the test of their sonship would consist, moreover, solely in their works, the works that the divine Word or Spirit had enabled them to do (10:38). This stress on works, on *karma-yoga*, accords with the utterances in the other Gospels where Christ recognizes as done for himself what was done for the least of his brothers and sisters. His commandment to love one's neighbor as oneself was for him inseparable from the commandment to render supreme love to the perfection which is God.

Chapter 11 is instructive as containing a supreme miracle which certainly never occurred, for, had it happened, it would have had an incalculably confounding effect, of which there is no record, not even in the other Gospels. John's immense miracle is that of the raising of Lazarus: that Jesus wept over his dear friend is perhaps the only fact of history in the story. The reason for telling this miraculous tale is that John wishes to affirm that what Jesus accomplished is the Resurrection and the Life, that by reliving this in oneself one may achieve identification with what cannot pass away. It must have been with a clear conscience, if not without a few mental reservations, that John weighed the eternal truth of what he was relating against the surface truth that it did not happen, and must have found the latter wanting in importance. The glorious declaration that John puts into the mouth of the incarnate Word is therefore one that Jesus could never have uttered, as it could only have been misunderstood.

The Gospel scene now shifts to the celebration of the Passover and the washing of the disciples' feet, a homage to the most tarnished, but also most serviceable aspect of the human person. It also involves the departure of Judas, whose incapacity to understand the meaning of the identification which John had understood so perfectly and the other disciples dimly, necessitated the "betrayal" which Jesus had long anticipated and accepted, and which he saw as part of the Great Rite of this-worldly rejection and of otherworldly glorification which was preordained eternally for himself as the Teacher of Righteousness and the Suffering Servant.

We now move to the glorious discourses which were certainly never uttered in time but whose sense is mystical and eternal. They relate to a House or a Kingdom which is not of this world, but which may at some time come down into this world. It is a House or a Kingdom to which Jesus provides the only entry: whoever arrives at that House or that Kingdom will have done so through the working of the Word that is now manifest in Jesus. The identification of Jesus with deity is asserted as unambiguously as similar identifications are asserted in the Vedic writings, with the wholly un-Vedic addition that anyone who finds it hard to believe that Jesus is in the Father, and the Father in him, should try to believe it for the works' sake, and in the hope of performing the same or greater works. The Divine Center of Unity is not for this Gospel merely a refuge from the storms of life: it is a source of light and power that can irradiate and transform everything earthly. The Divine Home is further declared to be a House of many mansions. It is, we may conjecture, not a single World where all things are crowded together, but rather a World of Worlds, each structured according to the lifestyle and aspirations of its blessed inhabitant, and with its own mountains, seas, skies, and vegetation, yet also tenanted by the visiting phantasms of the companion spirits that had significance for the inhabitant in question. It may also be likened to a realm where the sheep wander freely over their own hillsides, though always aware of the tinkling notes of their fellows, and the voice of their Shepherd. It is not, one may hope, a state where all will be congregated together, and involved in collective activities, a condition appropriate to the periphery, but hardly to the Center of Being. However this may be interpreted, the Divine Word asserts that he will now depart to his Father's house, but that he will also send forth from that house a blessed and holy spirit that will comfort those he is leaving. Through it they will come to experience in themselves what they have seen so gloriously realized in him. From this there will result a set of lifelines of identification linking peripheral beings with their point of unity at the center: the Divine Word will be in them, as the Father is in the Word, so that all will be made perfect in unity. We shall not attempt further paraphrases of passages so poignantly expressed.

The story of the Passion is now related in chapters 18 to 20. Judas, the unhappy victim of a misguided theology, betrays Christ's misunderstood identification with deity to the chief priests and Pharisees, who send men to apprehend him in the garden where he is known to resort. Jesus submits to arrest and to interrogation by the priests, but denies that he has taught anything in secret other than what was said in his public utterances (18:20). In this denial of esotericism, Jesus might be thought to be contradicting what he said about the mysteries of the Kingdom of God in the other Gospels, but arguably there is no contradiction. For Christ's identification with deity is not a proposition which can be endorsed as true, or rejected as false, but a living act made manifest in all that he did and said, and in which others could participate as they heard him in the synagogue, or were healed by him of some grievous infirmity. There was therefore nothing specially arcane about it, except as all spiritual acts are arcane to those who have never experienced or performed them. Pilate, to whom Jewish clericalism and Christ's mystical, otherworldly Kingdom were alike unintelligible, then hands Jesus over to his clerical enemies, being unable to find fault with him himself. We shall not here dwell on the agonizing

Rite which follows, in which the clerical dogmatists, on the one hand, and Jesus, the anointed Teacher of Righteousness, on the other, attach quite different meanings to what is done or suffered. The story is peculiarly agonizing on account of the unmystical conceptions which motivate it: the belief, on the one hand, that mystical union is religiously or politically subversive, and, on the other, that a *via dolorosa* is a necessary prelude to a mystical consummation. The Jesus of John is at least not agonized by the absence of a final miracle, but is simply glad that the sad Rite is over. The body of Jesus is then tranquilly laid to rest in a garden by Nicodemus and Joseph of Arimathea, from which garden it was probably never removed.

We shall not attempt to examine the various tomb visits and visionary encounters related by John: the discovery of the empty tomb by Peter and another disciple, and Mary's encounter with a gardener, whom she afterwards decided, or knew, to be her master. Nor need we consider the sense of presence that stirred the assembled disciples in a room in Jerusalem, nor its removal of the doubts of Thomas. And the last, beautiful Galilean appearance, with its miracle of the fishes, must be left unexamined: probably there was on this occasion an extraordinary draught of fishes to which a miraculous significance was subsequently attached. We do not fully understand the processes by which mystical experiences become visionary, and visionary for a number of persons, while some, who have not shared the vision, remain doubters, and yet others, who shared the experience, convince themselves that they too shared the vision. Nor have the processes been sufficiently studied through which experiences quite doubtful in character become transformed in memory into experiences quite indubitable, and are testified to as such by those to whom they have been merely reported. Nor have philosophers considered the possibility that minor miracles are always occurring, miracles springing from those regulative values which are as essential to the world as its laws, but which must never become so obvious that they shatter our faith in those laws. We at least believe that the deontic modalities are as much part of the world's structure as its nomological principles, and that both spring from the central unity in which all things and persons have their ground. Such possibilities are perhaps more credible to those who have had experience of cosmic regions nearer to the center, where legend becomes truth and *le songe est savoir.*

This essay is only a random series of mystical thoughts on a great religious document and is obviously open to many criticisms. Quite possibly the writer of the Gospel was more existentially Hebraic in his belief in the individual otherness of deity and in the sheerly marvelous character of the stream of light and grace that it sheds upon us and which became channeled to us through the extraordinary person of Jesus. Possibly he also entertained doubts as to the communication of such grace to such as were unable or unwilling to accept such a channeling. To the extent that this is the case, John's Gospel itself becomes unacceptable to us. For we are too irredeemably Hellenistic or Platonic to accept any unique channeling of the values of the Spirit into anything particular, anything that merely instantiates those values rather than absolutely *is* them, and so is essentially communicable. The idolatrous worship of particulars is, however, no more essentially characteristic of the Jews than of others, and in John, as in Isaiah the prophet, it is plainly breaking down. In any case, we, as confirmed Platonists, cannot deprive ourselves of the charisma of the three supremely transfigured members of our race, Socrates, Buddha, and Jesus. (The mention of these three together makes no attempt to compare them or to grade them, though the transfiguration was perhaps greater and deeper in the case of Jesus than in that of the others.)

Socrates was, of these three, the least extraordinary in his claims. His reaching up to the source of all values took the form of a searching enquiry into their nature and content, and their necessary differences and affinities, and he saw the only profit and blessedness of the soul in the realization of all those values conjointly, in a virtue which was inseparable from its own knowledge. The theology of this transfigured personality was worked out by Plato in the *Phaedo* and in other writings, and whatever spiritual heroism was achieved by Stoics, and by other noble Greeks and Romans, was a reflex of his intellectual spirituality. Buddha, on the other hand, reached out to the ultimate source of all values as a peace beyond all personal cravings, and beyond the perpetual frustration and misery of their attempted fulfillment. It was a peace in which an absolute, final insight would flood the mind, and put an end to its struggles, but it was also an insight that sprang from sources internal to the mind. All persons had a Buddha-eye within them and could be a lamp unto themselves, could work out their own salvation with diligence. But this message of wisdom and detachment was also a message of boundless love and compassion: the quest for the freedom from narrow, personal desire must be extended to everyone. And the theology implicit in Buddha's transformed life was then worked out in the many hypostases and spiritual states of the Mahāyāna. In the case of Jesus, however, the reaching up to the source of all values took the figurative form of a love among persons, whose doctrinal elaboration took many forms, and extended over many centuries. What, however, is distinctive of Christianity is the close bond that it weaves between what is transcendentally central and whatever is most humbly peripheral. It thus extends a transfiguring touch to all human relations, and especially to such as are cases of personal love. This touch extends even to the *pains* endured by love battling for the life or natural happiness of some beloved child, parent, friend, or mere fellow-human. Peripheral life is made radiantly good by Christianity as it is not by other religions, and in this it compensates for the stress on particular channels from which Buddhism is exempt. There are not, it seems, any perfect religious messages or messengers. Human access to the central source of all being and value must in the last resort remain internal to human beings. We must be lamps unto ourselves, as Buddha said in his last discourse, trusting to no external refuge, and we must worship the Father, as Christ said to the Samaritan woman, not in a mountain nor in Jerusalem, but in spirit and in truth.

NOTE

1. The title of a work on the Gnostics that I read in adolescence.

11

Religious Pluralism and Absolute Claims

JOHN HICK

THE TOPIC THAT I am going to pursue under this title is that of the absolute claims made by one religion over against others. Such a claim might be concerned with knowing and teaching the truth or with offering the final good of salvation/liberation. I suggest that in fact the truth-claim and the salvation-claim cohere closely together and should be treated as a single package. The valuable contents of this package, the goods conveyed, consist in salvation or liberation; and the packaging and labeling, with the identifying of the sender and the directing of the package to the recipient, are provided by the doctrine. Thus doctrines are secondary and yet essential to the vital matter of receiving salvation, somewhat as packaging and labeling are secondary and yet essential to transmitting the contents of a parcel.

What then is an absolute claim when made on behalf of such a religious package? In this context the term *absolute* is not, I think, being used as a precision instrument. Its operative meanings are revealed in its uses, which are in fact various. In one sense, the absoluteness of, say, Christianity means the salvific sufficiency of its gospel and its way for Christians, that is, for those whose religious life is determined by that gospel and that way. In this sense the absoluteness of Christianity is compatible with the absoluteness of Islam, or again of Hinduism, or Buddhism, or Judaism, as the salvific sufficiencies of these different messages and ways for those who have been spiritually formed by them. But since *absolute* so strongly suggests uniqueness, and the impossibility of being surpassed or even equaled, it seems inappropriate to apply it to this pluralistic conception. And in fact this plural sense is the polar opposite of the religious absolutism that I want to discuss. Let me approach it, however, through this opposite, namely, religious pluralism.

By this I mean the view that the great world faiths embody different perceptions and conceptions of, and correspondingly different responses to, the real or the ultimate from within the major variant cultural ways of being human; and that within each of them the transformation of human existence from self-centeredness to Reality-centeredness is manifestly taking place — and taking place, so far as human observation can tell, to much the same extent. Thus the great religious traditions are to be regarded as alternative soteriological spaces within which, or ways along which, men and women can find salvation/liberation/fulfillment.

From this point of view the proper understanding of one's own religious faith and commitment in comparison with others can be well expressed by adapting a phrase of Rosemary Radford Ruether's. She speaks of her own commitment as a Roman Catholic, rather than as some other kind of Christian, as a matter of "ecclesial ethnicity" rather than as involving a judgment that her church is superior to others.[1] Extending the idea, we may say that one's being a Muslim, or a Christian, or a Hindu, is a matter of religious ethnicity. That is to say, Christianity, or Buddhism, or Islam, or any other religion, is the religious community into which one was born, into whose norms and insights one has been inducted, and within which one can therefore most satisfactorily live and grow. There are of course spiritual immigrants; but they are very few in comparison with the vast populations through which each religious tradition is transmitted from generation to generation. And having been born into, say, the Christian religious world, one does not have to be able to prove that it is superior to the other religious worlds in order for it to be right and proper for one to be wholeheartedly a Christian. Realistically viewed, one's religious commitment is usually a matter of religious ethnicity rather than of deliberate judgment and choice.

But nevertheless each of the great traditions has long since developed a self-understanding which at some point jars, or even positively clashes, with this conception of religious pluralism.

Thus in the Hindu tradition one believes that one has access to the *sanātana Dharma*, the eternal truth, incarnated in human language in the Vedas. There is a general tolerance of other ways, often however combined with the assumption that sooner or later, each in his or her own time, and if not in the present life then in another, all will come to the fullness of the Vedic understanding. Further, in Advaitan philosophy it is often held that the theistic forms of religion represent a less advanced awareness of the ultimate Reality. Thus Hinduism is conscious, at least in many of its adherents, of its unique superiority among the religious movements of the world; and such a consciousness does not naturally encourage a genuine acceptance of religious pluralism.

In the Hebrew tradition it is held that the Jews are God's chosen people with whom God has made a special covenant, so that they may be God's means of revelation to all the human race. Thus, whilst to be a Jew has often involved special burdens and sufferings, sometimes of the most extreme and appalling kind, yet to be a Jew is also, from the Jewish point of view, to stand in a unique relationship to God. This does not lead to any general intolerance of other religions, nor to a feeling that their adherents must be converted to Judaism; but it does induce a sense of the privilege of having been born a Jew. However, religious pluralism implies that those who are on the other great ways of salvation are no less God's chosen people, although with different vocations; and a genuine acceptance of this is not naturally encouraged by the traditional Judaic self-understanding.

In the Buddhist tradition it is held that the true appreciation of our human situation occurs most clearly and effectively in the teachings of Gautama Buddha; and that any doctrine which denies the ceaselessly changing and insubstantial character of human life, or the possibility of attaining to the further shore of nirvana, is not conducive to liberation from the pervasive unsatisfactoriness of ordinary human existence. The *Dharma* is the full and saving truth, uniquely clear, effective, and final among the illuminations and revelations of the world. And, again, such an assurance does not naturally encourage a full acceptance of religious pluralism.

In Islam there is the firm belief that Mohammad was "the seal of the prophets," and that through the Qur'ān God has revealed to humankind the true religion, taking up into itself and fulfilling all previous revelations. Thus, whilst a Muslim should give friendly recognition to brothers and sisters within the other Abrahamic faiths and may even, in some recent interpretations, extend the Qur'ānic concept of the People of the Book to include those who encounter the divine through the Hindu, Buddhist, Confucian, and Taoist as well as Jewish and Christian scriptures, yet the Muslim will retain a strong sense of the unique status of the Qur'ānic revelation. Here is God's final, decisive, and commanding word which all must heed and obey. Such a conviction, again, does not naturally encourage a full and unqualified acceptance of religious pluralism.

And in the Christian tradition there is a powerful inbuilt basis for the sense of the unique superiority of the Christian faith in the doctrine that Jesus Christ, the founder and focus of the religion, was God in human form or, more precisely, the Second Person of the divine Trinity living a human life. Given this basic dogma, it has been a natural historical consequence for Christians to see theirs as the one and only true religion, founded by God in person and the locus of God's unique saving act — with the corollary that all the other supposed ways to the real are human structures, not to be compared with that which God has provided. From this has flowed the missionary imperative (though considerably muted today within large sections of the Church) to convert all humanity to the acceptance of the Christian gospel and to membership of the Church as the body of Christ's redeemed people.

Each of these great religious traditions, then, assumes in one way or another its own unique superiority. Psychologically, this may well only be an instance of the corporate self-respect that characterizes any viable human group. The nearest parallel is national pride. What American would wish to be other than American, or what Chinese person would wish to be other than Chinese, or Nigerian other than Nigerian, or Britisher other than British, or French man or woman other than French? And do not most people likewise take it unthinkingly for granted that their own mother tongue is the natural form of human speech and that their own culture, with its familiar food, manners, and art forms, its pervasive presuppositions and atmosphere, represents the proper way of being human; so that they find it hard to see foreign ways of life as other than peculiar and, when strikingly different from their own, either laughable or bizarre. The other side of this natural parochialism, however, is that we are what we are, and are poor creatures if we do not take some satisfaction and pride in our own ethnic or national or cultural identity, however critical we may also be of some of its particular manifestations. Further, it is largely this residual tribalism that prompts us to work and sacrifice for the good of our community. And the same principle will naturally produce a corporate pride in any religious group of which we are members, both the immediate local community and the vast historical tradition which gives the latter its character and imparts to it its aura of sacredness. For we have, in most cases, been formed from infancy by our tradition, absorbing its values and presuppositions. It has become as much a part of us as our nationality, our language, and our culture, and alien religious traditions can seem as peculiar or comic or bizarre as can foreign names or customs or foods.

Psychologically, then, the sense of the unique superiority of one's own religious tradition may be simply a natural form of pride in and ingrained preference for one's own familiar group and its ways. And thus far it is to be accepted, and taken into account, as an inevitable feature of human life; though it must not be allowed to inhibit the spiritual travel which has been called the imaginative passing over into another religious world and then coming back with new insight to one's own.[2]

But natural pride, despite its positive contribution to human life, becomes harmful when it is elevated to the level of dogma and is built into the belief system of a religious community. This happens when its sense of its own validity and worth is expressed in doctrines implying an exclusive or a decisively superior access to the truth or the power to save. A natural human tribal preference thereby receives the stamp of divine approval or the aura of a privileged relationship to the divine. The resulting sense of a special status has in turn, in some cases, either spontaneously motivated or been manipulated to motivate policies of persecution, coercion, repression, conquest, and exploitation, or a sense that others cannot be left to follow their own faith or insight but must be converted to our own gospel. It is at this point, at which the sense of the superiority of one's own tradition is enshrined in formal doctrines as an essential article of faith, that the idea of religious pluralism is felt as a challenge and may be resisted as a threat. It is also at this point however that the acceptance of religious pluralism may lead to creative doctrinal development, either in reinterpreting absolutist doctrines or in allowing them to fall into the background so that they become ideas of historical interest rather than of immediate practical concern.

It is for the adherents of each of the great traditions to look critically at their own dogmas in the light of their new experience within a religiously plural world. As a Christian I shall therefore direct my attention to Christian absolutism. In the past this has taken powerful forms, with immense human consequences, in the Roman Catholic dogma *Extra ecclesiam nulla sallus* ("outside the church, no salvation") and its nineteenth-century Protestant missionary equivalent, outside Christianity, no salvation. The former was expressed, for example, in the affirmation of the Council of Florence (1438–45) that "no one remaining outside the Catholic Church, not just pagans, but also Jews or heretics or schismatics, can become partakers of eternal life; but they will go to the 'everlasting fire which was prepared for the devil and his angels,' unless before the end of life they are joined to the Church" (Denzinger, no. 714); whilst the latter was expressed as recently as a message of the (Protestant) Congress on World Mission at Chicago in 1960, declaring that "in the days since the war, more than one billion souls have passed into eternity and more than half of these went to the torment of hell fire without even hearing of Jesus Christ, who he was, or why he died on the cross of Calvary."[3]

There are today some Roman Catholic traditionalists, pre-Vatican II in outlook, who adhere to the *Extra ecclesiam* dogma in its full logical rigor; and likewise there are some extreme right-wing Protestant fundamentalists who practice the nineteenth-century missionary faith in an unqualified form. Indeed if we look at the entire Catholic and Protestant worlds, and not only at the parts with which we tend to be most familiar, there may well today be large numbers and powerful groups of Christian absolutists. But nevertheless I think that historians of twentieth-century Christianity will see as the more striking fact the progressive decay of absolutism during this period within the more active and self-critical layers of the Christian mind. The clear trend of mainline Catholic and Protestant attitudes is away from the absolutism of the past.

But it is easier for this to happen at the level of practice than at the level of theological theory. For there can be no doubt that traditional Christian belief, as expressed in the Scriptures, the ecumenical creeds, and the major dogmatic pronouncements and confessions, has been understood as embodying an absolute claim for the Christian gospel and the Christian way of salvation. According to this system of belief, the historical Jesus was God the Son, the Second Person of the divine Trinity, living a human life; and by his death on the cross he has atoned for human sin, so that by responding to him in genuine repentance and faith, and gratefully accepting the benefits of his sacrifice, we may be reconciled to God and so become part of Christ's Church and heirs of eternal life.

Probably the majority of Christian theologians today want to remain loyal to the heart, at least, of this traditional teaching, centering upon the unique significance of Christ as God incarnate and as the source of human salvation, whilst at the same time renouncing the old Christian absolutism. And so it has become common to give the old doctrines a universal rather than a restrictive meaning. It is taught that the salvation won by Christ is available to all humankind, though whenever and wherever it occurs it has been made possible only by his atoning death. His sacrifice on the cross is thus the necessary condition of human salvation, but its benefits may nevertheless be enjoyed by people who know nothing of him, or even who consciously reject the Christian interpretation of his life and death. Again, the divine Logos which became personally incarnate within the Jewish stream of religious life as Jesus of Nazareth has also been at work within other streams of religious life, inspiring spiritual leaders and thus being actively present, though perhaps in varying degrees, in Hinduism, Buddhism, Islam, and so forth. Consequently there may well be significant religious lessons which Christians can learn from the people of these other traditions.

But I want to suggest that these moves, whilst admirably ecumenical in intent, only amount to epicycles added to a fundamentally absolutist structure of theory in order to obscure its incompatibility with the observed facts. In analogy with the old Ptolemaic picture of the universe, with our earth at its center, traditional Christian theology sees the religious universe as centered in the person of Christ and his gospel. In the history of astronomy, when new observations of the movements of the planets seemed to conflict with the Ptolemaic scheme, smaller circles were added to the theory, centering on the original circles, to complicate the projected planetary paths and bring them nearer to what was observed, and these epicycles enabled the old picture to be retained for a while longer. Analogously, the Ptolemaic theology, with Christianity at the center, is now being complicated by epicycles of theory to make it more compatible with our observations of the other great world faiths.

Purely theoretically, these moves can be successful. Further epicycles can be added indefinitely, as required, and the abandonment of the old scheme thereby indefinitely postponed. The problem is one not of logical possibility but of psychological plausibility. Natural human candidness sooner or later finds it unprofitable, and even perhaps undignified, to go on investing intellectual energy in defense of a dogma which seems to clash with the facts. And so when a simpler and more realistic model emerges there is liable to be a paradigm shift such as took place in the Copernican revolution from the earth-centered to the heliocentric conception of the universe. In the theology of religions a comparably simpler and more realistic model is today available in the theocentric or, better, Reality-centered conception, with its pluralistic implications. Here the religious universe centers upon the divine Reality, and Christianity is seen as one of a number of worlds of faith which circle around and reflect that Reality.

But a wholehearted shift to religious pluralism would mean abandoning not only the older and cruder Ptolemaic theology but also the more sophisticated versions, with their new epicycles. For to hold that divine grace reaches the other worlds of faith via the person and cross of Christ would be like holding that the light of the sun can only fall upon the other planets by being first reflected from the earth. To take a different analogy, it is as though there were a lifesaving medicine, the true chemical name of which is Christ. This medicine is available in its pure form only under the brand name of Christianity. But there are other products which, unknown to their purveyors, also contain Christ, though diluted with other elements and marketed under other names. In these circumstances a knowledgeable pharmacist would always recommend Christianity, if it is available. However, there may be places where it is not available; and there, for the time being at least, another product will serve as an adequate second-best. This, I would suggest, is essentially the theology of religions created by the currently favored theological epicycles.

But once these epicycles are seen for what they are, it is, I think, clear that a Christian acceptance of religious pluralism must involve the kind of rethinking of the doctrine of the Incarnation that has in fact been taking place during the last fifty years or so. Let me briefly illustrate this, first, from one of the most influential of living Roman Catholic thinkers, Karl Rahner. Although questions have been raised by traditionalists in Rome about his orthodoxy, Rahner's position as a Catholic theologian has never been successfully challenged, and he is widely regarded as a prime example of one who is faithful to his own tradition but at the same time accepts a responsibility to reformulate its affirmations in ways which are relevant and intelligible to the modern world.

In his much discussed article, "Current Problems in Christology,"[4] Rahner says that the Chalcedonian definition is not to be seen as ending christological thinking, for

> the clearest formulations, the most sanctified formulas, the classic condensations of the centuries-long work of the Church in prayer, reflection, and struggle concerning God's mysteries: all these derive their life from the fact that they are not end but beginning, not goal but means, truths which open the way to the — ever greater — Truth.[5]

Further, the traditional two-natures formula has often led in the past to "a conception, which undoubtedly dominates the popular mind (without of course reaching the stage of consciously formulated heresy), and which could be put rather as follows: 'When our Lord (= God) walked on earth with his disciples, still humble and unrecognized. . . .'"[6] As against what Rahner sees as this popular misconception — which is however barely distinguishable from the traditional Christian conception of Incarnation — we must, he writes, recognize the genuine humanity of Christ, which entails that

> the "human nature" of the Logos possesses a genuine, spontaneous, free, spiritual, active center, a human self-conscious-

ness, which as creaturely faces the eternal Word in a genuinely
human attitude of adoration, obedience, a most radical sense
of creaturehood.[7]

For otherwise Christ "would only be the God who is active among
us in human form, and not the true man who can be our Medi-
ator with respect to God in genuine human freedom."[8]

Accordingly, Rahner suggests that we should see the Incarnation not as the unique exception to God's normal relationship
to humanity, but rather as the uniquely perfect instance of that
relationship. For

> christological considerations have led the way back to the more
> general doctrine of God's relation to the creature and allowed
> Christology to appear as the clearly unique "specifically" dis-
> tinct perfection of this relation.[9]

Accordingly, the relation of created spiritual beings to God
"reaches its absolute peak in the case of Christ."[10] Indeed Rahner
suggests, in a striking phrase, that "Christology may be studied as
self-transcending anthropology, and anthropology as deficient
Christology."[11] Thus the Incarnation is not to be seen as a divine
intervention which lies apart from God's creative work in human
life, but as

> the *ontologically* (not merely "morally," an afterthought) un-
> ambiguous goal of the movement of creation as a whole, in
> relation to which everything prior is merely a preparation of
> the scene. . . . Consequently it is not pure fantasy (though the
> attempt must be made with caution) to conceive of the "evo-
> lution" of the world *towards Christ,* and to show how there
> is a gradual ascent which reaches a peak in him.[12]

Hence Rahner can even see the Incarnation as the supreme
instance of the operation of divine grace. For is not grace

> the unfolding within human nature of the union of the hu-
> man with the Logos . . . therefore, and *arising thence,* some-
> thing which can also be had in those who are not the ek-
> sistence of the Logos in time and history but who do belong
> to his necessary environment?[13]

And so Rahner is able to say:

> Suppose someone says: "Jesus is the man whose life is one of absolutely unique self-surrender to God." He may very well have stated the truth about the very depths of what Christ really is, *provided* that he has understood (a) that this self-abandonment presupposes a communication of God to the man; (b) that an absolute self-surrender implies an absolute self-communication of God to the man, one which makes what is produced by it into the reality of the producer himself; and (c) that such an existential statement does not signify something "mental," a fiction, but is in the most radical way a statement about being.[14]

In a later paper, Rahner develops this thought that human nature is essentially endowed with the possibility of self-transcendence, and that "the incarnation of God is therefore the unique, *supreme*, case of the total actualization of human reality, which consists of the fact that man *is* in so far as he gives up himself."[15] For

> God has taken on human nature, because it is essentially ready and adoptable, because it alone, in contrast to what is definable without transcendence, can exist in total dispossession of itself, and comes therein to the fulfillment of its own incomprehensible meaning.[16]

In other words, divine incarnation in human life is a general human possibility. As Rahner says in the context of a discussion of Christology in relation to the idea of evolution:

> It seems to me that we should have no particular difficulty in representing the history of the world and of the spirit to ourselves as the history of a self-transcendence into the life of God — a self-transcendence which, in this its final and highest phase, is identical with an absolute self-communication of God expressing the same process but now looked at from God's side.[17]

Thus incarnation is the ultimate human possibility and will constitute the eschatological human reality. But in this world it has only actually happened in one unique case: "It is only in Jesus of Nazareth that one can dare to believe such a thing has happened and happens eternally."[18]

Clearly one could pursue this line of thought further by understanding incarnation as a matter of degree. We should then say that whenever and wherever the grace of God is effective in men and women, evoking self-giving love for God and neighbor, to that extent God has become incarnate within human history. Such an enlarging or metaphoricalizing of the idea of divine incarnation would have important implications for the Christian theology of religions. For whereas a unique and absolute Incarnation defines a unique stream of salvation history, incarnation understood as taking place in many degrees of human openness to the divine has no such effect.

However, Rahner is bound to the Chalcedonian tradition, according to which Incarnation is unique and absolute. In Chalcedonian thinking this uniqueness and absoluteness are necessitated by the concept of substance. One is or is not of the eternal and uncreated substance of God; this cannot be a matter of degree; and among all human life only Jesus Christ has been of that divine substance. Thus against the prompting of his own insights Rahner insists that although Jesus was genuinely human yet also "this man . . . is God."[19] And in support of the traditional paradox that Jesus was unambiguously human yet unambiguously God, he propounds the following argument:

> only a *divine* Person can possess as its own a freedom really distinct from itself in such a way that this freedom does not cease to be truly free even with regard to the divine Person possessing it, while it continues to qualify this very Person as its ontological subject. For it is only in the case of God that it is conceivable at all that he himself can constitute something in a state of distinction from himself. This is precisely an attribute of his divinity as such and his intrinsic creativity: to be able, by himself and through his *own* act *as such*, to constitute something in being which by the very fact of its being radically dependent (because *wholly* constituted in being), also acquires autonomy, independent reality, and truth (precisely because it is constituted in being by the one, unique

God), and all this precisely with respect to the one God who constitutes it in being.[20]

Here Rahner attempts to render the paradox acceptable by the assertion that God, being God ("This is precisely an attribute of his divinity as such"),[21] can bring it about that, as incarnate, this person is both free, autonomous, finite, and human, and yet at the same time the infinite Creator of all things. But the tortuous complexity of his argument conceals the simple proposition that God, being God, can do anything, and therefore can become a genuinely free and independent human being whilst remaining God. This is merely, however, to reiterate the traditional dogma without doing anything either to recommend it or to make it intelligible. Rahner's faithfulness to his tradition, with its implied absolute claim, is reflected consistently in his own theology of religions. Here it is assumed, on the basis of tradition, that redemption is through Christ alone and that outside the Church there is no salvation; but devout and godly people within the other great world traditions are regarded as anonymous Christians. This has been Rahner's distinctive contribution to the spinning of epicycles in aid of a basically Ptolemaic theology. Given his adherence to the Chalcedonian Christology, despite exciting new insights which seem to point beyond it, the doctrine of the anonymous Christian is as far as he is able to go toward the alternative vision of religious pluralism.

However, let us turn at this point to the work of recent Protestant theologians who have also been trying to do justice to the genuinely human Jesus perceived by the modern historical reading of the Gospel records. The work of some of the more adventurous among them points to a way of understanding God's activity in the Christ event which does not in principle preclude an acceptance of religious pluralism. These theologians have not generally been primarily concerned with the question of other religions; and insofar as they touch upon it, most of them adhere to the traditional assumption of the unique superiority of Christianity. But it is an important feature of their work, even if one which was not always noticed by these authors themselves, that whereas the Chalcedonian Christology entailed the unique superiority of Christianity, these modern Christologies do not. Logically, they leave the comparative assessment of the Christian and other traditions to be determined by historical observation and spiritual judgment. Thus the superiority of Christianity loses its status as an *a priori* dogma and becomes a claim that could only be established by adequate historical evidence.

I shall illustrate this development from the work of the Presbyterian Donald Baillie and the Anglican Geoffrey Lampe. I select these because they may be less well known to you than American scholars such as John Knox, Norman Pittenger, and many others, who would have served my purpose equally well.

The late Donald Baillie's book *God Was in Christ* was described by Rudolf Bultmann as "the most significant book of our time in the field of Christology."[22] Not only the title but the entire tone of Baillie's book show that his intention was wholly orthodox. He was not criticizing the idea of divine incarnation in Jesus Christ but was trying to make it intelligible to our twentieth century. He did so by understanding incarnation in terms of what he called the paradox of grace. This is the paradoxical fact that when we do God's will it is true both that we are acting freely and responsibly, and also that God, through supernatural grace, is acting in and through us. The paradox is summed up in Paul's words, concerning his own labors, "it was not I, but the grace of God which is with me" (1 Cor. 15:10). As Baillie says, the essence of the paradox

> lies in the conviction which a Christian man possesses, that every good thing in him, every good thing he does, is somehow not wrought by himself but by God. This is a highly paradoxical conviction, for in ascribing all to God it does not abrogate human personality nor disclaim personal responsibility. Never is human action more truly and fully personal, never does the agent feel more perfectly free, than in those moments of which he can say as a Christian that whatever good was in them was not his but God's.[23]

Baillie now uses this paradox of grace as the clue to the yet greater paradox of the Incarnation: that the life of Jesus was an authentically human life and yet that in and through that life God was at work on earth. Baillie says:

> What I wish to suggest is that this paradox of grace points the way more clearly and makes a better approach than anything

else in our experience to the mystery of the Incarnation itself; that this paradox in its fragmentary form in our own Christian lives is a reflection of that perfect union of God and man in the Incarnation on which our whole Christian life depends, and may therefore be our best clue to the understanding of it. In the New Testament we see the man in whom God was incarnate surpassing all other men in refusing to claim anything for himself independently and ascribing all the goodness to God. We see him also desiring to take up other men into his own close union with God, that they might be as he was. And if these men, entering in some small measure through him into that union, experience the paradox of grace for themselves in fragmentary ways, and are constrained to say, "It was not I but God," may not this be a clue to the understanding of that perfect life in which the paradox is complete and absolute, that life of Jesus which, being the perfection of humanity, is also, and even in a deeper and prior sense, the very life of God himself? If the paradox is a reality in our poor imperfect lives at all, so far as there is any good in them, does not the same or a similar paradox, taken at the perfect and absolute pitch, appear as the mystery of the Incarnation?[24]

In other words, the union of divine and human action which occurs whenever God's grace works effectively in a man's or a woman's life, operated to an absolute extent in the life of Jesus.

Now Baillie's suggestion, which has its roots in the thought of Augustine, and earlier in Origen, and in Theodore of Mopsuestia and others of the later Antiochene school, does have the advantage that it offers some degree of understanding of what it means to say that the life of Jesus was a fully divine as well as a fully human event. But of course in making the idea of incarnation thus to some extent intelligible, Baillie discards the traditional Chalcedonian language of Jesus' having two natures, one human and the other divine, and of his being in his divine nature of one substance with God. That was a way of expressing it which made sense within the philosophical world of the early Christian centuries, but which has now become little more than a mysterious formula which is obediently repeated but no longer bears any intrinsic meaningfulness. Thus the kind of reinterpretation that Baillie offers should be seen as an attempt to bring the doctrine of the Incarnation to life in the modern mind, giving it meaning as a truth which connects with our human experience and which is at least to some extent intelligible in contemporary terms. For whilst few people today use the concept of substance, or find the idea of a person with two natures other than grotesque, all Christians have some experience and appreciation of the reality of divine grace operating in human life. Further, they can connect this reality with the extraordinary events of the New Testament.

The other recent Protestant theologian to whose work I should like to refer is the Anglican Geoffrey Lampe, who was Regius Professor of Divinity at Cambridge University until his death in 1980. I shall be referring in particular to his last book, *God as Spirit*. Lampe uses as his clue or model for the understanding of Christ the activity within human life of the Holy Spirit, the Spirit of God. And the Spirit of God, he says, "is to be understood, not as referring to a divine hypostasis distinct from God the Father and God the Son or Word, but as indicating God himself as active towards and in his human creation."[25] Further, "the Spirit of God is God disclosing himself as Spirit, that is to say, God creating and giving life to the spirit of man, inspiring him, renewing him, and making him whole."[26] The principal activity in relation to humanity of God as Spirit is inspiration; and accordingly the Christology which Lampe presents is "a Christology of inspiration."[27] For "the concept of the inspiration and indwelling of man by God as Spirit is particularly helpful in enabling us to speak of God's continuing creative relationship towards human persons and of his active presence in Jesus as the central and focal point within this relationship."[28] Again, "the use of this concept enables us to say that God indwelt and motivated the human spirit of Jesus in such a way that in him, uniquely, the relationship for which man is intended by his Creator was fully realized."[29]

Accordingly Lampe does not accept the traditional model of "the Incarnation of a preexistent divine being, the Logos who is God the Son."[30] For that model is bound up with the two complementary notions of the primal human fall from righteousness to sin, and then God's intervention by coming to earth in the person of Jesus of Nazareth to redeem humankind by the sacrifice of his own life upon the cross. Instead, Lampe prefers to follow the early

Greek-speaking Fathers of the Church, such as Irenaeus, in thinking of a continuous ongoing divine creation of human beings.

> Irenaeus speaks of the making of man according to God's image and likeness as a continuous creation. . . . Man gradually progresses until he attains the perfection of created humanity, which consists in likeness to the perfection of uncreated deity. . . . Man, according to Irenaeus, is first molded by God's hands, then he receives the infusion of the soul, the life-principle, and finally through Christ he is given the lifegiving Spirit that makes him God's son.[31]

Thus "the Spirit transforms man into that which he was not; yet this transformation is continuous with creation; it is the completion of creation."[32] On this view, the Spirit of God has always been active within the human spirit, inspiring men and women to open themselves freely to the divine presence and to respond in their lives to the divine purpose. This continuous creative activity of God as Spirit means that "God has always been incarnate in his human creatures, forming their spirits from within and revealing himself in and through them."[33] We must accordingly "speak of this continuum as a single creative and saving activity of God the Spirit towards, and within, the spirit of man, and of his presence in the person of Jesus as a particular moment within that continuous creativity."[34] For "a union of personal deity with human personality can only be a perfected form of inspiration."[35]

I suggest that in relation to the question of religious pluralism the momentous consequence of this kind of reinterpretation of the doctrine of the Incarnation is that it no longer necessarily involves the claim to the unique superiority of Christianity which the more traditional understanding involves. For if one says, with the older Christian formulations, that the divine substance was present on earth once and once only, namely in Jesus Christ, it follows as a corollary that the Christian religion, and no other, was founded by God in person; and it certainly seems in turn to follow from this that God must want all human beings to accept Christianity as the religion which God has created for them. From this starting point, all other religious traditions have to be regarded as in various ways preliminary or defective or inferior. This is, of course, the way in which the Church has in fact usually regarded them in the past. But if, with Baillie, we see in the life of Christ a supreme instance of that fusion of divine grace and creaturely freedom that occurs in all authentic human response and obedience to God, then the situation changes. For we are no longer speaking of an intersection of the divine and the human which only occurs in one unique case, but of an intersection which occurs, in many different ways and degrees, in all human openness and response to the divine initiative. There is now no difficulty in principle in acknowledging that the paradox of grace was also exemplified in other messengers of God or indeed, more broadly, in other human beings who are markedly Reality-centered rather than self-centered.

Of course Christians who feel impelled to claim superiority for their own tradition can still find a way to do so. For they can claim that the paradox of grace, which occurs whenever a human being freely responds to divine grace, was more fully exemplified in the life of Christ than in any other life. This indeed appears to have been Baillie's own view. But it is important to note that, whilst this is still a claim to a unique superiority, yet the epistemological nature of the claim has changed. It is no longer an *a priori* dogma but now is, or ought to be, a historical judgment, subject to all the difficulties and uncertainties of such judgments. Lampe also, given his understanding of God's action in Christ as the supreme instance of divine inspiration, is still able to make a unique claim for this particular moment of divine activity. For "this moment is," he says, "the fulfillment of all the divine activity which preceded it, and . . . it determines the mode in which God the Spirit is experienced in all subsequent history."[36] "The evidence," he continues, "that this claim is justified is the actual fact that Christians find in Christ their source of inspiration, they are attracted by him to reorient their lives towards faith in God and love towards their neighbors, and they see in him the pattern of this attitude of sonship and brotherhood."[37] However, that for which Lampe claims this unique significance is not the historical Jesus himself, in isolation, about whom our information is often fragmentary and uncertain, but the Christ event as a whole. "The Christ event . . . for which we claim so central a place in the history of the divine self-disclosure to man includes all human thought inspired by God which has Jesus as its primary reference point."[38] In other words, the uniquely

central inspiration event is virtually Christianity itself, as a historical tradition focused upon the person of Jesus Christ. Thus Lampe
says that

> if a saying in the Gospels, such as, for instance, one of the
> Beatitudes, touches the conscience and quickens the imagina-
> tion of the reader, it does not matter greatly whether it was
> originally spoken by Jesus himself or by some unknown Chris-
> tian prophet who shared "the mind of Christ." It is in either
> case a word of God communicated through a human mind.
> It is an utterance of man inspired by God the Spirit.[39]

Thus it is not vitally important whether the famous words of Christ
in the Gospels were actually spoken by the Jesus of history.

> We value them because we find truth in them and gain in-
> spiration from them, and we acknowledge Jesus to be uniquely
> significant because he is either their author or else the origi-
> nator of the impulse which evoked them from the minds of
> others — from people whose debt to him was so great that they
> composed them in his name, as his own.[40]

Here again, as in the case of Donald Baillie's paradox-of-grace
theory, we see a separating in principle of Christology from the
theology of religions. That is to say, the unique superiority of the
Christian revelation no longer follows as a logical corollary from
either Baillie's or Lampe's Christology. To see Jesus as exemplifying in a special degree what Baillie calls the paradox of grace, and
what Lampe calls the inspiration of God the Spirit, is thus far to
leave open the further question as to how this particular exemplification stands in relation to other exemplifications, such as those
that lie at the basis of some of the other great world religions. Baillie
believes that the realization of the paradox of grace in the life of
Jesus was unique because total and absolute. But the point I want
to stress is that this belief is no longer, in the light of either Baillie's
or Lampe's Christology, a necessary inference from the nature of
God's action in Jesus, but must instead be a judgment based upon
historical evidence. And the main question that arises, for any
Christian who is familiar with the modern scholarly study of the
New Testament, is whether we have a sufficiently complete knowledge of the historical Jesus to be able to affirm that his entire life

was a perfect exemplification of the paradox of grace or of divine inspiration.

We saw that in Lampe's thought there is a shift from the historical Jesus to the Christian movement as a whole as the locus of the uniquely central and focal revelatory event. But if we do not have enough historical information to attribute absolute religious value to the historical Jesus, we have, I would think, too much historical information to be able to make such a judgment about Christianity as a historical phenomenon. To Lampe it was self-evident that Christianity is the central and decisive strand of human history. But, clearly, this is not self-evident to others whose spiritual life has been developed in a different religious environment and whose relationship to the divine has been shaped by a different spirituality. At this point Lampe is left witnessing to an unargued presupposition.

It is thus an important feature of these modern Christologies that, without necessarily intending this, they can make it possible for Christians to think without basic inconsistency in terms of religious pluralism. And my plea is that we should have an integrated faith in which our Christology and our theology of religions cohere with one another.

NOTES

1. James M. Wall, ed., *Theologians in Transition* (New York: Crossroad, 1981), p. 163.
2. John S. Dunne, *The Way of All the Earth* (Notre Dame, Ind.: University of Notre Dame Press, rpt. 1978), p. ix.
3. John Ottley Percy, ed., *Facing the Unfinished Task: Messages Delivered at the Congress on World Mission* (Grand Rapids, Mich.: Zondervan, 1961), p. 9.
4. Karl Rahner, *Theological Investigations*, 2nd ed., trans. Cornelius Ernst et al., 20 vols. to date (London: Darton, Longman, & Todd, 1965–), 1: chap. 5
5. Ibid., 1:149.
6. Ibid., 1: 157.
7. Ibid., 1: 158.
8. Ibid., 1: 160.
9. Ibid., 1: 163.

10. Ibid., 1:164.

11. Ibid., 1:164, n. 1.

12. Ibid., 1:165.

13. Ibid., 1:199–200.

14. Ibid., 1:172.

15. Ibid., 4:110.

16. Ibid.

17. Ibid., 5:178–79.

18. Ibid., 4:111.

19. Ibid., 1:173.

20. Ibid., 1:162.

21. Ibid.

22. Rudolf Bultmann, quoted in John Baillie, *The Theology of the Sacraments* (New York: Scribner's, 1957), p. 35.

23. Donald M. Baillie, *God Was in Christ* (London: Faber & Faber; New York: Scribner's, 1948), p. 114.

24. Ibid., pp. 117–18.

25. Geoffrey Lampe, *God as Spirit* (Oxford: Clarendon Press, 1977), p. 11.

26. Ibid., p. 61.

27. Ibid., p. 96.

28. Ibid., p. 34.

29. Ibid., p. 11.

30. Ibid., p. 14.

31. Ibid., p. 18.

32. Ibid.

33. Ibid., p. 23.

34. Ibid., p. 100.

35. Ibid., p. 12.

36. Ibid., p. 100.

37. Ibid.

38. Ibid., p. 106.

39. Ibid.

40. Ibid., p. 107.

12

Commitment in a Pluralistic World

GEORGE E. RUPP

I

WE LIVE IN AN ERA when the traditional foundations for faith are severely shaken. In a sense the Protestant principle has triumphed. No individual or insitution has unquestioned authority.

In an extension of this Protestant principle beyond what the Reformers themsevles envisioned, the authority of the Bible itself has not gone unquestioned. Impressive numbers of people may still insist that they accept the Bible as the inerrant authority for their faith. Similarly, significant numbers of the faithful declare their submission to the teaching authority of the Church — to the Magisterium and to the Pope when he speaks *ex cathedra*. But the need to interpret and adapt authoritative pronouncements in their everyday application characterizes the behavior of even those who subscribe to inerrant authority in principle. Think of fundamentalist interpretations of the Sermon on the Mount that somehow still support American superpatriotism. Or consider birth control among devout Roman Catholics. In short, no authority remains unquestioned in practice.

The situation is analogous to that of true believers in the political realm. In recent years there has been no shortage of declarations of support for the United States Constitution as virtually sacrosanct. And yet every position on the political spectrum has its recommendations for improvement. In some instances, the proposed amendment is quite self-consciously advanced to rectify limitations in the time-bound and partial vision of the framers of the Constitution. The Equal Rights Amendment is a case in point. In other instances the change is presented as consistent with the intention of the framers of the Constitution; so the amendment is offered as a more specific application designed to address new issues and to counter intervening misinterpretations of fundamental rights. The proposal for a constitutional amendment to ban state support for abortions illustrates this pattern. But in each case, the effect is to propose amendment in what is a foundational authority of American political life.

Because we discount the excesses of political rhetoric, we are not overly surprised at the proposing of constitutional amendments. We know that there have been more than a few formal amendments and that there will be more over the years. But in our religious communities there is no similarly formalized procedure for amending the pronouncements of our foundational authorities. Nor is there a formally established record of those amendments over time. As a result, change in our religious traditions strikes us less as a process of orderly amendment and more as a shaking of the very foundations of faith.

II

Changes in belief and practice have occurred in the course of the history of all religious communities — even the most tenaciously conservative ones. But our sense of a shaking of the foundations of faith has an edge to it that distinguishes our situation from much of the past. The reason is that we are crossing the threshold into a new era in the history of human religious life. What characterizes this new era is an increasingly general recognition of our individual and corporate role in fashioning the religious worlds, the symbolic universes, in which we live.

Awareness of this role is not unprecedented. Exceptional individuals — both critics of religion and initiates in its mysteries — have for millennia insisted on this dynamic contribution of the human imagination to religious traditions. An intriguing Western example is the quite self-conscious recasting of Greek mythology in the late drama of Euripides. And in the East, both elaborate symbolic inventiveness and vigorous iconoclasm are evident among initiates in, for example, tantric or Zen Buddhism.

What is new in our situation is that not only exceptional individuals but rather also the prevailing culture as a whole is coming to recognize our collective role in fashioning religious symbols. The threshold into this new era is admittedly wide. In the West, we have been in the process of crossing it for at least several centuries. But the shift from the insight of exceptional individuals to a cultural ethos of general recognition is nonetheless a profoundly challenging transition for religious communities.

The challenge may be formulated quite simply: Are religious communities viable in this new situation of increased self-consciousness? Can religious communities survive in this situation? Religious communities provide symbolic universes for those of us who are their members: rituals, injunctions, images, and ideas through which we interpret our experience and which in turn shape that experience. The question is whether or not we can continue to live within such a symbolic universe once we recognize its status as a creation of collective human insight and imagination.

I do not think we have enough information about this question. We are in effect living out our various answers. For several centuries in the West, the presumption has been that the recognition of religious symbols as human artifacts requires a rejection of those symbols. But we have also come to see that we unavoidably live within one or another symbolic universe. Thus a rejection of religious symbols does not in itself settle the issue of what values we commit ourselves to and what meanings we affirm. That issue remains solidly grounded in all of our living no matter how severely the traditional foundations for faith are shaken.

III

Religious communities have for millennia been moving toward the periphery of society — or at the least toward a diffusion throughout the social structure. In the institutionally least complex cultures about which we have data, there is no differentiation of a religious group from the society as a whole. Instead, the tribe is a single political-economic-religious entity. In more complex societies, religious institutions typically are differentiated from political and economic ones. The priest and the king are no longer the same person. In our own tradition, in which this differentiation has become sharpest and most self-conscious, there is a church distinguished from the state. But separation of church and state as two more or less unified spheres mutually balancing and correcting each other is not the final stage in this line of development. Instead, as the process of differentiation continues, the dichotomy of state and church yields to a series of regions or dimensions of society that mutually influence each other: not only the political and the religious, but also the economic, the educational, the legal, the artistic, and so on.

The result of this process of differentiation is a sense of movement of religious communities toward the periphery of the social system. Religious life is not inescapably integral to our social existence, as in tribal culture. Nor is a unified religious community institutionalized as one of two central authorities that structure the social system, as in medieval Europe, for example. Instead, religious communities are among those voluntary associations to which we may belong as we struggle to orient our lives, to appraise competing value systems, and to commit ourselves to the causes that seem most compelling.

Viewed from the perspective of traditional religious authority, our situation is, then, doubly dubious: individuals are more and more aware of their role in shaping religious traditions, and religious communities are increasingly marginal in the social system as a whole. The two developments reinforce each other. The result is that our religious life is beset with the same dispirited individualism that plagues so much of contemporary society. Even those of us who affirm religious values as crucial to our identities may do so apart from any commitment to a self-consciously religious community. We Americans have a two-hundred-year tradition here: in the words of Thomas Paine, "My mind is my church"; or, as Thomas Jefferson put it, "I am a sect myself." A religious dimension to the culture available directly to individuals displaces religious institutions. Here, as elsewhere in our society, individualism threatens to run amok.

An effective response in this situation must engage the issues focused in modern Western individualism. This need is a religious imperative: central to the religious life is the struggle against our idolatrous glorification of the self. But the need to address the is-

sue of unchecked individualism also follows from considerations
of social psychology and the sociology of knowledge. Thomas Paine
and Thomas Jefferson to the contrary notwithstanding, every person is not and cannot be his or her own church.

In part because religious communities are no longer centrally
and unquestionably authoritative in contemporary society, we do
have an increased awareness of our role in shaping the symbolic
universes in which we live. But we do not simply invent our symbols. Instead, we participate in changing traditions and therefore
bear responsibility for the ongoing development of the symbolic
resources available through those traditions. In some cases, it may
be most responsible simply to reject a tradition. Even then we are
not, however, moving out of every symbolic universe. Nor are we
creating an entirely new one. Instead we are engaged in a process
of critical appropriation through which we assess and often reinterpret the symbols available to us.

To focus this general description of what I am calling critical appropriation, I want to sketch two contemporary illustrations
of the dynamics involved. The first is the impact of feminism on
contemporary religious life and thought. And the second is the religious and ethical challenge of limits to growth in our biosphere.

IV

The impact of feminism has made us painfully aware of how
deeply patriarchal are the symbolic forms and institutional patterns of Jewish and Christian traditions. In the most virulent expression of this sexism, women are simply barred from positions
of authority in the liturgical and administrative life of the community. But even when this extreme is rejected, there remains the
sexism that pervades the language and imagery of our churches
and synagogues. Those of us who have tried to locate biblical texts
or liturgies or hymns that do not have sexually exclusive language
know how pervasive is this sexism in virtually every aspect of our
religious traditions.

For significant numbers of contemporary Christians and Jews,
this pervasive presence of sexist language and imagery is simply
unacceptable. It is unacceptable in the straightforward sense that

it interferes with the very act of worship. Instead of being incorporated into a vital community that transcends the individual, we experience exclusion that vitiates any sense of a common and inclusive body.

This contemporary state of affairs is very much a product of historical development. For thousands of years participants in biblical traditions have been able to celebrate their common life without being conscious of the sexism that pervades those traditions. That third person singular masculine pronouns and nouns like *man* and *mankind* are intended as inclusive in reference was for our forebears a grammatical point that did not violate their conscious experience. Similarly, references to God as masculine were not perceived to be dignifying male as distinguished from female experience. But that is no longer the case for increasing numbers of women and men. In sum, authoritative traditions have come into direct conflict with our contemporary awareness of the role of gender in the symbolization and institutionalization of religious life.

In theory, we can envision three ideal typical responses to this situation. One is to insist on the inviolability of the authoritative traditions and therefore to reject the claims of contemporary awareness as illegitimate human self-exaltation. A second is to reject completely the pretensions of the tradition and to affirm the new awareness as alone having true authority — as exercising genuine power in our common life. The third response is to recognize that neither authoritative traditions nor contemporary awareness can be rejected completely and that, therefore, there is no alternative except to attempt to do justice to the power of both.

As this formulation suggests, the three theoretical responses in practice are points on a single spectrum. Even the most conservative traditions change over time; and even the most unqualified commitment to radically novel insight or awareness draws on the resources of the past. Responses to a specific issue may fall at multiple points on the spectrum. But none of them can fail to take a position with reference to both poles. To adapt an aphorism from Kant: exaltation of current awareness apart from the symbolic resources of the past is empty; fidelity to tradition without attention to contemporary experience is blind.

Specifically on the issues focused in contemporary feminism, a full spectrum of responses is represented. It ranges from modest renovation among those who want to continue to dwell in the house of traditional authority, through efforts at more systemic transformation, to emphatic rejection of Christian and Jewish traditions in their entirety. But in each case, there is the recognition of the need for at least some changes and there is also, despite protestations to the contrary, very substantial continuity. Commitment "beyond God the Father" is still heavily dependent on theological and philosophical images and ideas fundamentally shaped in Western patriarchal traditions.

In exemplifying the process of critical appropriation through which we assess and often reinterpret the symbols available to us, the feminist movement also illustrates the complex relationship between Western individualism and the increased self-consciousness about commitment today. In a sense, the movement in its contemporary form is itself a powerful expression of just this individualism. After centuries of accepting and affirming identities that subordinated their individuality to the prerogatives of others, women have insisted that they, too, must be able to do their own thing. At the same time, the feminist movement has had the greatest impact when it provides a community in which this new individuality is nourished and sustained. The broader culture can and does offer various stimuli to individuals, especially through the mass media. But this general cultural awareness is certainly not as effective in enabling change as is a community of shared commitment in support of that change.

In this respect also, the feminist movement exemplifies the general issues involved in contemporary commitment. Talk of assessing alternatives and reinterpreting traditional symbolism unavoidably sounds highly individualistic. But that process of critical appraisal in turn shapes our living most effectively when we participate in a community that shares our commitment. Through this active collaboration, both the symbolic resources of the tradition and the participants are changed.

V

Like the impact of feminism, the challenge of limits to growth in our biosphere has implications for both the symbolization and the institutionalization of our common life. In short, this challenge also affects both our ideas and our actions.

It is, I think, helpful to attempt to gain some historical perspective in viewing the impact on religious life of this sense of limits to growth. Most of the traditional forms of the great world religions generate their power through appeal to an order of reality that is the ultimate destiny of the human and in comparison to which this historical existence is radically deficient or even hopelessly corrupt. In much Christian piety, this realm is heaven over against earth or the liberating vision of God over against enslavement to the world. For the Theravāda Buddhist, this destiny is the attainment of the other shore, of nirvana over against *saṁsāra*; for the Pure Land Buddhist, it is rebirth in the western paradise of Amida. For virtually all Hindus, the goal of the religious life is the attainment of *mokṣa*: deliverance from the round of birth and death that constitutes ordinary historical life.

In popular piety, deliverance to this other realm — heaven, nirvana, the Pure Land, union with the ultimate through release from recurrent births — is often portrayed as the destiny of the faithful or disciplined or devoted individual. In the various religious traditions there are, however, also resources for interpreting this deliverance in less individualistic terms. Liberation from Egypt that leads to settlement in the promised land is a dramatic instance of corporate and this-worldly deliverance in biblical faith. So too are certain Mahāyāna Buddhist tendencies — for example, the vow of the *bodhisattva* to save all sentient beings rather than attain deliverance alone. But the predominant pattern is that such corporate or inclusive transformation is projected into the future or into an apocalyptic end time or is realized apart from all ordinary historical processes. In the end there is a transforming resurrection of all humankind. Or in a final vindication of divine power, the kingdom of God is established in utter discontinuity with the dynamics of human historical development. Or through rigorous spiritual discipline, enlightenment is attained and all of reality is seen to be Buddha-nature — even though to ordinary human vision it is unchanged. Or through renunciation of worldly involvements, the transtemporal identity of the self with the ultimate is realized in a single all-comprehending whole. In sum, even though in such instances the goal of the religious life is envisioned as a reality that transcends the individual, its realization is still viewed as discontinuous with ordinary historical life.

To this pattern of traditional religion in both its individual and universal forms, the post-Enlightenment West has posited a direct and quite simple alternative: human progress. The goal of human life is not envisioned as discontinuous with history. Instead human history itself is presumed to be progressing inexorably into, or at least is thought to be developing toward, even greater fulfillment. Like the pattern of traditional religion, this alternative is expressed in both individualistic and corporate forms, as is illustrated in the numerous versions of bourgeois individualism and Marxism. But in all of the variations, transformation discontinuous with ordinary life is replaced with hope for the future of human development. The vision of heaven above is translated into aspirations for the earth below.

Although it has been severely shaken by the cataclysms of our century, this presumption of continuing progress is still central to the cultural ethos of much of the West even today. It is a salient feature in the ideology of both laissez-faire capitalism and Marxism. It certainly has shaped the rhetoric and programs of parties at all points on the political spectrum. In alliance with traditional tendencies to ethical perfectionism and spiritual discipline, commitment to progress has also found expression in religious and philanthropic communities, as dedication to human welfare has become a goal significant in its own right rather than a temporary means to transtemporal salvation for both the donor and the recipient.

Because the presumption of progress has been central to so many post-Enlightenment cultural traditions, it unavoidably informs our current discussions of limits to growth in the biosphere. Indeed, those discussions become traumatic precisely because the very idea of limits to growth seems to contradict the tenet of indefinitely extended progress which is still central to much of our culture.

At first glance, threats to the ideology of progress might appear to signal a revival of what I have called the pattern of traditional religion. After all, the attractiveness of traditionally valued forms of religious development is only enhanced with the recognition that indefinite material progress cannot be sustained. Striving toward ethical improvement and disciplined spiritual attainment does not depend on the exploitation of limited resources. From this perspective, only the illegitimate secularized versions of religion that focus on this-worldly welfare are shown to be untenable. Traditional religion, in contrast, is vindicated through its refusal to compromise with secular culture in its preoccupation with material progress.

Despite the so-called moral majority and the resurgence of conservative religion, the situation is not that simple. The preoccupation of the post-Enlightenment West with progress is not simply an aberration. Nor does the impending collapse of that preoccupation signal a return to the simple truths of traditional religion. We are all children of the Enlightenment who cannot simply return to the comforting dualisms of traditional religion. Instead, for most of us, too, visions of heaven have come to represent hopes for our common life here on earth. To use Buddhist imagery, the land of Amida Buddha is our historical life transformed and purified.

In short, as it has been for the proponents of progress, the place for us is here; but in contrast to the future orientation of the proponents of progress, the time must be now. There must be a transformation in the personal, social, and cultural dynamics of our common life in history. But that transformation cannot be envisioned as only a future realization of all the ideals and aspirations that motivate present action. Instead, we must participate now in the corporate reality to which the symbols of religious traditions testify — in Christian imagery, the reality of spirit, the kingdom or commonwealth of God, the divine-human body of which we are all members.

For those of us who cannot return to the dualisms of traditional religion, there is a special urgency and also a sense of tragedy in our appropriation of such symbols of human destiny. This double sense of urgency and tragedy is with reference not only to the individual but also to humanity as a whole — indeed to all of life as we know it. Many of us cannot affirm individual survival of death in some other realm. As a result, we place a special premium on the contributions we are enabled to make and the satisfactions we are allowed to enjoy in all the dimensions of our daily living. A similar sense of tragedy and urgency seems to envelop our corporate existence. That is, there appears to be a final limit to the viability of the earth as an ecosystem capable of supporting life as we know it. So our corporate life also is lived in the face of a final death that accentuates the need to realize value here and now.

In this context of limits to growth in our biosphere and even a final term to the viability of our ecosystem, to affirm that we are all members of one body has definite implications for action. Any such affirmation calls for measures to redress the enormously uneven distribution of wealth that makes a mockery of all talk about an inclusive human community. And the fact that available resources are limited serves to accentuate the indefensibility of dramatically inequitable distribution. The easy answers of the recent past become less and less plausible: proportionately the same slices of an ever larger socio-economic pie may have some attractions even to those with small pieces; but if the pie cannot increase in size indefinitely or even for very long, then the alternative of reslicing it becomes compelling.

In sum, in the context of limits to growth, our appropriation of such religious images as the spiritual community, the kingdom or commonwealth of God, and the divine-human body of which we are all members entails a commitment to radical programs of redistribution rather than the easy gradualism that assumes indefinitely extended socio-economic growth. As we move increasingly to an integrated planetary culture, we must, therefore, press for policies that protect and further the interests of the third world. Similarly, as our society recognizes the long-term untenability of affluence driven through such devices as planned obsolescence and investment in superfluous armaments, we must struggle toward institutional patterns that reinforce simplicity and frugality rather than unnecessary production and consumption. Only through this double movement toward reduced consumption and redistribution of wealth can we be faithful to affirmations of inclusive community.

VI

The need for redistribution of resources in the context of limits to growth is not as directly a personal challenge as are the issues at the heart of the feminist critique. Yet both challenges call for a fundamental change in personal, social, and cultural patterns that must begin as particular communities actualize new or reaffirmed values in their common life. In both cases, there is a general cultural awareness of the need for this change. But also in both cases, the call for change is most effective when there is a community of shared commitment in support of that change.

A critical question focused through the examples of the feminist movement and the limits to growth in our biosphere is where this community of mutual support is to be located. More specifically, can it be located within religious communities?

This question brings us full circle to the issues involved in the collapse of traditional authorities. Not only the traditional foundations for faith but also other authorities are shaken. Yet the reverberations of the collapse seem especially pronounced in the case of religious communities. Religious life has so powerfully shaped human identities at least in part because it has engaged the deepest levels of the self at the earliest and perhaps the most formative stages of development. For precisely that reason, increased self-consciousness about our individual and corporate role in fashioning our symbolic universes constitutes a particularly acute threat in this case.

In the wake of the collapse of traditional authorities, religious communities will survive only if they conduct genuine power to their members — only if they provide a context in which individuals are delivered from their self-preoccupations for commitment to more inclusive causes. To this end, the rituals, injunctions, images, and ideas of particular communities must be represented effectively so that they both interpret the full range of contemporary experience and in turn shape that experience in ways that elicit affirmation.

This need is not just the expression of an abstract intellectual interest. Instead, it directly affects our living in all of its empirical concreteness. To refer again to the two illustrations I sketched, the issues focused in the feminist challenge to religious imagery and institutions affect not only our ideas but also our most fundamental individual and corporate identities. Similarly, our increased awareness of limits to growth in our biosphere affects every dimension of our living. Consequently, interpretations of contemporary experience through reference to traditional images and ideas must in turn shape our lives in ways that we affirm. In the case of the feminist challenge, we must realize the potential in biblical and other religious traditions for supporting inclusive communities that enhance the female as well as the male dimensions of the human. And in the instance of limits to growth, we must come to affirm our situation as finite moments integral to an order of being and value that is dynamic and has the capacity to be inclusive and just. In sum, for religious communities to survive, there must be an emotionally powerful and intellectually satisfying expression of post-conventional faith that is adequate to the full range of our developing experience.

The need to relate traditional symbols to the dynamics of contemporary life is certainly not a new imperative for religious communities. But our greater self-consciousness about this process of appropriation has both a threatening and a promising aspect. Our new awareness can inhibit or even block the energy generated through religious commitment. We can become self-conscious in the debilitating sense of looking only at ourselves and exaggerating our role as individual arbiters or even manipulators of traditional symbols. But recognition of the role of human insight and imagination in the fashioning of our religious worlds can also be liberating. It can release both our critical and our creative capacities as we seek to act out of a corporate vision that we are committed to making our own. Because we recognize our responsibility for this process, we must identify those places in the tradition that do not adequately interpret and acceptably shape our experience. We must enlarge those places so that they can accommodate all that we affirm. Only this inclusive commitment can be at one and the same time faithful to the past, adequate for orienting us in the present, and promising in projecting us and our world into the future.

Author Index

Subject Index

Absolute, 11, 193ff.
Absolute Knowledge, 82
Art, 8–9, 130–44

Block universe, 69–71
Buddhism, 9, 145ff., 175–77, 195

Christian theology, 3ff., 10, 21,
   26ff., 128
Christianity, 145ff., 161–78, 195–
   96
Commitment, 214–26
Cosmotheandric experience, 111
Covenant, 3–4, 34–37
Creativity, 131ff.

Dasein, 85
Death-of-God, 17
Determinism, 5–6, 54–74
Divine Principle, The, 40ff.

Eleatic School, 58–59
"Eternal Sentences," 6

Feminism, 218ff.
Freedom, 78ff.

Global City, 146ff.
God, 180ff.
Greek Tragedy, 55

Havurot, 20
Heresy, 38ff.

Hermeneutics of religion, 8,
   116ff.
Hinduism, 195
Historicity, 85
History, 6, 17, 20, 78ff.
Holocaust, 3, 17ff.

Incarnation, 183ff.
Islam, 195
Israel, 3, 18

Judaism, 3–4, 17ff., 23, 195

Kerygmatic theology, 162ff., 169

Liberation theology, 3, 28
Limit, 116ff.
Logos, 183ff., 201

Messianism, 46ff.
Metaphysics, 101
Missionaries, 12
Modernity, 6, 77–92
Moonies, 4–5, 39–51
Mormonism, 42ff.
Mysterium tremendum, 131

New Testament, 55ff., 118

Old Testament, 55ff.

Pantheism, 65
Physics, 72–73
Play, 131

229